To Barbara,
A beautiful person
& fellow violinist.
Love,
Maureen (and Joe)

The Living Art of
Violin Playing

The Living Art of Violin Playing

PROGRESSIVE FORM

Maureen Taranto-Pyatt
WITH PETER STICKEL

INDIANA UNIVERSITY PRESS

This book is a publication of

INDIANA UNIVERSITY PRESS
Office of Scholarly Publishing
Herman B Wells Library 350
1320 East 10th Street
Bloomington, Indiana 47405 USA

iupress.org

© 2023 by Maureen Taranto-Pyatt

All rights reserved
No part of this book may be reproduced or utilized in any form or by any means, electronic or mechanical, including photocopying and recording, or by any information storage and retrieval system, without permission in writing from the publisher. The paper used in this publication meets the minimum requirements of the American National Standard for Information Sciences—Permanence of Paper for Printed Library Materials, ANSI Z39.48–1992.

Manufactured in the United States of America

First printing 2023

Cataloging information is available from the Library of Congress.

ISBN 978-0-253-06660-2 (cloth)
ISBN 978-0-253-06661-9 (paperback)
ISBN 978-0-253-06662-6 (ebook)

Dedicated to

Lawrence Jeffrey Pyatt

*Our love—the worm in the earth, the bird in flight,
stars swirling the galaxies . . .*

Contents

PREFACE xv
ACKNOWLEDGMENTS xix

Introduction 1

Part One: Left Arm 5

1 Left Arm Overview 7
Setting Up the Violin 7
Positioning of the Elbow 8
Swinging Motion of the Left Elbow 8
Transporting the Hand 9
Fundamental Motion of the Forearm 14
Facilitation of the Hand in Passage Work 14
Reducing Hand-Shoulder Tension 16

2 Left Arm Subdivisions 18
Balance of the Forearm 18
Forearm Rotation—The Radius and the Ulna 20
Left Upper Arm 21
  Presentation and Directing Points 21
  Upper-Arm-to-Hand Balance 23
Left Shoulder 24
  Support through Passivity 24

3   Total Left Arm   27

    Forearm and Upper Arm Mutuality   27
    Strength versus Tension   31
    Balance and Suspension of the Violin   32
        Setting Up without Tension   32
        Positioning the Violin   34
        A Malleable Violin   35

4   Left Wrist   36

    Traveling the Fingerboard   36
    Wrist Motion in Position   37
    Side Roads and the Four Strings   38
    Wrist Response in Meandering Passages   39
    Hand-Weight Balance and Creative Imagery   39
    Wrist and Finger Collaboration   41
    Optimum Wrist Placement   42
    Suspension of the Wrist and Hand   45
    Hoisting and Propelling the Wrist   46
    Rebound Motion of the Wrist   47

5   Left Palm   49

    Palm Formation   49
    Stabilizing the Palm   51
    Palm Pliability   52
    Palm Height and Balance   55
    Palm-Base-to-Fingertip Balance   57
    Overall Balance and Mobility   59
    Migration of the Hand   60

6   Left-Hand Knuckles   62

    Structure and Weight   62
    Knuckle Support for the Articulating Finger   65
    Large Knuckles and Hand Rotation   67
    Large Knuckle Movement in Tandem with the Wrist   68

7   Left-Hand Fingers   70

    Finger Balance   70
    The Hand's Stabilization of the Fingers   73
    Direction of the Fingers   75

Finger Placement　77
　　　Leading with the Pad or the Nail Side　79
　　　The Conjoining of the Fingers and Palm　80

8　LEFT-HAND FINGER ACTION　84
　　　Finger Position　84
　　　Support for Finger Action　85
　　　A Dream　89
　　　Poised Fingers　89
　　　Imagery That Supports Finger Rebound　90

9　LEFT THUMB　94
　　　Balance of the Hand and Thumb　94
　　　Thumb Contact with the Neck　98
　　　Securing the Hand's Tunnel　98
　　　Thumb-to-Fingertip Rotation　99
　　　Invisible Props for Thumb Support　102
　　　The Thumb's Role in Hand Compression　103

10　FINER BALANCES OF THE LEFT HAND　104
　　　Thumb-to-Finger Balance　104
　　　Thumb-to-Finger and Thumb-to-Palm Rotational Relationships　104
　　　The Left-Hand Bow Hold　106
　　　The Thumb Lever　108
　　　The Thumb's Suspension of the Fingers　110
　　　The Thumb Axle　112
　　　Thumb and Fingerboard Usage and Imagery　114

11　LEFT HAND FORMATION　116
　　　Symmetry　116
　　　The Home Position　117
　　　Hand Angle Relative to the String　119
　　　Building Left-Hand Forms　121
　　　The Equator　123
　　　The Sphere of the Left Hand and Its Axes of Rotation　123
　　　Combining Weight Imagery with Hand Pressures　127
　　　Left-Hand Suspension　129
　　　Expansion and Contraction of the Hand　130
　　　Optimizing Hand Flexibility　131

12   Lower Outside Corner   132
Hand Balance   132
The Lower Outside Corner's Relationship to the Wrist   136
Lateral Hand Balance   137
Transporting the Hand via the Lower Corners   137
Structure and Rotational Pathways of the Hand   139

13   Shifts   141
Finger Shape and Hand Positioning   141
Strategies between Shifts   143
Lateral Movement   143
The Third-to-Fourth-Position Changeover   145
Descending Shifts   145
Stretching the Limits   147
Guiding Imagery Using the Violin String   148

14   Scales   150
Combining Imagery for Left-Hand Support   150
Arcing Paths above the Fingerboard   151
Catapulting the Hand from the Bottom Center   151
Escalating the Left Hand   152
Hand Mobility without Disruption of Form   153
Chords and Double Stops   156

15   Trills   157
Hand Position   157
Hand-Arm Balance   158
Presenting the Finger   158
Finger Shape and Articulation   159
Contrary Motion of the Base-Trill and Trill Fingers   160
Countermotions and Pressures within the Hand   161
Compressions That Support Trill Finger Rebound   163
Support for the Trill Finger   163
Coordinated Compressions within the Hand   165

16   Vibrato   168
Balancing the Hand   168
Bottom-of-Hand Balances   170
Inside the Square-Shaped Finger   171
The Palm   171

    The Inner Circle   172
    The Shoulder   173
    Rotational Interactions of the Arm and Hand   173
    Employing the Knuckles   174
    Optimal Support for the Vibrating Finger   178
    Aiming the Fingertips   180
    Finger Vibrato   180
    Hand Vibrato   182
    Wrist Vibrato   182
    The Finger-to-Thumb Relationship to Gravity   183
    Transitioning from Vibrato to Running Passages   183
    Compressions That Enhance the Motion of Vibrato   185

Part Two: Right Arm   187

17   Right Forearm   189
    Forearm Balance   189
    Locating the Balance Point   190
    Balance Point Functionality   192
    Forearm Suspension   196
    Forearm Application   198

18   Right Hand   203
    Stabilization of the Wrist   203
    Bow Hand   205
        Balancing the Hand   205
        The Right-Hand Spine   207
        Hand-to-Thumb Rotation   208
    Bow Fingers   208
        The Bow Hold   208
        Finger Action   211
        Projecting the Sense of Touch   211

19   Total Right Arm   212
    Right Arm Presentation and Directing Points   212
    Right Elbow   213
        Taking the Lead   213
    Right Shoulder   214
        Multiplicities of Suspension   214

Contents

    Comprehensive Right Arm   214
        An Overview   215
        Right Arm Suspension   215
        Know Thyself—The Bow Arm   217
        Arm Shape and a Coaster Full of Weight   218
        Weight Transference   219
        Hand and Arm Placement Relevant to the Violin   220
    Bow-Arm Rotation   222
        Right Forearm   222
        Three Points of Rotation for the Bow Arm   223
        Side Arm Rotation   225
    The Bow   226
        Rotations   226
        Integrating the Arms through Visualization   228

20   BOW FORM AND APPLICATION   231

Autonomy of the Bow Hand   231
Martelé   232
    Form and Application   232
Spiccato   234
    Fundamentals   234
Legato   237
Detaché   239
    Points of Rotation in the Hand   240
    Imagery with the Bow as a Conduit   241
String Crossings   242
    Circles and Figure Eights   242

21   THE BOW STROKE—SPEED, BALANCE, AND MENTAL PROJECTION   244

Bow Speed   244
Bow Imagery   244
Gravity's Influence on the Bow   246
Tracking the Bow   246
The Sounding Point   247
    Right- and Left-Hand Synthesis   249
Right-Hand Chords   251
    Two Hands Ascend   253

Part Three: Integration 255

22 Full Body Balance 257
    Arm-to-Body Expansion and Contraction 257
    Balancing the Body and Violin 259
    Application 262
    Creative Division of the Body 264
    Synchronized Compressions 265
    Elbow to Palm: Two-Way Compression 266
    Forearm to Hand: Four-Way Compression 266
    Restoring Force 266
    Coordinating the Periphery 268
    Supporting the Violin with Compression 270
    Creative Use of the Bow 270
    Using the Restoring Force of a Ball 272
    Performance Energy 272
    Energy and Balance 274
        Implied Spiral Motion of the Head and Torso 274
        Motion and Energy Pathways 274
        Forces of Nature in Motion 275

23 An Expanded Approach to Scales and Arpeggios 277
    Elaborating the E Major Scale 277
    The Thumb's Role in Supporting the Fingers 290

24 Mental Training and *Progressive Form* 291
    The Visually Balanced Violinist 291
    Visualization and the Bow Arm 293

APPENDIXES 299
GLOSSARY 305
INDEX 307

Preface

When I was eight years old, I heard a sound in a school auditorium that spoke to my very core. From that day forward, I knew I had found my calling. When I picked up the violin and drew the bow, each note resonated with ease. I found ecstatic freedom in motion and played effortlessly like the child I was—who ran, skipped, and climbed trees. For a time, circumstances led me away from the instrument, but my yearning to perform never waned. As a young adult, I returned to the violin, but now I clenched its neck, choking out the magical movement that in my younger years had happened so naturally. I spent my twenties developing technique in search of that naturalness.

During my postconservatory days, I studied violin for a number of years with Max Hobart, longtime associate concertmaster of the Boston Symphony Orchestra (BSO). As my comfort level with the instrument improved under Max's guidance, he invited me to join two orchestras that he conducted; one was a training ensemble. As a principal player, I was asked to play a mentoring role, helping music students and members of the community overcome technical limitations and obstacles in challenging passages.

Some years later in 2002, BSO violinist Victor Romanul performed a Mozart concerto with a chamber group in which I was playing. The fluidity of his performance magnified some remaining discontent with elements of my own technique, rekindling the still-lurking desire to recapture that early spontaneity and ease of form that was accessible to me as a child. I asked Victor if he would work with me, and he agreed.

Our lessons became fertile explorations of the fundamentals of violin playing. In July 2003, I began to tape and eventually transcribe our sessions to capture the insights arising from our time together. What started off as self-growth quickly developed into an intention to develop a system of visual analogies that could cultivate in other violinists a greater ease of playing. Based now on a deeper sense of purpose, I carried on the project of refining and recording the visual images described in this book, along with the technical observations that accompany them. To further evaluate components of Progressive Form, I also worked with professional musicians in many formal and informal settings, experimenting with the conceptualizations. From the accumulation of feedback from my teachers, students, orchestra members, and colleagues, I've learned which images seem to be most helpful to players.

The physical motions of elegant and effective violin playing are exquisitely complex and nuanced in their individual components as well as in combination. As a result, they are challenging to understand and devilishly difficult to describe. Visual images are easy to grasp and convey, however, so they impart information and guidance quickly and efficiently. As such, they have the power to help us realize principles that may be less accessible conceptually. Added to this utility is the personal power of visualization—the fact that we tend to manifest what we picture. You could say to a student, "Lift your arm," but offering a visual aid, such as the image of placing a ball under your left arm, can open up additional dimensions of consideration, in this case leading to other benefits from a more relaxed separation between the torso and upper arm. Ultimately, the goal is to engage more deeply on a feeling or experiential level as our relationship with the instrument becomes progressively more natural and therefore more intimate.

In *The Living Art of Violin Playing: Progressive Form,* the evolution of the left- and right-arm structures is designed to be intuitively systematic, building from micro-motions that feel natural to gestures that make sense as they are reconstructed into larger forms designed to serve high-level performance. It is common, for example, to see players drop their left arm while changing positions on the fingerboard or when playing for prolonged periods of time. When the elbow dips, the hand drops and disrupts the shape of the fingers. Recognizable objects and mechanisms can illuminate the interactive relationship of elbow position to hand facility, the imagery providing support for the elevation of the shifting hand as well as its continually changing configuration.

Students on a professional track usually approach their technical issues by practicing scales, arpeggios, and excerpts until the fingers absorb the lessons. Unless there is an optimum positioning of the arm and hand that supports a healthy follow-through of the fingers, the natural wear and tear of repetitive percussive movements through misaligned joints catches up to you. Then, the instinctual strategy is to make bodily adjustments to ease the burden of discomfort at the cost of further degradation of form.

The violin is arguably one of the most unwieldy instruments. Its awkwardness is not limited to the beginner, however. The veteran player may manage to get around the instrument with adequate proficiency yet with an ungainliness in form that can result in feeling continuously pushed against the upper limits of technical ability. This can undermine confidence as well as the joy of performance at all levels, sometimes leading to collapse under pressure or even to surrendering the instrument altogether.

Progressive Form is a system that can be used both as a reference for individual issues or as a guide to a revamping of technique. The latter requires serious study. The player who is willing and able to reconsider their technique as a seasoned performer may be very adaptable, especially if they have had an attitude of lifelong learning because that involves an array of psychophysical abilities, a developed sense of self, and with any luck physiological health. A comprehensive system of improvement, as opposed to a trial-and-error approach, can make a powerful difference.

Most teachers would agree that the fundamental goal is to help the student overcome the physical challenges of the instrument to achieve an unfettered artistry of expression. Offering a comprehensive structural framework is critical to that success. Adding the visualizations to the basic explanations and guidance—a little help to better see and incorporate the complex motions of violin playing—can move the player more effectively into alignment with the instrument and ultimately with the music.

Progressive Form can produce quick and consistent results because its principles are built on solid physics and anatomy, experienced through a nuanced and colorful kinesthetic landscape, and inspired by insights from the great violin pedagogues of the twentieth century. When well used, its lessons prove to be efficient, powerful, and additive.

Progressive Form builds methodically from the trunk through the left arm before addressing the bow arm. That linear development takes place in a holistic setting that acknowledges the connections of body with emotion, mind, and spirit and the even larger context of music making. To those ends, the following concepts are woven throughout the text:

Balance: using imagery to support healthy balances among bigger masses, such as between the trunk and the arm, or in smaller systems—within the hand, for instance. Practically speaking, staying in balance simplifies decision-making and creates more elegant transitions in everything from articulations to big shifts.

Gravity and Verticality: adjusting to the vertical orientation of our body as the foundation for its horizontal functioning. The reader is then invited to optimize the ability to perform from any point of balance, considering all the possible angles among three fundamental axes of rotation and imagining all possible playing positions.

Weight and Motion: using the feeling of weight to create momentum, such as in the shifting left hand, or simply to transfer relaxed weight—for instance, from the right arm to the string via the bow.

Presentation, Directing, and Balance Points: using anatomical locations that imply a more efficient use of resources. For example, locating a presentation point below the left shoulder blade to initiate the extension of the left arm engages trunk muscles that support that movement.

Anatomy, Physiology, and Health: gradually entraining the body to higher levels of integration for improved playing, but also for injury prevention.

Progressive Form provides a detailed concept of left arm and hand formation, as well as applications that serve the hand's migration on the fingerboard. Musical examples and photographs reinforce the modeling of hand structure, left and right. Visualizations situate the left hand such that the fingers are positioned to articulate efficiently with each string. Exercises without the instrument in hand support traveling from one fingerboard location to another to easily reengage with the instrument.

The hand transitions from a position of being upright to being essentially upside down during the third-to-fourth-position changeover and can fall out of form at this point because of the uncertainty of negotiating the shoulder. Supporting an effective left-hand mold during this transition prevents the inevitable loss of dexterity and all its consequences, including the time lost in refashioning the left hand.

A section on trills utilizes the concept of compressions, balances of natural, intrinsic pressures that can be consciously adjusted. Its imagery guides the trill finger's relationship to the base-trill finger.

Preface

The Progressive Form approach to vibrato offers a concrete system that regulates the speed and width of oscillation and assists in creating variation in tone color. Part One contains a variety of descriptions and examples that help secure the overall position of the left hand and arm that is particularly useful for vibrato.

Through the use of imaginative exercises, the martelé stroke is improved by moving from one note to the next in the most direct route. A precise view of spiccato is elucidated, and the proper arm balances for an effective stroke are achieved by way of props and visual tools.

There is a delicate balance between expanding sound volume and sustaining the quality of the sound. In the pursuit of a big, pleasing sound, the mechanics of drawing a whole bow are often underappreciated, but they separate one violinist's voice from another. Progressive Form's mechanisms guide the arm in drawing a whole bow that maintains good contact with the string, deepening the ability to produce a lengthy, beautiful tone with smooth bow changes.

Integrating the concept of bow weight and speed takes years to master, if it happens at all, and it is the very in-and-out breath of playing. A particularly powerful image assimilates the variables of string thickness, note values, and the amount of weight and speed applied to the bow. As a by-product, the contact of the bow to the string remains smooth, whether playing an on- or off-the-string bow stroke.

Knowing how to set up the hand relative to the bow and steer it with minimal effort requires a precise feel and a clear understanding. Progressive Form's imagery supports control of the bow's maneuvering in challenging string crossings without disruption to the shape and balance of the right hand.

The progression of carefully constructed systems that compartmentalize the forearm zero in on the exact motion necessary to implement detaché or spiccato bowing with multiple string crossings.

The methodology prescribed in *The Living Art of Violin Playing: Progressive Form* is harmonious with the teachings of the preceding masters. My most recent teacher, Victor Romanul, studied with Jascha Heifetz, Ivan Galamian, and Joseph Silverstein. My former teacher, Max Hobart, studied with Vera Barstow. And one of my first teachers, Leo Panasevich, was a student of both Louis Persinger and George Enescu. In significant ways, Heifetz, Galamian, Silverstein, Barstow, Enescu, and Persinger have all influenced methodologies my mentors have promoted. Much of my system has been weighed and measured against this existing knowledge.

Serious students of the violin frequently feel tremendous love and passion for the instrument, but stubborn technical challenges can undercut their enthusiasm. My hope through Progressive Form's method is to make more accessible the facility that allows us the joy of connecting our hearts to the notes.

Acknowledgments

To Max Hobart, performing artist, my teacher, and my friend: your ability to define sound in the realm of poetry awakened in me a lifelong conception of music as something living, breathing, here, yet not. I thank you also for the many years of affordable lessons; it is likely that I would not have continued if it hadn't been for your assistance and your making accessible to me tools that I needed to develop. Music is our shared religion.

Victor Romanul, I honor our beautiful exchange and am indebted to you for providing me with a strong foundation; a new methodology flourished from the roots of our exchange.

To my dear friend Peter Stickel, a professional violinist and practitioner of Structural Integration: thank you for working through Progressive Form in great detail, and for gifting me with your wonderful editorial insights. I appreciate your being the fussy critic to balance my creative enthusiasm. Not just any critic, of course: "a fiddle-playing, body-manipulating, language-loving, math-amorous, philosopher nerd," as you once shamelessly described yourself. Your benevolent perspicacity is just what the doctor ordered.

To John Bumstead: I thank you for the many sacrifices that you made and the responsibilities that you assumed while Peter and I navigated Progressive Form. You were truly selfless.

A special thank-you to my colleagues for their support:

My dear Barbara Lefkowitz, I value your musical insights, your incredible feedback, and, most importantly, our friendship.

Dear Kyung Yu, as a professional violinist and professor at Yale University, I especially value your insights on technical issues that commonly challenge the college-level violinist. I bless our friendship.

To Kristina Nilsson, a professional violinist: your editorial feedback in the initial stages of Progressive Form was a godsend.

Ruben Gregorian, a man of great dignity, a former teacher, and a mentor. Thank you!

For the visuals in Progressive Form:

My deep gratitude to Gail Taibbi, a professional photographer and friend who created half of the photo illustrations in this book as a volunteer (see the photo credits). Thank you for making the impossible possible.

To Eva Foxon Nicholas for your professionalism in taking the balance of the photographs for this book (see the photo credits). Your skills and kind manner were greatly appreciated.

To Gina Hagen for your graphic design work. It was truly a pleasure engaging with you in this process. Thank you for sharing your talents with me!

And finally, to my family:

To my parents, John M. and Marie Bernadette Williams, my greatest teachers and dearest friends.

Michael, Maria, Michael Jr., and Luciana (Taranto), I thank God daily for sending you to me.

Agnes Williams, my second mother, I thank you for your part in seeing me through a most challenging time.

My heart-filled love and appreciation to my dear niece, Ashton Williams, for being the model in some of the illustrations. Thank you for contributing your time and sophistication to this work.

To my dear sister Grace Williams: your conceptualism guided me inward, helping me bring to the forefront an overview of how I had come to develop Progressive Form. This and your editorial insights aided me in writing Progressive Form's introduction.

And to Paulette Saggio: I want to thank you here, as I promised I would if I were ever published, for letting me practice violin at 104 Summer Street—your home.

The Living Art of Violin Playing

Introduction

During private study with BSO violinist Victor Romanul, a transformation in my approach to the violin began. A pursuit of the naturalness I felt with the instrument as a child had taken me through conservatory training and into some fruitful years of study with Max Hobart. Influences from the established masters included Carl Flesch through *The Art of Violin Playing* (Books One and Two) and *Carl Flesch Scales System*; Yehudi Menuhin, who wrote *Unfinished Journey, Yehudi Menuhin Music Guides: Violin and Viola*, and *Violin: Six Lessons*, among other works; and Ivan Galamian, author of *Principles of Violin Playing and Teaching.* All three of these luminaries strongly influenced my own learning, but Galamian's encouragement of playing the violin according to what is most natural for the body particularly sparked my creativity and some growing conceptual explorations.

Then I began to wonder: What is natural that simultaneously serves playing the instrument? How does the rest of the body respond during the incorporation of any new adjustment? What has convention been trying to achieve? And how can students be assisted to become fully engaged with their instruments?

I noticed that even among the great violinists, hand positions varied. I thought about how, when leaning forward while balanced on one foot, a person heavier in the middle would have to adjust differently from a thin person and how the balancing in the body and with the violin is different for someone with longer arms than someone with shorter arms and longer legs. As I considered it further, it became clear that as each person's anatomy varies, so too does each point of balance. Given this diversity, did the idea of pursuing a common perfection of form make sense? What resonated in response was the serene image of a sphere, the only three-dimensional form with equilibrium in all positions. Maybe its equanimity could support our individual efforts.

This insight led to a shift of perspective. More and more, I realized that regardless of how odd it might seem, ironically speaking, perfectly round could very well be the best guide for overall balance with, and the perfect context for, our always oddly shaped body parts. Later, I would learn that the joints of the shoulder, wrist, and hand were all designed for circular motion, and that clinched it: now I could see that the neutral fullness of the sphere could encompass and support any particular functional unit—a hand, for example—and at the same time suggest the circular motion that integrates it with larger forms: the hand with the wrist, or perhaps with the full arm. In an effort to hone my technical skills using this strategy, I imagined holding a baseball while navigating passages, retaining a sensation not only of the hand but also of the ball's contact with the fingerboard and neck to assist in the hand's migration. I began to imagine props surrounding the instrument, illuminating the full three-dimensionality of each situation. For instance, I imagined encasing the neck inside a cylinder and navigating the fingerboard by way of the cylinder's surface. Through study and self-exploration, these nascent ideas helped clarify my technique and awakened in me a deeper consciousness of the reasons why that elusive sense of freedom was missing.

Students often migrate from one teacher to another. They may be told by one teacher with a particular methodology to place the tip of the right thumb against the second finger, or against the third by another; to bend or not to bend the thumb; and to tuck the elbow in like a wing or to avoid tucking the elbow in. The concept of Progressive Form evolved out of my curiosity about the principles underlying these seemingly contradictory directives.

When we think about our senses, generally we think about sight, taste, smell, touch, and hearing, which are designed primarily to perceive the outside world. There are other sensory modalities that are equally important, if more subtle, geared more to the awareness of ourselves. An example is kinesthesia, the ability to perceive the characteristics of movement, such as direction and extent as well as the feeling of weight. We can also feel where our various body parts are located in relation to each other with a sense called proprioception, slightly different from the kinesthetic sense of movement. Thanks to kinesthetic and proprioceptive awareness, we can learn to transfer weight while maintaining a good sense of balance and support. When you consciously combine frames of movement—in other words, when you become aware of how one functional unit corresponds to and integrates with another—your level of coordination is heightened and your facility is expanded. For example, the section under the heading "Forearm and Upper Arm Mutuality" suggests constructing images that demonstrate the simultaneous relationships of position and motion that exist between the left forearm and upper arm. Eventually, progressively larger forms can be constructed that lead to full-body synthesis.

Through visualization, Progressive Form supports the integrated development of technique with a foundation of body awareness and in a context of artistic sensibility. We begin with the left arm and focus on the left elbow. From there, we move to the forearm, the upper arm, the left shoulder, the wrist, and the hand. We break the hand into multiple components using imagery to facilitate balance and utility among the knuckles, the thumb, and the fingers, ultimately to optimize the moment of articulation. Then we move from the left arm to the right arm and develop the forearm's point of balance, first working outward toward the wrist, hand, and fingers and then to the elbow, upper arm, and shoulder. Once the shape and form of the right arm is established through suspension, the bow arm is set into motion. Some images allow us to effectively lengthen or shorten the bow; others to navigate the bow from a center point or alternatively from just one end. Just as the instrument needs to be stabilized, so too does the body relative to the violin. An example with a useful image is how the shift of weight in your feet while standing mirrors the response of the bridge's feet to the bow on the table of the violin.

Once mechanical motion becomes natural, finding something in nature (or some personal imagery) can unify the vast complexities of performing, moving us from acting on the violin into that place of being at one with the instrument. As each facet of balance and motion are brought into alignment and equilibrium is established, what shows up is the potential for releasing physicality and becoming a pure medium of response.

Progressive Form is an attempt to embrace a broad functional spectrum. Its fundamental concept is a balance image that is incorporated into a particular functional playing unit, each image over time adding to a more comprehensive understanding of technique and its potential metamorphosis into artistry. As an example of a balance image, visualize that the forearm is a seesaw. If there is a heavy weight on the elbow end and a light weight on the hand end, the hand ascends without effort, but then much effort is required to lift the heavier elbow end. If the weights are switched, with the heavier weight now on the hand, this time the elbow ascends with ease, but extra effort is required to lift the hand. Similarly, when bowing a detaché, martelé, or slower spiccato stroke with the fulcrum placed too close to the hand, the upbow is relatively effortless, but the downbow requires undue force. And in reverse, when the fulcrum is placed too close to the elbow and the surplus weight is near the hand, the downbow is effortless, but the upbow necessitates inordinate force. Adjusting these subtle balances is a way to liberate technique, clearing a path for deeper musical journeying.

Multiple images suggest shrinking or expanding the body, the bow, or the violin, as if each has the ability to solidify, evaporate, change shape, or have autonomous movement within a stationary frame. We break up the density of matter to eliminate the confines of our joints by imagining that the bones can bend or that areas of the body are without bone. These images begin to deconstruct any simplistic picture of our body's makeup and suggest a greater depth of its subtleties and a fuller use of its power, acknowledging the complexity of the soft tissues that are anchored to the relatively simple skeleton.

Some images address the full body more generally. To heighten a sense of the body's expansiveness, picture a breeze flowing through each of the joints, giving all the bony connection areas a sense of more volume—a larger space for the bones to relate, especially helpful for the vertebrae of the upper torso and neck, considering the tendency to compress the head, neck, and shoulder areas while securing the violin. Progressive Form's concepts are designed to ground an expanded range of possibilities in a realistic sense of the body, all toward the ultimate purpose of letting the music flourish.

The Progressive Form system aims to maximize potential through the use of props and imagery with which people can easily identify and from which they can draw inspiration. Pistons move faster than fingers, for example, and the velocity of wind is more rapid than the sweep of the bow arm. By visualizing a mechanical device that guides, or an image of nature that inspires, our playing motions become energized and integrated, while practical benefits follow, such as speed and facility.

After breaking the left hand into components—the palm, the knuckles, fingers, and thumb—we compare the balance and movement of each to motions of mechanical objects. Although these are inanimate objects, their shapes and their operations encourage proper positioning and balance, in turn supporting a more direct pathway to each finger's articulation. Once this foundation is established, we visualize the left hand as a ball settling down into the wrist, enabling the hand to establish and reestablish balance as it orbits the neck of the violin. Sometimes the hand shifts onto its lower outside corner, traveling the fingerboard length from that point of balance; other times, like a bead on a string, the hand rotates on an imaginary wire that is centered within the hand's tunnel, affecting E-to-G-string rotation.

Building the right arm structure gets underway with placement of the forearm on a fulcrum at its center of gravity, balanced longitudinally to enable the forearm to rotate within a larger context of the suspension of the whole arm. An awareness of the point of rotation, supported for instance by a rubber screw either from underneath or from the outer edge, enables the arm to rotate with ease and coordination either horizontally or vertically.

Comparisons between the right and left wrist identify a difference in the degree of firmness, and we explore a surprising similarity between the functioning of the two hands due in part to the independence of the thumb from the fingers. When dealing with the right forearm, we consider the influence of the upper arm, where the motions are both simpler and subservient to the progressively more complex motions toward the periphery. The bow arm is formatted into the shape of a suspension bridge, where a point on the elbow is the pinnacle from which the shoulder and hand suspend. The area from the balance point to the knuckles then becomes a slide through which gravity draws weight to the fingertips. During martelé or spiccato bowing or with string crossings, we imagine that sections of bone within the arm have the ability to separate and to rotate, or for one part to slide into another, all the while the flesh, like a rubber body suit, supports the return of each variation in motion to its original (centered) position. We change environments by visualizing that the arm is a Slinky that lengthens and shortens, and that the body of the violin is ghostlike, sometimes existing materially only as the neck and other times with the fingers playing to just a single string.

To conclude, I would emphasize that I did not start out to write a book in 2003, or even to theorize about violin technique, but rather to set out on a journey to explore the rocky road of my own deficiencies, strivings, and aspirations to better grow and create as a musician. It was only as I opened myself to the risky endeavor of unlearning and relearning that a metamorphosis occurred. Then in the winter of 2007, during a time when my mother was critically ill and I was particularly attuned to both the resiliency and fragility of life, against the backdrop of my many wonderful teachers and theirs, I became inspired to put to words and illustration the evolving concept of Progressive Form.

PART ONE

Left Arm

CHAPTER ONE

Left Arm Overview

Setting Up the Violin

Stand with your feet shoulder-width apart. Balance each foot as if it is on a tripod consisting of the big toe, the little toe, and the heel. Take a deep breath, let it all the way out, and wiggle your spine around to feel all parts of it. Then drop your tailbone and stack the vertebrae to the best of your ability, starting at the base of the spine, one upon another, until your head is balanced on top. To assist, visualize a one-pound weight hanging from your tailbone. Doing so grounds the spine the way that a weight tied to a string stabilizes a kite. Breathe easily and feel the way your weight can easily transfer back and forth from one leg to the other.

Rest the violin on top of your left collarbone and against your neck, with its long line (scroll to button) angled such that the end button is aimed toward the suprasternal notch in front of your neck. When the hand ascends a scale, the scroll swings slightly right to left, and during the hand's descent, it drifts back left to right. These motions are subtle and more noticeable when the shoulder moves freely, unencumbered by the shoulder rest. The idea is to keep your stance with the instrument stable but fluid. It is also helpful to consider whether the violin is in comfortable proximity when you present the bow arm, which means adjusting the rotational angle to avoid reaching across the body. Taken together, the positioning of the right arm and shoulder in conjunction with the bow and violin outlines the shape of a square. (Refer to chapter 19, "Hand and Arm Placement Relevant to the Violin.")

Position the violin so that it is level on its long axis. The instrument rotates somewhat around that axis, but be careful not to rotate too much on the perpendicular axis of the collarbone and lose altitude at the scroll. From time to time, lift the scroll end above the vertical, if necessary, to help secure a good connection to the instrument. Even though the violin rests on top of the left collarbone, it helps to imagine it centered and resting on both the right and left collarbones/clavicles. The process of imagining the weight of the instrument as evenly distributed frees up the left shoulder, which tends to tighten in an attempt to support the instrument from underneath.

Positioning of the Elbow

Good support from the left arm facilitates a suitable suspension of the left hand above the fingerboard, so after stabilizing the violin, the next step to building good playing form is to consider the height of the elbow. The arm is continually moving, so there is no fixed position for the elbow, but proper height is crucial to supporting both the instrument and the hand. To be aware of generating sufficient support, begin by initiating arm movement from a point several inches below the shoulder blade. Then direct the left arm by lifting it up and forward from a point behind the arm, approximately four inches below the shoulder socket, to a height that places the wrist at a location approximately level with your chin. To get the sense of maintaining a good height, place an imaginary vertical pole (or platform) underneath the elbow. Via the upper arm, the elbow's altitude becomes the foundation of the hand in playing position; the hand destabilizes during transport and then gets reinforced by the deliberate repositioning of the elbow. But always remember that the disposition of the elbow is a process, not a rigid placement.

Swinging Motion of the Left Elbow

After establishing arm position (its restrictions) to support the hand, we want to consider the nature of arm movement (its freedom) and how that serves the playing. Imagine tying a string to the inside bone of the elbow; pull it to the right and release. Effort is required to swing the arm underneath the instrument, partly because the direction is "uphill," but mostly because the arm is shifting and rotating against some built-in resistance. To minimize the arm's effort, always share the lateral rotation between the whole arm at the shoulder and the forearm at the wrist; the latter is known as supination (see fig. 1.1). Pronation is turning away of the palm with medial rotation.

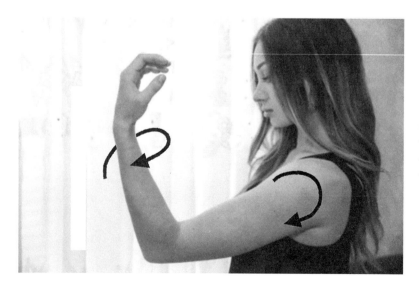

Figure 1.1 Lateral rotation of the shoulder and wrist. *Photo credit to Eva Foxon Nicholas.*

Transporting the Hand

Creating structures and providing a landscape or pathways that support the arm's elevation and the hand's smooth transit all take place in service to the hand's balance because they then confer stability and dexterity to the fingers. The motion of the elbow point is always curved, but to avoid losing elevation, when transporting the hand lengthwise along the fingerboard, think of it traveling closer to a level plane, corresponding to the path the hand travels (see fig. 1.2). Always maintain altitude.

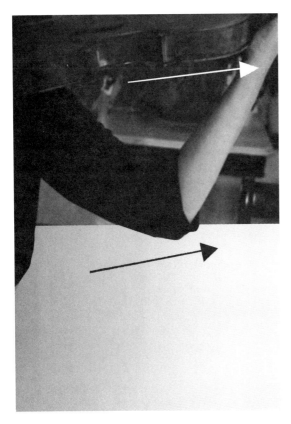

Figure 1.2 Imagining the elbow traveling in a level plane supports the hand's smooth migration along the length of fingerboard. *Photo credit to Gail Taibbi.*

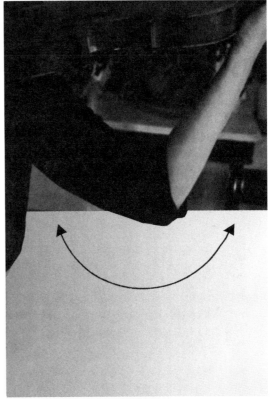

Figure 1.3 The elbow traces a more circular path to steer the hand across the fingerboard. *Photo credit to Gail Taibbi.*

Lateral motions across the fingerboard trace a more circular path and draw more support from the trunk and shoulder muscles (see fig. 1.3). To feed more energy to the hand or lend additional weight to the fingers, experiment with steering the elbow point along its circular path, adding energy, support, or a slight shift of direction.

Because juggling both the arm and the instrument is a delicate balancing act, and playing is therefore easily destabilized, try leaning the scroll on a dresser or shelf at a height that supports level placement of the instrument underneath your chin.

Steadying the instrument eliminates the need to control a major variable of motion, liberating the left arm and allowing you to experiment more effectively with it.

Visualize placing your bent elbow on a vertical pole at a height that supports a balanced hold of the violin. Attach a pull string midpole; then imagine someone off to the side pulling the pole with the elbow on top toward the midline of your body (see fig. 1.4). When the string is released, the arm swings away. The musculature of the arm itself is not the driving force, but it is responding to forces deeper in the body. Implementing motions by imagining an outside activating force—something that relieves your direct effort—has a relaxing effect and facilitates speed and agility. To experiment without using this image, feel the various tensions when you simply pull your elbow toward your body while focusing on speed in the left hand. Then rest your elbow on the pole and again visualize someone pulling the string to move your arm for you. You'll notice that the left hand feels freer and has more dexterity than when the motion is initiated by your effort.

Figure 1.4 Let a string pull the arm and elbow toward your body. *Photo credit to Gail Taibbi.*

Next, because of how far the hand extends and rotates away from the torso as it crosses or ascends the fingerboard, it helps to envision the arm navigating the contour of a sphere, actively carving a path with the elbow point that at first scoops slightly lower and away but then quickly moves higher up as the hand ascends the scale (see fig. 1.5).

Figure 1.5 The elbow's active engagement inside a sphere when ascending or descending the fingerboard. *Photo credit to Eva Foxon Nicholas.*

Even though it is closer by a straight-line measure, the farther the hand migrates across or up the fingerboard, the more remote it becomes on its curved path from its attachments to the torso. Think of that curved path and diminishing proportions as similar in design to a nautilus shell (see fig. 1.6). To keep the connection of the migrating hand closer to its source of strength and guidance as it ascends the scale, maintain an active extension of the elbow. Deliberately tracing this path of the sphere engages the torso muscles and helps prevent weak moments that would allow significant dips of the arm—interruptions of the hand's transit that create a ride on a road filled with potholes.

When moving up from first to higher positions as in a three-octave scale, the arm's ascent is gradual; coming down, the descent follows the reverse of that same path, but the arm remains coiled until the last moment, at which point it rapidly decompresses, quickly ushering the hand from fourth or third position into first, the elbow point once more projected underneath the scroll. On the ascent, the gradual

Figure 1.6 The shape of the hand's migration on the fingerboard mimics the growth spiral of the nautilus shell. *Photo credit to Eva Foxon Nicholas.*

coiling of the arm supports continual finger placements as the string becomes more challenging to reach. If the arm uncoils prematurely on the descent, the fingers may stray from the string, requiring the arm to tighten its compression once more to regain contact, interfering with a smooth, rhythmic transition.

When leaping from a high position to a low one—as in the first movement of the Bruch *Scottish Fantasy*, m.37, beat 1 (see ex. 1.1)—rather than transitioning more gradually (as in a scale passage), call to mind an image of someone using their fingers to lift the area between the elbow point and the triceps on the back of the arm upward and out, causing the hand to catapult in the direction of the scroll (see fig. 1.7).

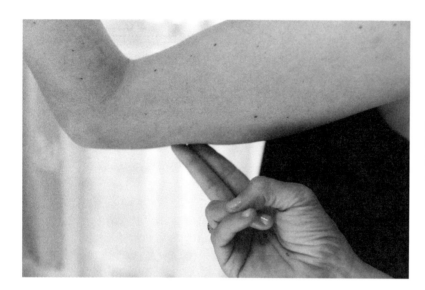

Figure 1.7 Lifting the area between the elbow point and the triceps. *Photo credit to Eva Foxon Nicholas.*

Example 1.1 First movement of the Bruch Scottish Fantasy, m.37, beat 1.

As the first impetus of motion during descending shifts, it is helpful to imagine tossing the ball of the shoulder above the violin and into the hand, as if the hand moving down the fingerboard is running to the outfield to make a catch. To lock the arm into a deep alignment and unification during the descending shift, the humerus (upper arm bone) then follows or tries to catch up with the forearm. When ascending, the forearm likewise energetically follows or chases after the humerus, each segment of the arm respectively engaging in this back-and-forth interplay.

This playfulness creates a healthy kinesthetic sense of motion of the arm, which is normally more gradual, as the involvement of the triceps in extending the arm and the countermeasures of the biceps continuously interweave. During the passage descent, mentally lengthening the violin's neck helps the hand maintain its natural shape by thwarting the tendency to scrunch the hand to avoid hitting the pegs.

The relationship of the forearm to the upper arm is one of continuous communication. Imagine that the left arm is a compass (drawing instrument) with the elbow representing its apex; the forearm-hand is the pencil, and the upper arm is the other "leg" of the compass with its metal point end at the shoulder (see fig. 1.8). Turn toward the wall on your left. Envision a rubber band fastened between the feet of the compass (to your wrist and shoulder) and plant those feet against the wall, pushing the apex at the left elbow toward the wall to widen the distance between the hand and shoulder. As the angle of the compass expands, the elastic band (representing the elasticity of the muscles and connective tissue) supports the interactive mobility of the hand and shoulder during the hand's change of position (besides its give, elastic has a restoring force that returns attached objects back to pre-stretch positions). In the first movement of the Mendelssohn Violin Concerto in E minor, from the pickup to m.37 to the downbeat of m.40 (see ex. 1.2), the left arm / compass contracts on beats 2 and 4 of the first two measures, expands to play beats 3 and 4 of the third measure, and then contracts to play the high G.

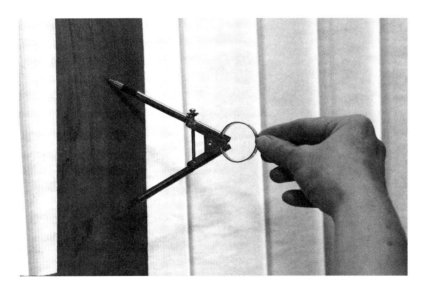

Figure 1.8 The left arm as compass with the elbow its apex, the hand its pencil point, and the shoulder its metal point. *Photo credit to Gail Taibbi.*

Example 1.2 First movement of the Mendelssohn Violin Concerto in E minor from the pickup to m.37.

Fundamental Motion of the Forearm

Place the violin in performance position. Then put the elbow on a stable platform in a location that allows the forearm to easily transport the hand from one point to another within a certain defined range along the fingerboard. Like most other arm movements, this simplified motion is still a combination of rotation at the shoulder and flexing at the elbow. It begins at the mid-forearm and causes the hand to fishtail, moving side to side in *a vertical plane,* the hand always seeking upright balance via adjustments in the wrist. This windshield wiper motion—with the forearm oscillating effortlessly back and forth while carrying the hand on a larger curve above the neck along a line between the scroll and bridge—applies generally to shifting. To enhance the image, imagine the inner forearm as a wiper blade moving against glass, brushing along a wet pane that extends from the scroll out to the shoulder of the violin.

Facilitation of the Hand in Passage Work

When the forearm is relatively vertical, the hand naturally establishes alignment, but when the forearm is more tilted, it is important to maintain a sense of continuity to the hand from underneath. If the hand loses that connection and fails to easily readjust itself to an upright position as necessary, the loss of their reciprocal relationship potentially impedes the ease with which the fingers articulate. While playing first position passages, if you visualize the upper arm extending beyond its actual length to a location underneath the scroll, it can more easily provide support to the forearm and lend stability to the hand.

Imagine balancing a vertical pole with a ball on top on the open palm of your left hand. Now capture that feeling in your arm in playing position, beginning with simple support through your elbow that allows the hand to float freely on top of your forearm (see fig. 1.9). The placement of the elbow point together with the angle of its joint determines the height and location of the forearm, with the hand's position and distribution of weight counterbalancing the angle of the forearm. The wrist cradles the hand. This image provides a dual awareness of the elbow and wrist, so as the angles change, the arm and hand is encouraged to stay very fluid, the hand continually adjusting its position vis-à-vis the elbow to stay vertical on top.

Depending on the situation, decide whether to maintain a more fixed elbow position or to release the arm, giving the upper arm and forearm the chance to choreograph their own sequences. The pole and ball image, with the upper arm extending and retreating, demonstrates the sense of freedom needed to steer the hand in meandering passages, whereas a stationary elbow–upper arm supports the forearm carrying the hand up and down the fingerboard as illustrated by the windshield wiper visualization. The left elbow remains more stationary during rapid ascending and descending scales and arpeggios, so the hand can rebound and return to its original position without effort.

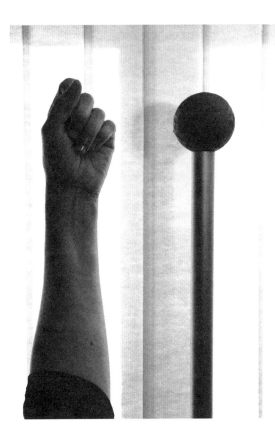

Figure 1.9 The elbow is the base of the pole; the hand, the ball. *Photo credit to Gail Taibbi.*

During rapid, ascending three-octave scales, imagine placing a vertical pole underneath the left elbow, where it would be at the midpoint of the scale/fingerboard, and maintaining that fixed position of the pole and elbow for the second half of the scale. To implement the wiper blade motion of the forearm, center the elbow so the ends of the arc delineate the full range of the scale. In the D-string passage at mm.35–36 in the Gnomus movement of Mussorgsky's *Pictures at an Exhibition* (see ex. 1.3), project the stationary elbow underneath the violin at the midpoint of the glissando so the hand has equal access to each end of the octave. The hand is balanced such that it can easily fall back or lean forward (waving motion). If the elbow-hand is poised in third position at the beginning of the glissando rather than midway through it, the hand can move easily only in a forward direction and will be less likely to encompass the full octave without some difficulty. When working in a smaller range of the fingerboard, the same procedure applies: position the elbow such that the hand's arc bridges the full range of the arpeggio, passage, or scale.

Example 1.3
Mussorgsky's *Pictures at an Exhibition* in B Major, Gnomus, mm.35–36.

Reducing Hand-Shoulder Tension

The greatest obstacle to effective violin playing is grasping the instrument. When the body gets too involved in supporting the instrument, that muscular effort constricts the playing apparatus, starting with the ability of the left arm to relax when and where necessary. Raising the height of an imaginary vertical pole underneath the left elbow relaxes the full arm from shoulder to hand while supporting the fingers' articulation from an above-the-fingerboard position. Now imagine that the pole supporting the elbow is a pogo stick: ease the elbow downward on the pogo stick; then on the pogo stick's rebound, quickly ascend and descend the scale. This effectively reduces left-arm tension while feeding continuity to the passage.

When fatigue sets in, there is a tendency to lower the left arm, and as a result, the large knuckles sink below the fingerboard and cause the fingers to reach, become misshapen, and bog down. Placing an imaginary ball under your left arm helps you maintain separation between the torso and upper arm and supports a relatively stationary elbow while sustaining its height and location. The size of the ball varies depending on the position played.

To alleviate overall tension, visualize a giant ball encasing the suspended instrument. Then drape your body around and on top of the ball, as if in a hug. The ball supports the weight and roundedness of good form while reducing distress in the torso, the jaw, the neck, the shoulders, the arms, and the hands.

When sitting, picture hugging a large exercise-sized ball that is on your lap, with your face and body again leaning into the ball. The ball image is more effective in combating tension than by focusing on the jaw, the neck, the torso, or any other part individually (see fig. 1.10).

To create a sensation of expansion of the spine, which in turn transfers a feeling of relaxation, increased strength, and mechanical advantage to the upper and lower extremities, affix a string to the crown of the head and suspend the body from the string while imagining a one-pound weight tied to a string dangling from the tailbone.

Figure 1.10 Sitting and relaxing with the ball, decompressing into a better sense of form. *Photo credit to Eva Foxon Nicholas.*

Figure 1.11 An elastic band that wraps and supports the rib cage encourages diaphragmatic breathing. *Photo credit to Eva Foxon Nicholas.*

Now envision an elastic band that wraps and supports the rib cage, encouraging diaphragmatic breathing. This wrapping sensation also supports and strengthens the core, which in turn generates greater facility and strength in the arms (see fig. 1.11).

We all have events in our lives that strongly influence who we are today. If they are traumatic and unresolved, these experiences tend to predispose us to certain physical postures and somewhat predictable emotional responses (for example, if we experience feelings of being ill at ease as an adolescent and integrate that relatively permanently into our bodies, expressed in our connective tissue and muscle memory). If we're lucky, we begin at some point to contend with the disparity between our chronic, contracted posture and our ideal form that enables a healthy reciprocity with the instrument. Exercises such as draping your body around and on top of the ball, as if in a hug, help us to begin to become aware of our acquired character and can start to neutralize bodily distortions. Making a project of dealing with our fundamental makeup with the assistance of teachers of disciplines such as yoga and tai chi and practitioners of body-oriented modalities is a necessity for most of us. As unwanted tension is dispersed and neuromuscular organization becomes more elegant, the mind begins to release its self-limiting thoughts and defensive responses, making room for a degree of clarity and the sense of possibility necessary to properly integrate the violin with the body and maintain a free-flowing energy in the playing.

CHAPTER TWO

Left Arm Subdivisions

Balance of the Forearm

Now that the arm's support of the hand via the elbow is established, transfer your awareness to the forearm. Fourth position is the comfort zone on the violin because the forearm is most vertical, and the hand is easily balanced on top. If the forearm is tilted too much to play in first position, the hand has to overflex to find its verticality and bring the fingers in closer to the fingerboard. But that break in the wrist weakens the good connection between the arm and hand, reduces its range of motion, promotes holding the neck with the palm, and compromises the facility and independence of the fingers. Just as it is easier to balance a ball on an upright pole, the comfort experienced in the higher positions on the fingerboard comes from the easy balance of the hand on the conveniently vertical forearm. Care should be taken to maintain as much of an upright forearm position as is comfortable in the lower positions.

Conversely, a substantial break in the wrist with the hand extending too far back detracts weight from the fingers, shifting it into the palm, where it weighs down the hand. The ultimate goal in positioning the arm and the hand is to encourage weight to migrate to the fingers so they can drop with ease onto the string. A slightly flexed wrist supports this migration, especially during rapid passages in lower positions.

In the first movement of the Mozart Violin Concerto No. 4 in D Major, 32 measures after the solo entrance (see ex. 2.1), unless you extend the elbow in support of a more vertical forearm, the hand has to overreach, breaking at the wrist such that the fingers are left on their own without support to reach around to first position on the G. When the hand is in any extreme angle to the forearm, it risks becoming ineffectual due to a lack of mobility in one direction or another, with this loss of range of motion restricting the ability to balance and rebalance on the moving forearm. This is especially noticeable either when trying to cross strings, as in the previous passage, or when vibrating, where too little finger-play in one direction and an overabundance of motion in the other creates a warped vibratory oscillation. To demonstrate this unequivocally, imagine holding a weighted ball in your extended (bent back) hand, subsequently dropping the ball, but retaining the tensions of that position while you consider articulating with the string (see fig. 2.1).

Left Arm Subdivisions

Example 2.1 First movement of the Mozart Violin Concerto in D, 32 measures after the solo entrance.

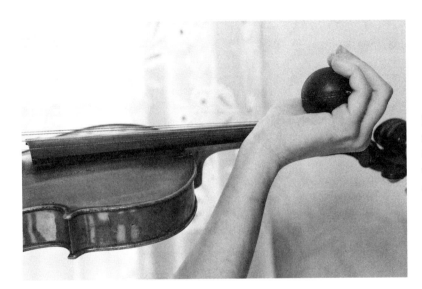

Figure 2.1 Improper transference of weight with an unhealthy break in the wrist. *Photo credit to Eva Foxon Nicholas.*

Now let the weight of that ball roll forward out of the hand and down the arm, with the fingers suspended from a hand supported at the wrist from the elbow (see fig. 2.2). This promotes a more vertical alignment, but more importantly, it relocates the primary foundation of support for the hand to a position underneath, in that way freeing the fingers to better express themselves.

Figure 2.2 Now let the weight of that ball restore a balanced hand position as it rolls down the arm. *Photo credit to Eva Foxon Nicholas.*

Forearm Rotation—The Radius and the Ulna

The interactive relationship of the two parallel bones of the forearm, the radius and the ulna, is one of the body's most complex and intriguing mechanical designs, and an awareness of its functionality is helpful to ensure good application of the left arm and hand. (See appendix A.) Thanks to the radius, the forearm has the ability to rotate the hand on the long axis of the forearm, movement variations important to carrying the fingers to their destinations. From a fixed point near the elbow, the radius rotates next to the relatively stationary ulna, completing a half circle around it at the wrist and affecting the relationships among the hand, forearm, and elbow (see appendix diagram A.1).

There is an unfortunate tendency to rotate the forearm on the longitudinal midline, involving the fourth finger side of the arm (the ulna) in that rotation. Because it is a hinge joint, the ulna does not want to rotate like an axle, and to do so puts strain on its joint's surrounding ligaments, creating tension at the joint and throughout the arm and hand. Just as an actual hinge resists movements that angle off from its functional midplane, to use a human hinge joint outside of its job description increases the risk of injury. (See appendix B.)

Besides damaging the elbow, twisting the forearm in an unnatural way leads to distortion around the shoulder, a disadvantageous forearm angle, and too much effort throughout the hand and arm. Distribute rotation evenly between the upper (full) arm at the shoulder and the forearm at the wrist (see fig. 1.1) to avoid overtaxing the major joints while optimizing wrist and finger placement. During prolonged periods of same position passages, there is a negative tendency to relax or release rotation of the left arm, which in turn causes the fourth finger to fly away from the neck. Stay aware of both the twofold rotation of the arm and sources of support for the arm in the torso to avoid having to struggle and strain to maintain good left-arm position.

To incorporate this understanding, try using the radius to lead or to steer the hand around the instrument. It is an effective way to retrain the arm to move in a relaxed suspension and specifically to learn to initiate forearm rotation from the base of the thumb.

Now that the hand is presented to the violin with relaxed and integrated support from the torso and arm, think of the radius and ulna bones as a pair of columns that balance the lower outside corners of the hand. These bones support an even distribution of hand weight that sustains the hand's one-four finger balance for an octave. The radius and ulna effectively support the hand in many positions. The caution is to avoid rocking the hand too far one way or the other when firing the fingers; keep the hand well centered to retain a sensation of the outer corners balancing equally on the wrist and the relatively vertically positioned forearm. Extend that balance out to the first and fourth fingers on the string to provide the moving fingers equally easy access to their articulations. Sustain weight in the fourth-finger part of the hand to maintain the balance and prevent the hand from wobbling.

It is common for the hand to spin away from the neck after each fourth-finger articulation, making it necessary for that fourth finger to find its way back to the string. It is typical to compensate by overrotating within the hand on the pinky side and freezing the hand in that position, locking that corner of the wrist. To avoid this, return to the fundamentals: initiate support from your back and then set up the hand with a balanced rotation in the arm. This allows the fourth-finger portion of the hand to stay relaxed yet in position, without the tendency to fly away from the neck.

Alternatively, you can also work to energetically secure the hand's position via the thumb, which acts as an extension of the radius. Imagine that the thumb is longer than it actually is and tuck it in between the second and third fingers (or in between whichever two fingers feel most comfortable for you). It acts as a barrier or wedge that minimizes rotational slippage and prevents collapse of the tunnel formed by the first finger and opposing thumb, both of which result in the fourth finger falling away from the fingerboard.

Left Upper Arm

Because careful positioning of the elbow helps to stabilize the forearm and hand, it is useful to back up and consider how the upper arm, which determines the position of the elbow, extends and retracts, elevates and drops, and rotates clockwise and counter, all in subservience to the forearm's placement of the hand.

Presentation and Directing Points

As first described in chapter 1, initiate the elevation of the left arm from the presentation point (see fig. 2.3), engaging trunk muscles to support the lifting—and

Figure 2.3 Initiating the elevation of the left arm from the presentation point. *Photo credit to Eva Foxon Nicholas.*

Left Arm

other fundamental movements—of the arm. The more efficiently—and initially, consciously—the trunk muscles are used to initiate and support arm movement, the more relaxed can be the more peripheral muscles that are designed for fine motor control. Direct the left arm by continuing the lift from a *directing point* underneath the upper arm, several inches from the shoulder socket (see fig. 2.4). The arm elevates the hand, eventually freeing it from the responsibility of holding by tilting the bulk of the instrument's weight into your neck/body.

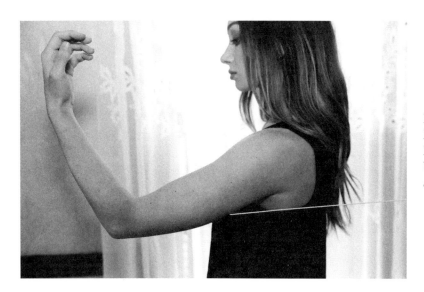

Figure 2.4 Direct the left arm by continuing the lift from a directing point behind the upper arm. *Photo credit to Eva Foxon Nicholas.*

If the impetus of arm placement comes primarily from the muscles of the forearm, especially when extending the arm toward the scroll (as when descending a scale) or when rotating the whole arm (swinging of the elbow), unwanted burden is placed on these smaller muscles designed for finer movement, and an overall constriction, likely with a feeling of weakness and disintegration, occurs. Deliberately engaging trunk muscles in arm movements, such as the latissimus dorsi (the lats) that wrap from the back around the sides (see appendix C) and the serratus anterior muscles that rotate the shoulder blades forward, will secure a feeling of strength and integration with the total limb. (See appendix D.) As a demonstration, consider lobbing a ball using only the arm itself without drawing on backup support from your trunk; there is no real power behind the throw. Similarly, if you extend the left hand into first position without maintaining the support of your torso, it is likely to lose altitude and surrender the strength and balance needed to support its fine motor movements. Involving the trunk muscles gives a feeling of cohesion among all segments of the arm and hand.

Using the directing point engages the lats and the anterior serratus to liberate the forearm while setting up and monitoring the height of the hand. Besides undermining support for the violin, too low a hand suspension (from the wrist) disorients the fingers the way body movements are affected when riding on a swing too close to the ground. When the wrist is set too high to the fingerboard, the fingers compensate by overextending. The properly supported hand eliminates strain from the fingers by providing them easy access to the fingerboard with enough height to rebound.

In slower passages or while vibrating, slightly lowering the arm allows the fingers to sink more deeply into the fingerboard. Like an airplane's cozy landing on the ground with heavy cargo, lowering or relaxing the weight in the left arm also heightens the tactile contact of the fingers to the string.

Upper-Arm-to-Hand Balance

Maintain an interactive awareness between the hand and the upper arm when shifting positions, especially from third to fourth. Without it, there is often a scramble to seek (reestablish) balance each time the hand arrives in a new location. Lift the arm from the directing point to a comfortable height for the fingers. Then feel a direct connection between a stable upper arm and the left hand strongly perched on the wrist. Establish a biceps and triceps balance of tension, and then flex your elbow, bringing the forearm toward your body. The biceps muscle contracts to close the arm angle, and the triceps contracts to open the angle.

To get a better feel for this balance, call to mind an image of holding a ball in your left palm (face up) while imagining that the left biceps muscle of your upper arm is a ball (see fig. 2.5). Sense a direct correlation of balance between the biceps-ball and the hand-ball while negotiating ascending and descending passages. In lower positions (first through third), simply keep an awareness of the weight and position of both the upper arm muscle–ball and the ball in the faceup palm. During the third-to-fourth-position changeover, maintain the awareness while lifting the ball in the hand from underneath to on top of the instrument; the motion is like waving to yourself.

Figure 2.5 Imagine holding a ball in your left palm while transforming the left biceps muscle into a ball. *Photo credit to Eva Foxon Nicholas.*

In higher positions (fourth position and higher), center your biceps underneath the midback of the violin, with the hand's ball secured in the facedown palm. To add fluidity to the motion during the third-to-fourth-position changeover, imagine that the hand flips palm side down as if doing a belly flop in a body of water from a level high enough over the fingerboard.

Taking the first cadenza in the Paganini Caprice No. 5 in A minor as an example (see ex. 2.2), while sinking into the initial A, picture both the biceps as a perched ball and an imaginary ball in your hand. The hand is leaning slightly back, but then you quickly shift into fourth position on the next A and avoid the shoulder/wall of the violin by grasping and securing the ball before flipping over and on top of the violin. The bottom of the hand catapults the entire hand including the base of the thumb. Maintain the ball shape of the hand to avoid, for example, the breakdown of the finger-to-thumb relationship, where the foundation of the thumb gets left behind, energetically speaking. Imagine a force field emanating from within the hand that preserves its organization, preventing any collapse or lean or distortion during transit. If the rounding of the hand collapses, various balances of strength and awareness in the hand are disrupted.

Example 2.2 First cadenza sequence in the Paganini Caprice No. 5.

When crossing the fingerboard, envision draping the fingers over the somewhat cylindrical thumb, with the fingers gently drawing the thumb toward themselves and into the palm, and then allow it to release as the fingers relax. Getting comfortable with this motion increases the facility of the hand by providing easier access to both the E and the G string. Also, because the thumb tends to go rogue when the fingers spread out while navigating (crossing or ascending) the fingerboard, this drawing back into the fold helps keep the overall integrity of the hand.

Left Shoulder

The arm determines its position in the shoulder socket. The shoulder contributes by not getting involved.

Support through Passivity

When you present your left arm, even though the arm is integrated into the shoulder, the shoulder is not active but rather is minimally reactive to what happens in the rest of the arm. In other words, the shoulder responds as needed by adjusting to the arm's positioning of the hand, which ultimately supports the fingers. As the hand ascends the fingerboard, the arm needs to rotate freely in the joint, avoiding the kinds of contractions designed for other efforts.

When presenting the left or right arms, it is tempting to tense up and raise either one or both shoulders. To support overall posture and relaxation of the body, imagine attaching two eye screws with a connecting string that is suspended from the heavens, one to the top of your left shoulder and the other to the right shoulder; then suspend and relax both shoulders as if hanging midair from a parachute (see fig. 2.6). Let your shoulders spread out in this relaxed suspension. This image creates the best balance of strength and relaxation, poising the shoulders to support the most efficient use of the arms. Ultimately, as they lighten up and extricate themselves from the torso, the shoulders should spread out from each other and seat themselves with their own weight, each becoming a foundation and a fulcrum for arm movement.

Think of the shoulders as a seesaw and weight as a ball that migrates, rolling downhill, either toward the right shoulder or the left depending on the musical requirements. For instance, when you want to achieve lightness in left-hand passages in conjunction with an active bow, allow the ball to migrate downhill toward the right shoulder; when you want a supple vibrato in the context of less volume, allow the ball to roll downhill toward the left shoulder; and when you want intensity in both the left-hand and bow applications, as in the opening of the Brahms Violin Concerto in D (see ex. 2.3), amplify the weight on both ends.

Figure 2.6 Suspend each shoulder from a string attached above. *Photo credit to Eva Foxon Nicholas.*

Left Arm

Example 2.3 Solo entrance of the first movement of the Brahms Violin Concerto in D.

Imagine transferring weight down and around the loop of the left arm toward the fingertips the way a cart travels on a roller-coaster track. The flow of that weight is interrupted if you lift the shoulder while extending the arm and presenting the hand. Also, leaning any part of the hand against the neck or body of the instrument impedes this desirable transfer of weight. With a continuity of weight flowing to the fingers, all kinds of finger movements, hand mobilities, and shifts are fostered without disrupting the intimate contact of the fingers with the string.

CHAPTER THREE

Total Left Arm

The primary function of the left arm is to set up the hand such that the fingers articulate with the string with ease. Coordinating the forearm and upper arm to support effective hand suspension is fundamental to achieving that goal.

Forearm and Upper Arm Mutuality

The positions of the forearm and upper arm individually hold many possibilities of movement in playing, but effective hand balance is achieved only through an awareness of their collaborative interaction. To form a good alliance of the forearm with the upper arm, conceive of two imaginary bones in the upper arm aligned with the two forearm bones. Be sure to continue the alignment past the wrist into the lateral edges of the hand and fingers (see fig. 3.1).

Because the wrist and hand follow the position of the ends of the radius and ulna, as much as possible, keep a sense of the radius and ulna bones of both arms in a larger frame of parallel lines of force and support and sensitivity that are relatively continuous with the upper arm in one direction and the hand in the other (see appendix E). When poised, the upper arm acts as a platform of foundational support for the forearm (and hand).

Place the violin underneath your chin and set up the left hand to play. Extend your upper arm as if to position the hand to play in first position. In your imagination, flex the forearm toward the upper arm until the violin is pressed in between. During ascending and descending passages, this feeling of the arm's unity creates a stable platform for the hand while better supporting the instrument, as a result averting the danger of the hand getting involved with holding onto the neck. Staying with this image, try stabilizing the position of the upper arm via the presentation point, and then allow the weight of the forearm to completely relax as it drapes over the upper arm. The resting forearm helps to isolate the weight of the hand, enhancing its potency and mobility via unencumbered muscularity. When situating the fourth finger above the string after a change of positions, especially in higher positions on the G string, flex the forearm while coaxing the upper arm to the right with a slight lateral rotation.

Left Arm

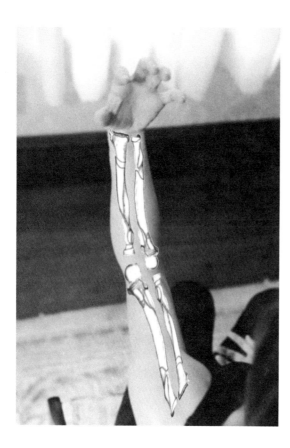

Figure 3.1 Conceive of two imaginary bones in the upper arm aligned with the two forearm bones. *Photo credit to Eva Foxon Nicholas.*

During the expansion and contraction of the left arm, there is a tendency to lose the continuity of the arm from the shoulder to the hand, primarily because the lateral rotation necessary for hand placement requires some effort for most players and is therefore easily lost. Without an active engagement from the shoulder extending through the elbow and into the wrist, both the hand's position and its integrity are likely compromised: the fingers walk as though they have joint dysplasia, and the third and fourth fingers are apt to have difficulty reaching the string. Beware of compensating by laterally twisting the elbow, a hinge joint that is not meant to be rotated on the longitudinal axis or deviated sideways.

To counter that tendency, imagine a ball that can expand and contract while cradled in your arm (see fig. 3.2). Even as the arm extends and contracts in conjunction with the size of the ball, the frames of the upper arm and forearm through all three joints should keep communicating and never fall far out of alignment with each other. To maximize the upper arm's extension, picture placing the triceps—the underside of the laterally rotated upper arm—on a table.

Imagine that the bone in the upper arm is bendable; then in higher positions that are less comfortable to access, energetically curve the upper third of the upper arm—the segment from the shoulder point to where the biceps begins to bulge. Doing so assists the transfer of weight to the rest of the arm while supporting a balanced suspension of the hand above the instrument (see fig. 3.3).

Figure 3.2 A medium-sized ball cradled in your left arm. *Photo credit to Gail Taibbi.*

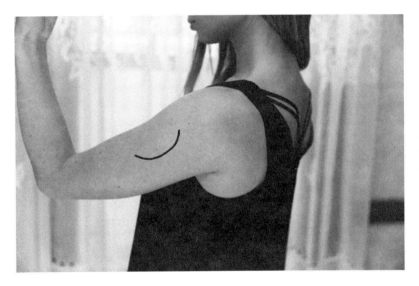

Figure 3.3 Energetically curve the upper third of the upper arm. *Photo credit to Eva Foxon Nicholas.*

This time, imagine wrapping the upper arm around a bicycle wheel frame that encircles the violin diagonally (see fig. 3.4); the elbow easily extends and elevates with the rounded shape of the overall arm. The circular frame encourages a healthy alignment of the forearm to the upper arm and supports an easy balancing of the first and the fourth finger on the fingerboard, which feels similar to an even application of weight to the first and fourth fingers on two piano keys.

Extend the upper arm and then flex in this order: the elbow, the wrist, and the large, middle, and small knuckles of the fingers. Consciously building finer contractions on top of more fundamental ones becomes a counterpoint to the simultaneous extension of the arm, the combination constituting an overall hand and arm readiness. In other words, zeroing in on the compressing (contracting) inner loop of the hand and arm while generating extension of the whole arm creates an overall

Figure 3.4 A vertical bicycle wheel frame that encircles the violin diagonally in alignment with the arm. *Photo credit to Eva Foxon Nicholas.*

dynamic tension that supports potent violin playing (see appendix F). This rounded feeling of muscular continuity reduces stress on the joints, whereas an uneven use of tension creates a more angular, often inflexible motion resulting in wear and tear on the joints and a stifled sound.

During the arm's presentation, you should always initially feel an overall lateral expansion of the hand and arm, an outward extension from the vertical midline of the body (akin to the expanded neck of a cobra). Feel the arm growing out of the shoulder, ultimately to fully embrace the instrument (including the scroll) and to provide the hand, the furthest extension of that circular expansion, with wide access to the fingerboard for maximal facility and minimal need for adaptation. When the hand and arm are conceived and set up as circular, the poised and responsive hand falls back easily but is ready to immediately rebound forward, whereas if the visual conception of the arm is V-shaped, when the hand extends back, it likely requires more conscious effort to bring it forward.

Starting with the hand in first position on the E string, picture the left arm rotating internally as the hand ascends a scale passage. Imagine a zipper assisting the forearm (ulna, pinkie side) and upper arm (humerus) in their flexing motion, with that support energizing and strengthening the fourth finger (see fig. 3.5).

Regardless of the alignment of the forearm and upper arm with each other, unless the arm and hand are well configured relative to the position of the string, the hand will still suffer limited mobility. Increasing the lateral rotation of both the forearm and upper arm as you approach passages on the G string establishes the position of the fourth finger above the string. Decreasing the rotation by degrees establishes the hand's alignment with the D, A, or E string.

Given that all four strings, but especially the G and E, are slightly fanned rather than parallel to one another, precise rotation of the arm is critical for positioning the wrist parallel to each string played. For example, with descending E-to-G-string passages, the mid-forearm aims for a destination that is challenging not only for its distance but also for the exaggerated angle of the G string. The move benefits by

Figure 3.5 On the ascent, the anterior of the arm feels as if it is being zippered up. *Photo credit to Gail Taibbi.*

imagining that the neck and other three strings (E, A, and D) are nonexistent. When playing in higher positions on the E string, even though the string is fanned outward toward the fourth finger, because the body of the instrument imposes distances between the hand and the strings, it is necessary to compensate by extending the arm and rotating it as if playing on a lower string.

Strength versus Tension

Adding strength to the left hand without adding tension is a perpetual challenge. One strategy is to secure a strong formation of the arm and hand. Envision pressing a ball in your hand against the fingerboard. Then imagine bending the forearm at its longitudinal midpoint (akin to a backhoe's arm) and using this leverage and angle to grasp the ball until it is drawn through the center of the palm and into the forearm. The resistance from the ball dissipates tension in the fingers but leaves the hand with a feeling of great strength. The implied bending or folding of the backhoe-like forearm enables exerting pressure without constricting the shoulder, elbow, wrist, and fingers by creating the illusion that the mid-forearm is poised above the hand. Like the backhoe, the forearm now bends (energetically), and in so doing allows the fingers (like the bucket part of the backhoe) to dig into the fingerboard, and it drags them into the hand (see fig. 3.6). The backhoe image supports the equalization of healthy tensions throughout the shoulder, elbow, wrist, and knuckle joints. Exaggerated or

Figure 3.6 The forearm bends like a backhoe and the fingers drag the fingertips into the hand. *Photo credit to Gail Taibbi.*

chronic flexing of the muscles of the arm can create unwanted pressures in the joints. The backhoe image serves to liberate the hand, releasing it from unwanted influences of the arm, which in turn frees up the finger and thumb interactions.

Balance and Suspension of the Violin

Setting Up without Tension

When holding the violin between the chin and the left shoulder, if equipment isn't dovetailed to the shoulder space below the instrument and to the height of the chin above, excessive tension tends to gather in the neck and shoulder areas. An ill-fitted shoulder rest can cause the chin to contract, and misaligned height and shape of the chinrest similarly provokes shoulder constriction. Permanently removing the chinrest puts flesh against wood that hinders the instrument's vibration more than cork or wood against wood, but imagining or simulating playing without both chin and shoulder rests awakens the top of the shoulder and areas underneath the chin and invites the involvement of both in the full mechanics of violin playing. Let the freedom of mobility be a priority that guides decisions about the height of the equipment and staging used. Be comfortable playing without the shoulder rest before thinking about removing the chinrest.

During descending shifts (as in fifth position to first), especially when playing without a shoulder rest, there is a moment when the violin feels as if it is going to slip. At this point, it is common to secure the instrument by compressing the chin and the shoulder and clutching the neck with the hand, but that instinctual response restricts the mobility of the fingers. More desirably, if you are able to trust that the violin will not fall, try securing the instrument first at the near end by slightly pressing the chin against the chin rest and tucking it into the collarbone. Then at the scroll end, think of the contact of the thumb more as a fulcrum for the hand, with its itinerant light touch supporting the remainder of the instrument's weight, some of which disappears with deliberate pressure into the neck. The fingers are then liberated to shift and fire freely.

To prevent that precarious feeling, again call to mind an image of someone using their fingers to lift the area between the elbow point and the triceps (the back of the arm) up and forward, causing the hand to catapult scroll direction. The upward motion of the lift counters the violin's tendency to drop during descending shifts by sending weight toward your neck, minimizing the need to involve the chin or support from the hand as a result.

The collarbone provides support without restricting the natural rotation of the shoulder with the instrument. The role of the shoulder rest needs to be minimal and unrestrictive. With or without a shoulder rest, the violin is supported on a solid platform only from one end, which puts the burden on the scroll end to counteract the combined forces of the left-hand fingers and the bow, both pressing down. To get a feeling of shoring up the middle of the instrument without overworking at both ends, contemplate that the midback of the violin balances on the top of a giant ball; the ball supports the violin while providing a buoyant response to the bow, its shape allowing the instrument to rock equally in all directions. The arms move through the ball, as if its sides are ghostlike.

When the hand becomes too involved in holding the neck, tension creeps in and the fingers become distorted, compromising their mobility and speed. If the scroll begins to lose altitude, instead of grabbing it with your hand, picture water rising underneath, in that way leveling the platform of the instrument without a rescue from the hand.

Again, picture being submerged in water up to your chin; now imagine that your two arms form an opening around the instrument that is similar to a tunnel: the violin floats inside, bumping into the sides of your arms (akin to a log floating inside a big drainage pipe), with the arms ignoring the violin's imposition. Likewise, picture the neck of the violin floating inside the tunnel of the postured hand. Or try enclosing the body of the violin inside a horizontally positioned cylinder (see fig. 3.7). The violin's encasement allows the arm to coast on a smooth, curved surface while preventing the hand from collapsing onto the instrument.

Figure 3.7 The body of the violin inside a horizontally positioned cylinder. *Photo credit to Eva Foxon Nicholas.*

Imagine that your left arm from the shoulder to the hand has the capacity to expand, contract, and wrap around the cylinder like a Slinky, with equal distribution, engaging the instrument from all points (see fig. 3.8). Hand destination determines the degree of arm expansion and contraction.

A snake coils around a branch while poising its head, and the underside of its body maintains contact with the branch. To generate an overall experience of bal-

Figure 3.8 Your left arm is like a Slinky. *Photo credit to Gail Taibbi.*

ance, flexibility, and sensitivity in the left arm and hand, imagine that the arm is the body of a snake and the hand is the head. Again, envision encasing the violin inside a cylinder. Then coil the arm around the cylinder like the snake around the branch from the biceps of the upper arm to the palm of the hand, appreciating this continuous touch with the anterior aspects of the limb. If, instead of combining them into one spiral motion, you isolate the lifting and lowering of the violin from the extending out and contracting back motions of the arm, then the arm unwittingly participates in holding the instrument and tension results. Ideally, if you imagine embracing a cylindrically shaped, supple body of matter, this enhanced image with softened edges lends a complex elegance to the movements, further supporting its balance.

This time, encase the violin inside a ball and navigate the instrument by way of the outer surface. The spherical barrier prevents the arm from collapsing in and around the instrument. The surface of the ball also helps bypass the crook of the neck, a place where the hand often gets trapped when ascending a three-octave scale.

Positioning the Violin

There is a common predicament when setting yourself up to play: each time you pick up the violin, the alignment of the body relative to the instrument can feel different. Consistent placement of the instrument supports consistency of form, but sometimes the hand falls comfortably into position, and other times it feels incongruous. One common variable to assess is the distance from your neck to the violin, which affects the distance the left arm has to extend. If there is an extra inch of space between the violin and your neck, the arm has to extend farther to accommodate the fingers, consequently changing the relational feel of the instrument.

To establish a consistent and reliable proximity of the instrument to your body, picture that your cervical spine (the neck portion of your spine) is a vertical pole about three inches in diameter. Visualize the soft tissue of your neck as ghostlike, and imagine that the violin can slide between your head and shoulders and lean directly against the spine/pole. Then picture the scroll swinging right to left in a slow, pendulumlike motion when the hand ascends a scale and left to right during the hand's descent.

A Malleable Violin

Creative visualization can affect real results. For instance, imagining that the instrument has extraordinary capabilities can assist in navigating the fingerboard. Imagine attaching a motor to the scroll end of the violin as you would to a raft and driving into the barrier of the neck (attempting to move through it) to support the descending shifts; back up or reverse direction to support the fingers as they ascend. Steering the violin in a horizontal plane provides a stable platform for the fingers to travel while supporting the direction that the fingers are migrating.

Imagine that the fingerboard is a rubber mat that moves forward and backward on rollers, scroll to bridge, the way a moving walkway assists foot travel at the airport. The direction of motion adds to the fingers' momentum in that direction. For same-finger shifts from one position to another, imagine that the strings travel scroll to bridge and back like cables on pulley tracks, aiding the forward or reverse direction of the fingers.

On same-string scale ascensions, imagine that the base of your hand is the wheel of a pulley, rolling on a track. As the bottom of the hand travels toward the bridge or toward the scroll, the string assists by moving in the other direction, like a rope on an actual pulley (see fig. 3.9).

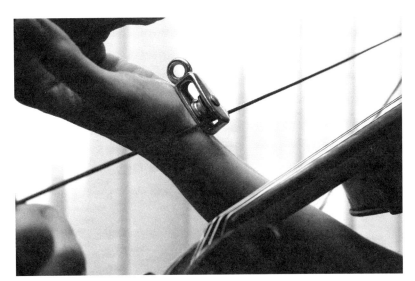

Figure 3.9 The base of your hand is the wheel part of a pulley. *Photo credit to Gail Taibbi.*

CHAPTER FOUR

Left Wrist

Many picture the wrist as a stationary part of the anatomy, but the wrist holds a world of secret motions. I say *secret* because its movements are seen mostly indirectly, visible largely in the hand's world of rotational possibilities. These motions allow us to maintain a consistent hand position throughout a long bow stroke or to pursue left-hand string crossings that set up the fingertips to easily seek out notes.

There is little written about the role the wrist plays in the hand's migration along the fingerboard. Movement in the wrist supports the exact placement of the fingers on the fingerboard, making all passages approachable. The fundamental motions of the left hand on the wrist are these rotations: forward to back (flexion to extension), side to side (abduction and adduction), and clockwise to counterclockwise (supination to pronation).

Traveling the Fingerboard

The wrist mediates balances and relays impulses between the arm and hand. Imagine that the base of the hand is a snow coaster and that the wrist area below dovetails with it. With this image, consider that the forearm portion of the wrist is concave (a concave cap on the end of the forearm), comfortably supporting the convex shape of the other part of the wrist that we think of as the bottom of the hand (see fig. 4.1).

Picture the bottom of the hand-coaster traversing the fingerboard, with the shifting body weight of the fingers riding inside. The coaster or base of the hand leads the way from the E string to the G, navigating the change of landscape and providing a foundation for the fingers to easily balance. Think of the base of the hand as leading the fingers the way a person leads with their feet while waterskiing. Just as a water-skier leads with the heels to avoid tumbling, leading with the top of the wrist (bottom of hand) prevents the fingers and hand from toppling forward prematurely.

Figure 4.1 Imagine that the base of the hand is a snow coaster or saucer. *Photo credit to Eva Foxon Nicholas.*

Wrist Motion in Position

The two lines of wrist bones (carpals) together enable the hand to rotate easily side to side in the plane of the palm—toward the thumb (abduction) or toward the fourth finger (adduction). This is a fundamental motion with which to become familiar in shifting, but it is equally important when staying in position. When the fingers are firing away in position, the side-to-side rocking motion of the hand on the wrist lends speed and snap to the drop and release of the fingers. Visualize the bottom of your hand as the bottom of a rocking chair, rocking lengthwise on top of the fingerboard (see fig. 4.2). Feel the fingertips flowing side to side in conjunction with the initiation of that motion in the wrist.

Figure 4.2 Visualize the bottom of your hand as the bottom of a rocking chair, rocking on the fingerboard. *Photo credit to Eva Foxon Nicholas.*

Imagining articulating in order fingers one, two, three, four, three, two, one in the same position gives a feel for the rocking chair. In the third movement of the Tchaikovsky Symphony No. 6 in B minor, from the pickup to 14 measures before the end (see ex. 4.1), the pattern of four, three, two, one, four (on the A string), one, two, three, four, three, et cetera benefits from the shift of weight initiated and continued inside the bottom of the hand as suggested by the rocker image. Specifically, in the descending four-note pickup, the hand rotates sideways from bridge to scroll; on the downbeat, the hand snaps toward the bridge for the G-natural (on the A string), and then toward the scroll to play the second note. For notes B-natural, C-natural, and D-natural (on the E string), the hand rocks sideways toward the bridge, and then back again for the descending sixteenth notes on beat two (toward the scroll). Feel the correlation between the notation on the staff (musical graph) and the rocking motion of the hand on the string. Just as the note pattern is repetitive, the side-to-side motion of the bottom of the hand also expresses and can be experienced in that same rhythmic pattern. To intensify the motion, turn the rocker blade upside down, this time rocking the bottom of the hand along the now-convex arc.

Example 4.1 Third movement of Tchaikovsky's Symphony No. 6 in B minor, the pickup to 14 measures before the end.

This time, try isolating the rocking motion of the hand to the area of the large knuckles with minimal follow-through motion at the wrist. The miniaturized motion allows the fingers to better navigate rapid passages, whereas visualizing the bottom of your hand as the bottom of a rocking chair serves a grander, more sweeping gesture. When playing nonsequential passages, it is better to avoid the rocking motion as there is not enough time between notes to reestablish balance.

Side Roads and the Four Strings

New roads are built in open land areas to provide pathways to otherwise unsettled terrain. The strings are our main roads, but what do we use for the territory in between? Where are our side roads? The side roads are for us to design. Using an A major scale as an example, span the end points of a three-octave scale by sticking an imaginary tack into the fingerboard at the low A on the G string and another where high A is located on the E; then imagine connecting a wire from the low A to the high A (see fig. 4.3). Following that line provides an unflagging sense of destination while allowing space to contemplate the hand's changing shape.

Imagine that the bottom of your left hand is grooved, as a wheel on a train, and that it rides back and forth along the wire. Whether you are ascending a scale on an established string or diagonally on an imaginary string, the grooved wheel engages

Figure 4.3 A wire connects the beginning and end of an A major/minor three-octave scale. *Photo credit to Gail Taibbi.*

the wire for a smooth journey. This image supports the hand's migration throughout the fingerboard, offering a direct route from the beginning of a shift, scale, or arpeggio to its end destination.

The wire image is particularly effective in shifting from one location to another when bypassing a string in between. When crossing from one string to the next, shifting on the line of the original string can be the most efficient method; then once the palm is properly situated, quickly rotate the hand to drop the finger on the neighboring string.

Wrist Response in Meandering Passages

The wrist coordinates with the elbow to position the fingers above the string. In general, as demonstrated by the forearm/pole image with the hand/ball on top, the hand responds in counterbalance to the angle of the forearm. But in faster, more contained passages, where wrist motion is small, the wrist is less dependent on the elbow. Think of centering the bottom of your hand on top of a unicycle that transports your hand across the fingerboard or longitudinally from scroll to bridge, allowing you to quickly adjust and readjust to the shift in hand weight with rapid micromotions while sustaining balance and mobility.

Hand-Weight Balance and Creative Imagery

Awareness of hand balance and mobility is crucial in establishing the equilibrium of the fingers. The hand has an infinite combination of its three primary motions: flexion and extension, side to side, and rotation on the long line of the forearm.

There are consequences for failing to exploit the full range of motion in order to optimize the position of the hand vis-à-vis the fingerboard: if the hand strays toward the thumb or loses its axial rotation, the fourth finger is distanced from the fingerboard; with a chronic tilting toward the fourth finger, the first finger is alienated; if the hand leans too far back, the fingertips are distracted from the string; and when falling too far forward, the fingers become misshapen. To maintain a continuous balance of the hand, imagine that it is weighted at the bottom like the counterweight of a smiley-face punching bag. After you whack the punching bag, it returns to its upright position—as does the hand via the weighted wrist. With this feeling of low-hanging weight, when you tilt the hand to lend support to an articulated finger, feel the base of the hand returning to an upright position of balance on reaching its string destination.

Managing the distribution of weight in the hand is a way to improve the balance of forces and the effectiveness of the fingers. Think of dropping weight down inside the palm and sensing a subtle sideways shift of that weight that creates a slight sidewise rotation of the palm, further enabling each finger to articulate more easily in its straight-up-and-down position. To demonstrate this, imagine four kangaroo pouches inside the palm of the hand on top of the wrist. Drop a metal weight inside each pouch one at a time, noticing the shift in the hand's balance. Start by dropping a weight in the first finger pouch, causing the whole palm to rotate slightly toward that first finger, and urging the base of that finger forward and down; the finger will be simultaneously prompted to begin to extend up. Remove the weight and drop it into the pouch corresponding to the second finger, in that way tilting the balance of weight toward the second finger, which feels the impulse to extend, and so on. Now optimally aligned with musculature around the base of its own metacarpal (see appendix diagram A.2), each finger so designated is engaged with its foundational strength and will articulate with clean precision. By dropping weight in the pouches underneath the second and third fingers, the hand becomes centered on the wrist, positioning all the fingers above the fingerboard in a balanced format. Another image that supports the extending of the finger is to imagine a weight attached to each metacarpal in the way that a large weight is attached to a rope inside the older windows. When the weight drops, it supports the opening or lifting of the window.

It is common for the fingers to experience a feeling of being disconnected from the rest of the hand, especially in fourth position and higher. Experience a sensation

Figure 4.4 Experience a sensation of the bones (metacarpals) in the palm moving like pistons. *Photo credit to Eva Foxon Nicholas.*

of the metacarpal bones in the hand moving like pistons, driven by the pulsating rotations in the base of the palm, those impulses translating through to the articulation of each finger with the string (see fig. 4.4). Or imagine sinking each metacarpal into the center of the palm as its finger flexes to restore the foundation of the fingers and engage the full strength of the frame of the hand. When crossing strings on a scale descent, for example, plant the metacarpal of the last finger remaining on the higher pitched string (usually the first) simultaneously with the finger that leads (usually the fourth) to maintain the hand's sense of balance and connection to all the fingers during their migration across strings.

Wrist and Finger Collaboration

The metacarpals are cylindrical bones inside the palm between the fingers and the layer of wrist bones (carpals) at the bottom of the hand. With the violin in hand, envision the top of the wrist as a pedal similar to the one on a trash can. When you press down the pedal, the bottom of the hand rotates down and the metacarpal leaps forward, almost as if out of the palm, helping extend the finger before the now-cocked finger can snap down onto the fingerboard from its heightened position. On the release of the pedal, the hand returns to its neutral, flexed position. While playing scales, instead of thinking of each finger individually, roll your foot back and forth on the four imaginary pedals, tipping over and releasing the fingers using counter pressures and motions from the wrist.

When lacking adequate awareness of the wrist-to-finger interaction, the fingers tend to overextend to reach their destination. As a result, the left hand eventually releases its shape during the migration of the fingers, and like a ball with no air, the hand and fingers fall flat. To avoid this, secure the hand's shape by coordinating the movement of each finger with the bottom part of the hand. Envision four shoes inside the heel of the hand, one underneath each finger, and imagine that the hand is a four-footed creature wearing these shoes, seated and strapped to a seat that rotates forward, waiting for brief moments where it can stand on one of its feet, reach out, and hit a drum. During a string change, the part of this upper wrist area (shoed foot) that corresponds to the finger about to change strings thrusts forward and down (the creature stomps a foot down as it stands up, drawing the seat forward with it) as the finger (creature's arm) is raised to make its move. Then as the finger (creature's arm) accomplishes its quick striking motion, the heel of the hand (seat) simultaneously closes back up (rotates right up under the creature), placing it in a new seated position.

To add buoyancy to the articulating finger, envision four tiny feet growing out of the bottom of the left hand, each foot corresponding to one of the four fingers above (see fig. 4.5). This time, tie a bungee cord around the (upright) hand just below the large knuckles and suspend the bottom of the hand above the fingerboard. The feet, barely able to reach, kick off from the fingerboard, pushing the bottom of the hand up and onto the foot underneath the next finger to be articulated, and that foot pushes the hand onto the next, and so on. The feet reposition the hand step by step by creating continuity between the last finger articulated and the next.

Figure 4.5 Envision four tiny feet growing out of the bottom of the left hand. *Photo credit to Eva Foxon Nicholas.*

Similarly, think of the curved bottom of the hand as the bottom of a ball. Position the ball so that the exact bottom point of the ball is underneath the finger articulated. The base of the hand secures the articulating finger by establishing a supportive platform on which each finger balances, whereas by carelessly positioning the wrist underneath the first finger while articulating the fourth, for example, a sensation of weakness results.

Because tension tends to accrue in the left hand and arm during same-position rotations around the neck, imagine that the hand is a super ball on a string affixed to the wrist's center; then manage the high energy of the bouncing ball from string to string. Doing so has a freeing effect throughout the arm and hand.

Optimum Wrist Placement

It is essential to experience the wrist's stabilized position as being above the fingerboard (see fig. 4.6); otherwise, feeling the wrist sinking below the fingerboard creates a sense of horizontal division within the hand, causing the fingers to lose some of their agility and forcing them to work too hard. Envision four strings above the four real strings (see fig. 4.7); imagine the wrist either resting on the actual strings in lower positions or suspending from the four imaginary strings in higher positions.

To prevent the thumb from losing a connection with the rest of the hand during scales and vibrato, imagine slipping a metal disc into the wrist, separating the hand from the forearm, with the thumb centered and counterbalanced on the same foundational plane as the fingers. Any deviation of the disc's placement misadjusts the form. For example, tension results if the thumb ends up underneath the disc, leaving the fingers an entity unto themselves.

To further reinforce the hand as an entity separate from the forearm, which is especially important for passages with a lot of horizontal motion across the width of the fingerboard, imagine that the open space between forearm and hand in this image allows the neck to pass through, enabling you to move your arm to either side of

Figure 4.6 Project the wrist's stabilized position above the fingerboard. *Photo credit to Eva Foxon Nicholas.*

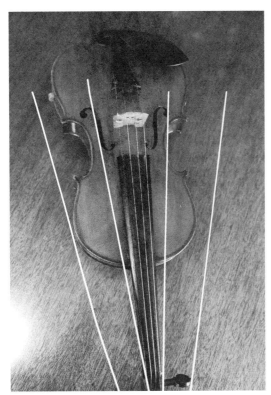

Figure 4.7 Four imaginary strings above the four actual strings. *Photo credit to Eva Foxon Nicholas.*

the neck. The plane of the fingerboard then acts as a wedge between the base of the hand and forearm: on the fourth-finger side of the wrist when ascending from the G to the E string, and on the thumb side when descending from the E string to the G (see fig. 4.8 and fig. 4.9).

In first position, imagine balancing the center base of the hand between the D and the A string, with the left hand angled so that the first finger touches the G string and the fourth finger touches the E (in an exaggerated octave position). Try

Figure 4.8 The fingerboard acts as a wedge between the base of the hand and forearm on the fourth-finger side. *Photo credit to Gail Taibbi.*

Figure 4.9 The fingerboard acts as a wedge between the base of the hand and forearm on the thumb side. *Photo credit to Gail Taibbi.*

reversing the angle, placing the first finger on the E string and the fourth on the G. This is helpful where notes descend from the E string to the G (as in a two-octave G major descending scale). By holding the hand in this quasi-octave position, the hand angle takes into account the outward fanning of the G string—its destination. It is also helpful to think of the outer strings as a corral to the fingers, with the fingers articulating in a more confined area, in that way minimizing excessive transference of weight that can throw the hand out of balance.

When you play rapid passages that encompass the use of all four strings, as in the first movement of the Brahms violin concerto, eight-note pickup to 16 measures after the solo entrance (see ex. 4.2), if you perceive that the space between the D and A string is home for the wrist, then the hand can simply flex forward (toward the left side of the fingerboard), causing the fingers to expand accordingly to support G-string finger access, or it can fall back, with the fingers dropping naturally into the palm to position the fingers above the E string.

Example 4.2 First movement of the Brahms Violin Concerto in D, pickup to m.16 of the opening solo.

Figure 4.10 Feel the presence of two horizontal poles supporting the hand, one in front and the other behind. *Photo credit to Eva Foxon Nicholas.*

Feel the presence of two horizontal poles, one supporting the hand in front of itself when leaning forward, and the other behind the hand when leaning back (see fig. 4.10). With these restraints, the hand can carry the fingers back and forth without allowing weight to shift away from the fingertips and into the palm. A substantial break in the wrist with the hand relaxing back guarantees a distraction of weight from the fingers. Feel a continuous coursing of weight through the arm and into the fingers.

Suspension of the Wrist and Hand

Expanding the wrist—the area between the forearm and metacarpals—allows for breadth of motion in the hand. Think of the hand positioned on a triangular platform in the plane of the wrist with the following vertexes: the base of the thumb metacarpal, the base of the first finger metacarpal, and base of the fourth finger metacarpal (see fig. 4.11). If you imagine centering the thumb between the lower outside and inside corners, the triangle has three equal sides. Attach three strings, one to each corner, suspending the triangle, creating one apex at a time (see fig. 4.12).

Try suspending the hand from the apex that best serves its positioning, always allowing the two lowered corners of the triangle to soften into position, maybe even rotating a bit horizontally, clockwise or counter. For example, when suspending from the hand's lower outside corner, the thumb and first finger apexes relax down evenly; when suspending from the thumb, let the area underneath the first finger and lower outside corner dangle; and when suspending from the bottom of the hand underneath the first finger, the thumb and lower outside corner drop where they will. Try suspending the bottom of the hand from various points (one at a time), releasing suspension from one and latching on to another, akin to swinging from a rope by releasing it first before grabbing hold of the next. Suspending the hand creates profound relaxation so when you slip the neck of the violin inside the hand, the fingers are free to contract and release without relying on the fingerboard for stability.

Left, **Figure 4.11** Think of the hand positioned on a triangular platform in the plane of the wrist. *Photo credit to Gail Taibbi.*

Above, **Figure 4.12** Attach three strings, one to each corner, suspending the triangle one apex at a time. *Photo credit to Gail Taibbi.*

Hoisting and Propelling the Wrist

Superimpose the bottom of the hand above the fingerboard; then lasso a string around your wrist to support an awareness of the division of the limb at the wrist. When traveling up the fingerboard, hoist and drag the thumb corner that runs behind the advancing hand; on descending passages, traveling in a bridge-to-scroll direction, lift and drag the lower outside corner of the hand down the fingerboard behind the advancing thumb. Pulling the lasso results in the hand extending early so that all the fingers have to do is drop and rebound.

Moving the hand across the width of the fingerboard in first position can be especially challenging because both the arm and the hand are in a more extended position. On passages where the hand migrates across the fingerboard, drag the imaginary lasso either toward the G or the E string. When crossing strings, lead with the heavier bottom of the hand; then thrust the large knuckles over the wrist or fingerboard to present the fingers to the string.

Notice the shape of the fingerboard: most narrow at the scroll end before it fans out more widely toward the bridge (mirroring the fanning of the inner and outer pairs of strings). Picture two horizontal tightropes above the fingerboard that are connected at a peak and projected out beyond and above the scroll, creating a larger outline of the fingerboard (see fig. 4.13). Now imagine someone at the bridge end holding the other end of each tightrope and directing the left wrist, either from the palm or posterior side, across the four-string terrain of the fingerboard. At times the

Figure 4.13 Picture two horizontal tightropes above the fingerboard connected at a peak beyond the scroll. *Photo credit to Gail Taibbi.*

person drags the tightrope that is to the right of the neck, carrying the wrist to the G-string side during E-to-G-string scale descents, or the reverse, with the tightrope to the left of the G string transporting the wrist from the G string to the E in ascending scales. Because there is a tendency for the third and fourth fingers to get left behind during same position E-to-G-string descents, this image is especially advantageous with the tightrope on the right pulling left, making contact with the back of the wrist in the area corresponding to the third and fourth fingers. During same position G-to-E-string ascents, the tightrope on the left (being directed to the right) then makes contact with the anterior side of the wrist at the first- and second-finger corner, again securing a healthy rotational position of the hand.

Rebound Motion of the Wrist

Visual imagery can help create a dynamic of resistance and rebound that propels the hand either up the scale or back down. On the ascent of a three-octave scale beginning on the G (or D) string, contemplate in the imagination that the back side of the

Figure 4.14 Contemplate that the back side of the wrist drags the G string to the right of the E. *Photo credit to Eva Foxon Nicholas.*

Left Arm

wrist drags the G string to the right of the E. The hand ascends and descends the E string (see fig. 4.14), and then for the rest of the scale descent, the restoring force of the G string snaps the wrist from the E string to the left of the G, the fingers articulating the notes en route.

The wrist can play off the strings as a wrestler bounces off ropes to enhance the fluidity of hand movement in both directions of the scale. When you descend from a high position on the E string to a lower position, then over to the G (or D) string, and ascend again to the E—as in a three-octave scale—the front of the wrist drags the E string to the left of the G (or D) string; then the string shoots the hand back over and up the scale again. Also use the leverage of the strings during same-position, E-to-G-to-E-string hand migration. Navigate the ropes with the mid-forearm to further support hand projection above the fingerboard.

CHAPTER FIVE

Left Palm

We have explored the hand's motions on the wrist and how hand position via the wrist translates into finger stability. In this chapter, we mold the palm in ways that add to the continuum of support for the fingers.

Palm Formation

In addition to affecting sheer strength, the disposition of the palm also determines finger efficiency. Inside the palm, there is a crease line below the large knuckles and another crease outlining the base of the thumb. Draw a circle approximately the size of a quarter in the center of the palm that intercepts the two lines. Around the now circular juncture of these lines, the hand folds up like a map or a shirt, forming a core of support for the left hand (see appendix G). Think of the hand closing in around the quarter-sized washer (see fig. 5.1), and then transfer that feeling to your hand cradling the neck of the violin.

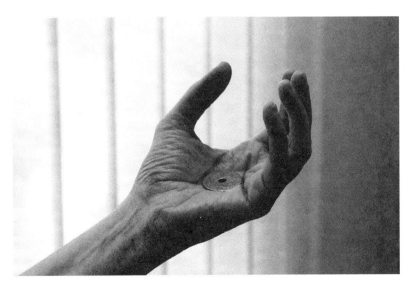

Figure 5.1 Two areas of the hand close in around the quarter-sized washer. *Photo credit to Gail Taibbi.*

As you play, form a visual image of holding a small ball in the palm's center. The action of fingers is enhanced as the hand maneuvers around this useful intrusion. There is a particular tendency for the thumb joints to fold passively, rather than maintaining enough extension (active flexion) vis-à-vis the palm. If that happens, the infrastructure of the hand collapses, causing constriction in the fingers. The small ball shores up the palm, helping the thumb maintain its agency.

Another image that helps ensure the hand's integrity without necessary tension is a gathering and securing the perimeter of the palm. With an incoherent perimeter, the fingers can lose their ability to effectively rebound from articulation, and unwanted tension creeps in as a result of the ensuing struggle. Contemplate in the imagination that the perimeter of your left palm is the top opening of a sock; slip the palm/sock partly over a ball, the elastic rim of the sock gathering equally around the circumference of the ball. If you release awareness of the elastic connection, or if you lose the feeling of grasping the ball with the palm, the fingers flail. To suggest another metaphor, they become feet running with shoes untied, with the lack of structural support from the palm undercutting the readiness of the fingers for quick action.

Alternatively, bending inward all together the first- and fourth-finger large knuckles with the lower corners secures the mold (ball shape) of the hand (see fig. 5.2 and fig. 5.3). Because a sturdy palm provides a foundation for the articulating fingers, connect one end of a wire to the large knuckle of the first finger (palm side) and the other end to the lower outside corner; then cross that with a second wire, one end to the fourth-finger large knuckle and the other end to the lower inside corner. Pulling the corners closer together molds a coherent configuration while it differentiates the fingers as it liberates them from the palm.

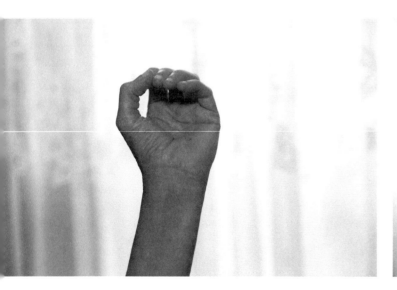

Figure 5.2 Reinforce an energized curvature of all the hand's joints. *Photo credit to Eva Foxon Nicholas.*

Figure 5.3 Bend the first- and fourth-finger large knuckles and lower corners inward. *Photo credit to Eva Foxon Nicholas.*

Stabilizing the Palm

The longest of the five metacarpals is only about two inches long in an average adult hand, with this fundamental part of each finger and the thumb occupying most of what we think of as the palm. The metacarpals float in between the fingers and the wrist, moving minimally in the longitudinal direction but much more laterally. An example is the contraction of the hand with the combination of the articulating fourth finger and the adduction (closing in) of the thumb to support it. Because of the way the thumb, rotating from its saddle joint, cozies in under the other fingers, the bass of the thumb and the large knuckles are good landmarks for monitoring the shape and movement of the palm.

Stabilizing the palm in a balanced format steadies the fingers. Place the heel of your hand against the shoulder of the violin (at fourth position). This reinforces the natural curve of the palm while supporting the center balance of the hand in the wrist. To use this image while playing, especially in lower positions, imagine a shoulder that is conveniently close to the hand. As it did in the fourth position exercise, the projected shoulder supports the palm, giving it something against which to leverage itself while articulating notes, offering the same sense of stability that exists in fourth position.

Just as the shoulder of the violin stabilizes the hand, stabilize the forearm by leaning the two forearm bones against the shoulder of an imaginary violin placed underneath. The shoulder of the top violin stabilizes the palm, and the violin underneath balances the two bones in the forearm (see fig. 5.4).

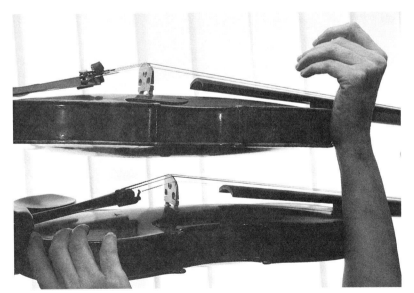

Figure 5.4 The shoulder of one violin stabilizes the palm while the other balances the two bones in the forearm. *Photo credit to Gail Taibbi.*

In the first movement of the Tchaikovsky Symphony No. 6, mm.173–174 (see ex. 5.1), starting on beat 4 after ascending the G string in the first three beats, align and stabilize the hand and arm, first by balancing the forearm bones against the

Left Arm

Example 5.1 First movement of Tchaikovsky's Symphony No. 6, mm.173 to 174.

imaginary violin (underneath the actual) and then by projecting the shoulder to first position. As a result, both the forearm and palm are balanced in a way that allows the fingers to articulate without disruption during the G-to-A-string transition.

Another way to provide this same kind of stability is to mentally bypass the violin in higher positions and instead imagine that the lower outside corner of the hand is leaning into the base of the thumb. Imagine that the base of the thumb is the strung head of a lacrosse stick and the lower outside corner of the hand is a ball. When shifting downward, lob the lower outside corner of the hand/ball to its desired destination with the base of the thumb / head of the lacrosse stick, anticipating the catch. This interplay supports a healthy formation of the hand that serves to stabilize the moving fingers in all positions. It is also a strategy for making a smooth transition from one position to another.

Palm Pliability

There is an elegance of motion that, if expressed between the notes, lends a sensual quality to the playing while creating an expanded sense of time—a space for movement and for the reverberation of the soul. Look for that openness in the hand itself. The importance of shape and strength notwithstanding, the palm also needs the flexibility to breathe for a more nuanced expressiveness. Technically speaking, experiencing this motility (passive motion) is especially important with shifts, string crossings, and vibrato. Imagine that the frame of the hand is made from a wire coat hanger and acts as a U frame, reinforcing the U shape down the thumb and over and out through the fourth finger. Cut a piece of balloon material the size and shape of your palm and secure its outer edges to the frame (see fig. 5.5). If you were to drag it back and forth in a sink filled with water, the give would be concave, then convex, with just the feeling of elasticity you want to feel in your palm. Maintain a sense of the hand's frame while feeling this fluidity to maximize its effectiveness.

For every closing or flexing of anything, there is also an opening, an extension, and with it a potential letting go into freedom and spaciousness. Exploring and appreciating the rhythms of these reciprocations is fundamental to creating a dynamic balance of compressions and decompressions that can reliably sustain your playing. Live in the exquisite realization that every particular tension or release is ready to transpose into its opposite at any moment. And now consider the overlay of forms and frames that our Progressive Form system is adding to mix, for example, the delicate interplay between preserving the hand's formation with a held image and allowing a natural expansion and contraction during passage work. For rapid scales passages and arpeggios, envision a horseshoe-shaped wire that reinforces the U-shaped thumb and fourth-finger hand frame. Then imagine that the fingers are webbed as

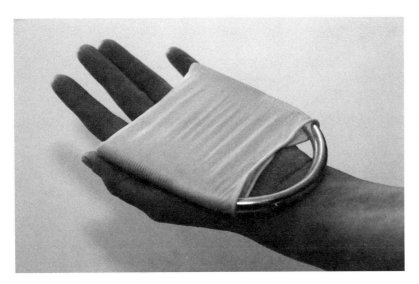

Figure 5.5 Balloon material on a U frame illustrates the palm's pliability. *Photo credit to Gail Taibbi.*

a duck's foot and moving through water. On ascending scales, the hand (palm and fingers) expands as it scoops water. On the descent, the back of the hand pushes against the water environment, which then returns the hand/matter to its original shape and size. Unless there is acquiescence in hand movement during transport, the finger rebound is ineffectual and the shifts boxy. Ideally, while it is held, the image guides and reminds and enhances the natural functions until they become automatic and are no longer needed.

Place the violin in playing position, and then imagine holding the scroll with a rubberized left palm. As the hand ascends the fingerboard to play a scale, the rubber palm remains pressed against the scroll, causing the material to stretch. With the neck now inside the center of the palm, the palm and fingers expand to envelop the neck and then the body of the instrument. The palm retracts on the scale's descent due to the resistance of the scroll and the restoring force of the rubber. This image supports the hand's continued sense of involvement with the instrument.

Envision—or view a video of—an octopus in the ocean, well above the sandy bottom, propelling itself horizontally through jet propulsion. The octopus backs up, storing potential energy, with the underside of the body becoming convex. Then it propels itself forward with the bottom body rapidly morphing into a concave shape, legs trailing. Now imagine that the left hand is the octopus—the palm the body and the fingers the legs. During same position G-to-E-string ascents, the palm shape is concave with the fingers trailing behind, and when playing same position, E- to G-string descents, the shape becomes more convex (as does the octopus when storing up). Mentally project the hand above the sea floor of the fingerboard, all the while mimicking this motion. This image supports fluidity of movement and appropriate placement of the neck inside the hand during the articulation of the fingers with each of the four strings.

This time, picture that the whole hand is a fish net enclosed around the periphery (including the fingertips) by a metal frame and immersed in water (see fig. 5.6). During ascending and descending passages, the fingers drag through the water, moving forward and backward through the frame the way fish netting would drag against the resistance of water in the ocean. If the hand's frame is misshapen, the back-and-forth transition of the netting/shifting fingers is met with interference and the path is distorted. On scale descents, as in the second movement of the Bruch *Scottish Fantasy*, from pickup to 18 measures after the solo entrance (see ex. 5.2), superimpose the outer pair of thumb and fourth finger onto the hoop, with fingers three, two, and one moving through its center. On scale ascents, as in the following measure, the thumb and first finger now constitute the hoop's frame, dragging the remaining fingers and hand through its center opening.

Figure 5.6 Picture the whole hand as a fishnet enclosed around the periphery by a metal frame. *Photo credit to Eva Foxon Nicholas.*

Example 5.2 Bruch's Scottish Fantasy, second movement, the pickup to 18 bars after the solo entrance.

To create a sense of buoyancy in the palm, imagine that the perimeter of the palm is a rubber tube. Picture sinking the tube / outer palm into a body of water by pressing on the midpoint of the back of the hand, palm down. Notice the outer palm's resilience and its countermotion to the palm's center. Again, on submerging the palm/tube into the water, focus your awareness on the follow-through response of the fingers and thumb. The submersion and release of the palm reveals a rebound effect to inspire the shifting hand while ascending the fingerboard atop arcing paths: the fingers and palm can breathe while in transition. The buoyant palm dispels knuckle tension before it coagulates, especially in the thumb, freeing the hand from the negative consequences of clutching the neck.

Palm Height and Balance

Unless a consistent distance is sustained between the palm and the fingerboard, the fingers at times will either collide with the fingerboard or fail to reach it, and they are forced to continually adjust their shape and position. To find that consistency, relax the palm back into the shape of a domed ceiling and then sustain that shape by resting the center of the palm on an imaginary post projecting up from the fingerboard (see fig. 5.7).

Figure 5.7 Rest the center of your palm on an imaginary post. *Photo credit to Gail Taibbi.*

Maintain the height of the post, determined by individual anatomy, as the hand orbits the neck, for instance with the palm traveling on a three-inch post in all positions. That consistency from any location to the next, such as from third position to fourth, reinforces a reliable relationship of the fingers to the fingerboard. Center the post to accommodate the balance of the hand and the position of the fingers above the string so each finger can articulate without disrupting the palm's point of balance on the post. The objective is to support the hand so the center of the palm does not cave in onto the neck and all four fingers dangle in a nice curvature (retaining similarity of shape and balance) above the string in any position.

Picture a circular dartboard. Now imagine superimposing the dartboard onto your palm (see fig. 5.8) and placing the point of contact with the post at the bullseye. Feel the weight progression as the concentric circles of mass surrounding the bullseye/hand expand. The heavier perimeter steadies the center of the palm on top of the post while regulating the transfer of weight to the fingers through levels of large-knuckle suspension. For a lighter articulation of the finger with the string, distribute the concentric circles of mass more evenly, with the palm balanced on a taller post.

The post can also travel along the pathway of the strings, transporting the balanced hand with it. The palm balances such that the large knuckles are able to expand and contract laterally; if the knuckles stay constricted, they can't assist the fingers in

Left Arm

Figure 5.8 Superimpose the dartboard onto your palm. *Photo credit to Eva Foxon Nicholas.*

synchronizing interval spaces, and intonation suffers as a result. As you balance the center of the palm on a post, imagine that the fourth finger (digit and metacarpal) is made out of heavy metal so that the thumb and fourth finger drape down equally, or else lighten the thumb by imagining it filled with helium. Combining the third and fourth fingers into a single unit also offsets the thickness/weight of the thumb.

There are times to create an off-center balancing of the palm. Lowering the arm sinks the hand more deeply into the fingerboard, in that way maximizing tone in slow legato passages. But during agile passages that use intermittent vibrato, as in the Mendelssohn mm.28–29 (see ex. 5.3), lowering the arm for vibrato bogs down the fast passages. In this latter instance, balance the heel of the hand on a post (see fig. 5.9);

Example 5.3
Mendelssohn's E minor concerto, mm.28–29.

Figure 5.9 Balance the left-hand base of the palm on an imaginary post. *Photo credit to Eva Foxon Nicholas.*

the placement of the post wristward from the palm's center enables an easier shift of weight to the fingers, allowing them to extend down closer to the fingerboard, in that way providing them with easy access. The relaxed weight and freedom in this hand position serves vibrato and allows for minimal adjustment with running the notes, and it is especially helpful in higher positions. Think of the weight transferring from the wrist to the large knuckles and down the fingers to their point of contact on the string. The wrist isn't literally the highest point, but it is helpful to experience it as the point from which the rest of the hand is suspended, a sensation of being functionally or energetically higher. Similarly, when using a more economical musculature of the hand, as in rapid passages, it helps to experience the weight of the large knuckles as being higher than the fingers.

The degree to which the supported hand drapes (or gives in to gravity) is based on two factors: the positioning of the post around the neck and the particular part of the palm (centered on the longitudinal midline or off-center) that is balanced on the post. When jump-starting a passage, visualize that the post is a miniaturized pogo stick (without handles), with the palm leaping up and onto the vertical stick. In response, the large knuckles rebound, smacking down and bouncing back, with the pogo stick supporting the hand's buoyancy while providing resistance. As the fingers articulate, the pogo stick prevents the hand from crashing onto the fingerboard.

Palm-Base-to-Fingertip Balance

To avoid imbalance in the hand, it is crucial to understand how the palm can align with the fingertips. When the fingertips and base of the palm are on a level plane, the knuckles relax and fall into balance, optimizing the efficiency of the fingers.

Try cutting a ball in half and placing it on a platform with the flat side down (see fig. 5.10); then rest your hand on top of the half-ball (see fig. 5.11). Doing so helps to

Figure 5.10 A half-ball is on a platform with the flat side down. *Photo credit to Gail Taibbi.*

Figure 5.11 Your hand is on top of the half-ball. *Photo credit to Gail Taibbi.*

frame up the hand, promotes good finger-to-palm connections, improves the distribution of hand angles, and supports a more balanced hand placement on the fingerboard. The half ball helps to maintain the shape of the hand, while leaning the heel of the hand against an imaginary platform reinforces the palm, in turn steadying the fingers during their up and down motion.

Envision cutting a light bulb in half vertically and resting the flat side on the platform. Then superimpose your hand onto that shape. Similar to the off-center post image, the center of the palm is elevated so the bulk of the weight tilts onto the fingertips. With this image, the heel of the hand is also supported by the metal sleeve that screws in the bulb, with the electrical connections representing the way that part of the hand energetically hugs the neck in all positions.

This time superimpose your hand onto the light bulb while imagining that the metal base (the part that screws in) is the base of the thumb (the big muscular segment). When navigating the fingerboard, experience the interrelatedness and sense of physical contact among the components of the hand, in this case with the more mobile two segments of the thumb and its base in the palm continually connecting with one another.

Now, imagine that the heel of the hand is one foot and that the fingertips comprise the other foot. Balance the palm and fingertips on a snowboard. Then with heel and fingertips tight to the board, leap up and bounce the midpoint of the board off the string played, with the fingertips and heel staying with each other in the same plane and at the same angle to the string. When descending E- to G-string passages, the bottom center of the board aims for the G-string destination as if the neck and other three strings (E, A, and D) are nonexistent. For instance, in the Mendelssohn, mm.33–36 (see ex. 5.4), the first three beats are on the E string, so the fingertips and palm lean the midpoint of the snowboard against the E string. In the next measure, because beats one and two are on the A string, fire the center of the board against that string before pushing through the A string and up against the D to play the third-finger G on the third beat; then rebound off that string to propel the balanced hand back to the E string to play beat four. In m.35, aim for the G string and play beats one and two on the A string and beats 3 and 4 on the D string before landing against the G in m.36 for the remaining passage. To support better hand suspension, try playing off imaginary strings above the actual strings.

Example 5.4 Mendelssohn's E minor concerto, mm.33–36.

Overall Balance and Mobility

When ascending or descending a scale or arpeggio, the movement of the *frame of the hand* (see fig. 5.5) is similar in motion to a Frisbee or discus in that all three—the hand, Frisbee, and discus—rotate while tracking distance. To get a feel for this, rotate the hand along its perimeter in the plane of the palm, leading from either the tip of the thumb or the fourth finger while maintaining the integrity of the hand's frame. Start clockwise, and then go counterclockwise. Ascending from first position to third, the fourth fingertip leads the hand's frame, rotating counterclockwise to keep the hand upright on the progressively leaning forearm. As the hand moves farther up into position, some clockwise rotation added to the equation and led by the tip of the thumb puts the hand up on its lower outside corner to improve the range of the articulating fingertips. Now hovering above the fingerboard like a horizontally positioned Frisbee, the hand makes the opposite moves when descending back to first position. At times, especially when playing passages in a localized area of the fingerboard, there is minimal play in the arm, with most of the adjustment from rotation of the hand in the plane of the palm. During a three-octave scale, the adjustments are incremental, with the arm informing the rotating hand. And when navigating larger steps as in an arpeggio, there is a grander sweep to the overall motion as the arm and Frisbee/hand comes around and over the top of the instrument and back. Despite the various subtle rotations, maintaining a relatively level palm provides all four fingers with equal access to the fingerboard.

Maintaining hand formation, hand height, and finger-to-palm alignment while moving from one position to another is a lot to juggle. The following image combines these four considerations into one representation. Place a ball on top of the fingerboard and then put an upside-down bowl on top of the ball. The ball rolls freely inside the bowl. Now place your left hand on top of the upside-down bowl; the bowl and ball suspend the hand such that the center of the palm never caves in onto the neck, and the fingers dangle in a nice curvature above the string. Akin to the bottom of a car frame following the contour of the road, the upside-down bowl maintains a continuous relationship to the fingerboard. To assist the migration of the hand during descending shifts, a direction that seems more challenging, imagine gently sweeping or coddling the bowl down the fingerboard and toward the scroll using the edge of the hand on the fourth-finger side.

This time, remove the bowl and place your palm directly on top of the ball. Now imagine that the ball has the capacity to spin directly inside the rounded palm like a ball inside a pocket. Coax the ball up the fingerboard using the other edge of the palm on the first-finger side, and then roll it back down engaging the fourth-finger edge. For same-position string crossings, either drag or coax the ball toward the E string from the G string with the large knuckles and the heel of the palm simultaneously, and when descending from the E string to the G, push the ball to the G string with the heel of the palm. Guiding the ball via the various aspects of the palm with minimal involvement of the fingers is an efficient way to properly situate the fingers while allowing them the freedom to move rapidly up and down on the string. When guiding the ball with the palm's periphery, avoid the tendency to start gripping the ball with the fingers. Picture the palm with webbing or a kangaroo pocket that secures the ball in such a way that only the palm is in communication with the ball; the fingers are liberated.

When traveling in a motor vehicle, your body can stay relatively relaxed because it is not involved in providing the locomotive power but instead is free to execute the fine motor activity of steering it. Similarly, if you take the upside-down bowl image and imagine that the ball part is motorized and rolls without the hand's input, the transporting of the hand on the fingerboard is now without effort, leaving the much lighter function of finger placement. When the impetus or agency is in some sense outside of direct control, the approach is more as a responder to forces than as an initiator. It is easier to relax with this attitude of allowing rather than one of manipulating.

Imagine a ball that is slippery and pliable. Now visualize the palm pouncing on the ball (the fingers articulating the notes) and the ball slipping out from the hand's tunnel in the direction of the subsequent hand position. Both left-hand string crossings and shifts benefit from this image. As the ball arrives in its new location, the palm leaps on top (again with the fingers articulating the next cluster of notes), and again the ball escapes from underneath the hand, miraculously in the direction of the musical passage. The image of the palm chasing and trapping the ball removes the necessity of having to think about the mechanics involved—arm rotation, elbow position, and so forth—keeping the focus on the palm's interaction with the body of the violin by proxy of the imaginary ball.

Migration of the Hand

The following visualization synthesizes several motions into one image. Balance the hand on its bottom center. Imagine that your hand is a bird: the thumb and fourth-finger sides are the wings, and the middle of the hand is the body. Attach an eye screw with a string to the base of your palm (midpoint) and drag the hand up the fingerboard in ascending passages (see fig. 5.12). The wings (thumb and fourth finger) fall back as the body/palm is pulled forward.

Figure 5.12 Attach a string to the base of your palm and drag the hand up the fingerboard. *Photo credit to Eva Foxon Nicholas.*

On the return, attach the eye screw with the string to the lower-middle back of the hand; then drag the hand (bird) down the fingerboard backward: the wings (thumb and fourth finger) tuck into the sides of the palm; the hand (bird) then relaxes at the bottom of the scale, perched to once more to ascend the fingerboard. In lower positions on the E-to-G-string descent, reattach the eye screw with the string to the base of your palm. On the E-to-G-string ascent, attach it to the lower middle back of the hand. During passage work, picture the palm flying like a bird around the perimeter of the neck without landing prematurely on top of the fingers. Without some suspension of the palm, the fingers become earthbound and bog down the passage.

This time, envision the bird wearing a straitjacket with the fingers-wing in one sleeve and the thumb-wing in the other. Now crisscross the sleeves. Regardless of how loose or tight the sleeves are pulled, the idea is to balance the wingtips (the thumb and four fingers) with one another from this wrapped-around extension. Doing so is a way to not only align the fingers to the string but also steady the hand while the fingers are articulating.

CHAPTER SIX

Left-Hand Knuckles

Here we shift focus from the palm more generally to the knuckles and illustrate their role in supporting optimal finger functioning. The left-hand knuckles are joints that serve as fulcrums for the articulating fingers. More than that, they can be seen as center points of the hand's springs, the very pliant and responsive mechanical action of the hand. At the same time, they are the nexus of lateral expansion and contraction. As such, their positioning crucially determines the balance and intervallic placement of each finger. And finally, due to extra mass at the flared ends of the bones at these joints, we can use a sense of that weight to add momentum to the follow-through motion of the hand's rotation.

Structure and Weight

It is common practice for the young student to stretch the hand by widening between the tips of the thumb and fourth finger. But to maintain strength and control while expanding the fingers, initiate the stretch via the large knuckles (see fig. 6.1). Randomly stretching the hand using peripheral points creates diagonal distortions that disrupt the coherent frame of the hand. For instance, stretching from the thumb tip to the fourth finger's large knuckle or from the large knuckle of the thumb to the middle knuckle of the fourth finger creates an unevenness of articulation patterns because the amount of support accessed along diagonal lines varies from finger to finger.

To create natural expansion of the fingers and thumb as a group, superimpose your hand on an imaginary ball above the line of the string. If note intervals are close, gather your fingers around a smaller ball; if the intervals are far apart, then expand the size of the ball, fanning out the large knuckles (along the line of the string) relative to the larger interval size. Similar to a pulsating heart, think of the ball rhythmically expanding and contracting the hand to accommodate the differential in interval size from one group of notes to another.

For large intervals, the large knuckles determine placement of the fingers, not the other way around. In other words, anticipate the expansion and contraction of the knuckles as a function of the musical need so the fingers can simply drop when they

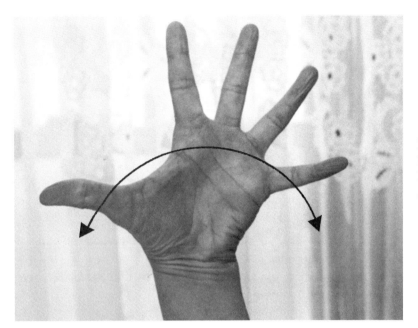

Figure 6.1 Expand the hand by stretching through the large knuckles. *Photo credit to Eva Foxon Nicholas.*

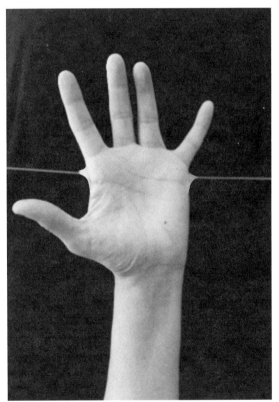

Figure 6.2 Connect string to the first-finger large knuckle and another to the fourth-finger knuckle. *Photo credit to Eva Foxon Nicholas.*

reach their destination. When transitioning from one intervallic setup to another, the hand morphs in fluid increments, adapting to each cluster of notes during the hand's migration over the fingerboard.

Picturing two elastic strings, connect one to the radial (thumb) side of the first-finger large knuckle and the other one to the ulnar (pinkie) side of the fourth finger (see fig. 6.2). Then imagine a force pulling them laterally while you play. This fosters an artificially expanded state in the hand, with the large knuckles contracting for half-step intervals and the fingertips following in compliance. With the hand poised in playing position, envision the large knuckles strung and knotted like pearls on an elastic string; then lift and pull the string laterally (as if tightening a slackened rope). Doing so elevates the knuckles and expands them sideways, in that way supporting a suspended position for the

Left Arm

articulating fingers. When you release the ends (as when playing chromatics or other half-step intervals), the hand returns to its naturally unexpanded state.

With the hand in playing position, drop the large knuckles down close to the string; feel their weight above the played string so that they lend backup support to the articulating fingers without creating a disruption of form. When you place all four fingers on one string, allow the large knuckles to fan open. Experience the first- and fourth-finger knuckles dropping with equal weight to the outsides of the hand. Any two knuckles representing a half step will naturally contract.

If the hand is in balance but the four fingers still fail to balance well above the string, try putting the hand in playing position while holding a rubber ball. Then visualize a bar positioned against the top of the hand just beyond the large knuckles (see fig. 6.3). With some weight against the knuckles, this bar restrains the large knuckles, preventing them from lifting up with the fingertips. Because the ball has give to it, the pressure applied centers weight in the second and third fingers—the middle of the hand—while energizing the area where finger motion originates. For example, in the Scherzo movement of Schumann's Symphony No. 2 in C Major, beat 1 of m.47 (see ex. 6.1), do not lift (throw away) the fourth finger on the downward shift. The bar acts as a ceiling, restricting excess motion by containing the fingers close to the string.

Figure 6.3 A bar is positioned against the top of the hand just beyond the large knuckles. *Photo credit to Gail Taibbi.*

Example 6.1 Scherzo from the Schumann Symphony No. 2, m.47.

Think of the large knuckles as the fulcrum in lifting and dropping the fingers onto the fingerboard, with the power coming from the hand to leave the finger relaxed in and around its other joints for fine tuning the nature of the contact with the string. Then when the fingertip hits the string, the weight at the second knuckle continues to drop after the fingertip strikes, similar to the body of a landing plane that continues to drop after the wheels have touched down. After the fingertip hits the fingerboard and the full finger (body) lands, the fingertip rebounds due to the buoyancy at the second knuckle.

The arm can be supporting the hand optimally and the hand properly balanced, but without a clear understanding of how weight is distributed within the hand, the fingers may still respond poorly. Be sure to avoid holding on by shifting weight back and forth between the fingers and the thumb. When the thumb becomes overly involved, the fingers constrict in response. To keep the fingers efficient, bend (flex) them at the middle and small knuckles so the inside forms a square room; then conceive of weight in the form of a ball bouncing around its infrastructure. Let the weight jockey around off the walls of the square room formed by the fingers alone (inclusive of the large knuckles), but not inside the cylindrical room formed by looping the fingertips to the thumb (see fig. 6.4). It is helpful if all the joints are relaxed, but especially those in the fourth finger and thumb, two digits that tend to hold tension.

Figure 6.4 Weight jockeys back and forth off the walls of the square room inside each finger alone. *Photo credit to Gail Taibbi.*

Knuckle Support for the Articulating Finger

There is a twofold interaction between the large knuckle and the fingertip during the fingers' articulations with the string. Inadequate awareness of it can result in a sluggish rebound. Think of each large knuckle as a ball, and then imagine bouncing that knuckle/ball off the string; then use the feeling of that bouncing force to articulate each finger. The limited motion from the joints at the large knuckles in a flexed hand provides for a fast knuckle bounce, which translates into rapid finger articulation. When bouncing the large-knuckle balls, either maintain the thumb's solid connection to the neck or picture resting the thumb on the same side of the fingerboard as the fingers so the thumb does not drop with the knuckles; otherwise, there is no fixed resistance away from which the knuckles can rebound.

Left Arm

Just as it is necessary to maintain the height of the hand to support a healthy suspension of the fingers through conscious support at the elbow, it is also essential to focus on the integrity of the palm itself in this regard. Problems arise for the articulating fingers if the palm progressively collapses or sinks too low on the downward motion of the fingers. Despite the relentless up-and-down motion of the fingers from the joint at the large knuckles, keep the palm moving horizontally, maintaining a steadfast height.

As a way to maintain the altitude of the palm, picture a rubber band with one end attached to the elbow and the other end affixed to the center back of the hand (see fig. 6.5). When the fingers are flexing toward the string, the rubber band urges the back of the hand upward, in that way dissuading the palm from dropping with the fingers to the point of articulation.

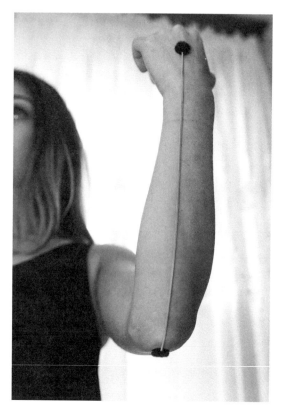

Figure 6.5 A rubber band stretching from the elbow to the center back of the hand. *Photo credit to Eva Foxon Nicholas.*

Just as the core of the body supports our migrating limbs, the forearm similarly acts as a core of support to the hand, and on an even smaller scale, the palm always sustains the fingers. Furthermore, even though the fingertips are deliberately weighted for rapid articulations, the large knuckles counterbalance the fingertips such that the hand remains poised during each dropping motion of the finger. Think of that weight as not fully transferred to the fingertips but perhaps just lent to them. The feeling of the rubber band stretching from the elbow to the center back of the hand allows the fingers to articulate with the string without a sense of the hand tipping over or falling off its base of support onto or otherwise losing any independence to the fingers. The support structure remains the foundation, the center of gravity, for the more active elements.

When you need a quick, lateral expansion of the large knuckles, as in fourth finger extensions or an up-tempo shift to whole step intervals, throw the large knuckle/ball sideways. With proper positioning, a finger that stretches for an extension snaps back in place as soon as the extension is complete. Imagine artificially elongating the extending finger.

For large shifts, lead with the wrist and then thrust the shift finger's large knuckle above the others in the direction of the shift to propel the hand up and down the string. On a scale ascent, the large knuckle of the shift finger propels the lateral part of the hand further to the right of the thumb, essentially extending and expanding the palm. On the scale descent, the large knuckle of the new shift finger leads the hand back toward the thumb as it rotates more into a flexed position. When the descending shift is with the third finger, experiment with firing both the third- and fourth-finger large knuckles above, below, or against the others along the line of the string.

When shifting up in smaller increments, as in scale passages, fire the first-finger large knuckle underneath the second-, third-, and fourth-finger large knuckles, akin to a baseball player sliding under a catcher into home plate; on the descent, thrust the fourth-finger large knuckle under the third-, second-, and first-finger large knuckles. Taken together, this technique supports transporting the hand up and down the fingerboard without compromising the hand's shape and balance.

Large Knuckles and Hand Rotation

An awareness of the large knuckles can assist the rotation of the hand around the fingerboard, supporting the position of the fingers. The first finger can use the string as a barrier when hurling the large knuckles to the subsequent string, preventing the hand from flying out of control. On E-to-G-string descents, toss the third- and fourth-finger large knuckles from the E string to the A, play the A string notes, and then throw the third- and fourth-finger large knuckles from the A string to the D; then on completion of those notes, hurl the third- and fourth-finger large knuckles from the D string to the G. When rotating the hand, as in same position ascending or descending scales, think of the large knuckles dropping with gravity in the direction they are headed. With chords, toss the large knuckles that are compatible with the note configurations.

Without a sense of large-knuckle backup to the fingers, the fingers lack grounding and can flounder, akin to a kite without a stabilizing weight. Form an image of the neck of the violin running through the center of a ball (creating an axis). Put your hand on top of the ball and your thumb underneath. Drape the large knuckles on top and roll the ball counterclockwise (to the left of the fingerboard). This shifts the knuckle weight on the ball's slope to the left toward the G string. Then roll the ball back (clockwise), in that way shifting the knuckle weight in the direction of the E string. The wrist rotates the ball, in turn transporting the large knuckles back and forth across the width of the fingerboard. When the knuckles are positioned above the string played, the fingers are able to articulate without extending.

Large Knuckle Movement in Tandem with the Wrist

Large-knuckle weight can be used effectively in tandem with the bottom of the hand. Just as a water-skier has to keep the feet in front of the body not to tumble, leading with the wrist (bottom of hand) as the water-skier would lead the body with the heels prevents the fingers from toppling forward; otherwise, the hand loses its balance.

A twofold communication between the bottom and top of the hand supports *left-hand string crossings*. Lead the way with the heavier bottom of the hand (see fig. 6.6); then accompany it by throwing the knuckle weight, which completes the positioning of the hand (see fig. 6.7).

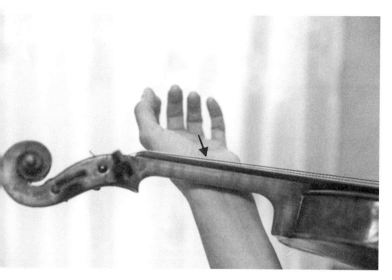

Figure 6.6 Lead the way with the heavier bottom of the hand. *Photo credit to Eva Foxon Nicholas.*

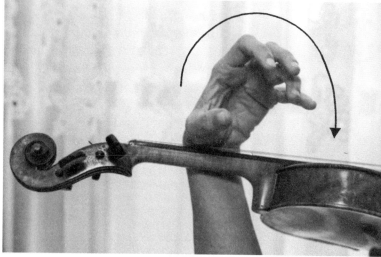

Figure 6.7 Throw the knuckle weight to propel the fingers into position. *Photo credit to Eva Foxon Nicholas.*

Catapulting the left hand, with the impetus of motion coming from the wrist, propels the hand without distorting its shape. To explore this, imagine attaching a clasp to the bottom center of your hand (see fig. 6.8); then approach the G string by leading with the bottom of the hand until the clasp energetically connects to the string; then thrust the large knuckles over the wrist. Imagining securing the base of the hand to the string enables the wrist to effectively catapult the top of the hand above that same string.

Because it is easier to articulate fingertips that are comfortably close to the palm (rather than having to reach), leading with the heel of the hand before thrusting the large knuckles over the wrist allows the fingers to stay close, always ready to drop down to their string destinations, with the palm in a continuous couching of the fingers. The following image displays the motions involved in guiding the fingers. When descending a scale in first position from the E string to the G, the wrist aims directly for the G string (instead of incrementally to the A, to the D, and then to the

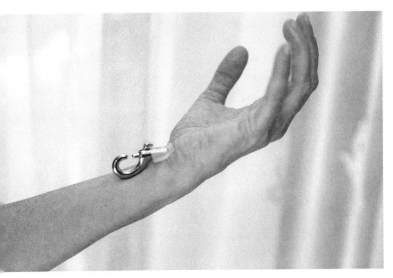 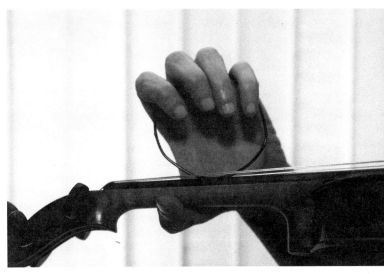

Figure 6.8 Imagine attaching a clasp to the bottom center of your hand. *Photo credit to Eva Foxon Nicholas.*

Figure 6.9 Center the area between the second- and third-finger large knuckles on the top of the circular wire. *Photo credit to Gail Taibbi.*

G) and lands on the G, with the bottom of the hand catapulting the top of the hand over the G so all the fingers have to do is to drop when they get there.

Take a circular wire and stand it up like a tire, aligning it with the track of the string. Suspend the large knuckles on the wire with the second and third on top (see fig. 6.9). With the foundation of the wire stationary, thrust the large knuckles to lean the wire one way and the other, allowing the bottom of the hand to swing through the opening. Enlarging it will carry the hand farther. Use the wire image to maintain a good distance from the fingerboard as well as remembering to relax the thumb and rest the hand.

Each time there is a cluster of notes, visualize the circular wire's proper location and angle; then engage the hand with the wire. When the wire shifts locations, the hand scrambles to catch up, and then it leaps on top of the wire in perfect balance, with the weight of the large knuckles placed over the string played. This process reinforces the importance of always thinking one step ahead, through to the completion of the piece.

The wire prop supports the sensation of the large knuckles as the apex of the hand while reinforcing an energetic placement of the palm above the fingerboard. During passage work, maintaining a globelike shape of the hand, with focus on the interaction between the flexed large knuckles and the padded bottom of the hand, allows the fingers to move with ease.

CHAPTER SEVEN

Left-Hand Fingers

Achieving an efficient left hand and arm formation is worthwhile for the primary purpose of securing the balance, shape, and proper position of the fingers above the string in anticipation of their next articulation. Here, we address the configuration of those fingers.

Finger Balance

An effective strategy to get set up for a persuasive performance is to center balance each component of the hand. To find individual finger balance, draw two lines lengthwise, dividing each finger into quarters using an ink marker (see fig. 7.1). In the center of the fingertip where the cross-cuts intersect is a point of balance that gives maximum strength and stability for the articulating finger.

Figure 7.1 Divide each finger lengthwise into quarters. *Photo credit to Eva Foxon Nicholas.*

Visualize each fingertip centered on a vertical toothpick on top of the fingerboard (see fig. 7.2); the motion of the fingertip is similar to a ballerina on one toe, balancing with microrotations. In left-hand string crossings, the last fingertip to leave the string transports the remaining fingers from one string to another by rotating briefly on the toothpick. When shifting, carry the circular motion of the fingertip into a rotation of the whole hand with the large knuckle of the shift finger leading and steering the remaining large knuckles, with the fingertips following and the curved line of the hand in counterpoint to the line of the string.

Figure 7.2 The first fingertip centered on a vertical toothpick on top of the fingerboard. *Photo credit to Eva Foxon Nicholas.*

When articulating the fingers with the fingerboard, imagine that as a finger drops down, a vertical toothpick projects up and out of the fingerboard, meeting it midpoint, with the finger landing on top in balance. When grouping the fingers into a chord, collectively lift the fingers up between shifts and onto two, three, or four imaginary toothpicks—depending on the chord configuration—in perfect balance. Decreasing the distance to articulation with this image allows a refining of the motion that improves dexterity. And because less movement requires less effort, it also has a freeing effect on the mind and body.

Versus simultaneous notes as chords, organizing consecutive notes as chords can preempt getting bogged down in a fast passage. It helps not only in huddling the fingers closer to the string but also in evenly distributing weight among the strings involved. In this example from the Finale of the Dvořák String Quartet No. 12 in F Major, Op. 96 (see ex. 7.1), distribute the weight of the hand in the first measure

Example 7.1 From the Finale of Dvořák's American quartet, mm.111–114.

between finger one on the D string and finger two on the G. In m.112, the weight can be distributed among the four fingers on the D string. In m.113, distribute evenly between finger one on the A string and finger three on the D to articulate from that vantage point. And in m.114, hand weight is allocated between the E and A strings, with emphasis on finger one on the E string and finger two on the A.

The more efficient articulating fingers described earlier improve the synaptic pathways and the muscular response. Consideration of thumb and finger angles will also lead to improved coordination. To support proper finger alignment, lean a pencil against the ends of the thumbnail and fingernails. Or imagine poking your fingers and thumb through balloon material under the neck; the membrane holds the neck, relieving the fingers from that burden to allow their natural alignment (see fig. 7.3).

Figure 7.3 Maintaining good alignment using balloon material.
Photo credit to Gail Taibbi.

Imagine holding four small balls, one inside each square-shaped finger, so the finger does not release its shape during the upward motion following articulation. Do not squeeze the fingers/balls; constricting the finger muscles impedes the motion.

To access the hand's potential energy while maintaining agility in the fingers, picture that the fingers and thumb form a cone-shaped coil. To get that feeling, try wrapping your hand around an actual cone, with the first finger around the narrow end. To determine the diameter of each finger coil, place the first finger on the E string, the second on the A, the third on the D, and the fourth on the G—or the reverse, with the first on the G, the second on D, the third on A, and the fourth on E. To support rapid finger articulation, tighten the coil by urging the thumb tip upward and the fingertips down, narrowing the opening to the spiral. In this position, each finger is more rounded, curling tightly into itself. Winding the fingers too tightly constricts them, such as when tucking the fingertips into the corresponding large knuckles.

The Hand's Stabilization of the Fingers

Once you get a feel for how the fingers balance with each other more generally, to stabilize the hand, try adding weight to the lower outside corner to support the fourth finger. Or elevate the medial corner until the first segment of the finger is perpendicular to the string. Leaning the left side of the first finger against an imaginary wall to its left also secures its vertical position, optimizing its ability to articulate with the string.

Think of the hand as a ball grounded in the wrist. Attach a string to the bottom center of the hand (the string exits the back of the hand). Lift the string, flipping the hand onto the fingertips while maintaining a suspension of the hand. Rest the weight of the hand either on fingers two and three or on one and four to evenly balance all four fingers on the string. To stabilize the overall left hand, shift the base of the thumb energetically into the center of the base of the palm across from the second and third fingers, placing all three around the extension of a line that splits the forearm bones, the radius and the ulna; the thumb's weight and strength counterbalances the fingers on top of the properly positioned forearm. Fingers two and three in conjunction with the thumb can form a subsection, a C-shaped band, within the hand.

To solidify the balance of the overall hand, position your hand and arm as if to play, and again picture the hand as a ball planted in the wrist. This time, imagine pressing the hand/ball down in between the radius and ulna while imagining the forearm bones extending up and out (see fig. 7.4). Doing so creates a sensation of the hand/ball being lodged between the bones, with the radius and ulna acting as

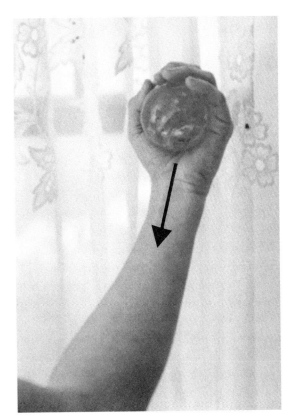

Figure 7.4 Imagine pressing the hand/ball down in between the radius and ulna. *Photo credit to Eva Foxon Nicholas.*

Left Arm

somewhat vertical barriers that hold the thumb and fourth finger sides of the hand in place. This thwarts the unsupportive tendency of the hand to roll around without regard for what the fingers are doing.

To stabilize the upright position of the hand during a continuum of passage work, visualize pulling a string that is attached to the center bottom of the hand through the center of the wrist and down the hollow of the forearm, securing it to the elbow (see fig. 7.5). For a deeper sense of hand and arm unity, compress the center of the palm toward the elbow (see fig. 7.6).

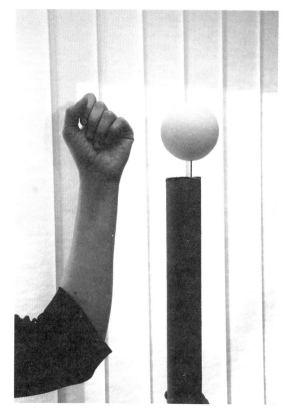

Figure 7.5 Pull a string attached to the hand down the hollow of the forearm, securing it to the elbow. *Photo credit to Gail Taibbi.*

Figure 7.6 Compress the center of the palm inward toward the elbow. *Photo credit to Gail Taibbi.*

It is helpful to balance the first and fourth fingers around the second or the third finger. Establish one or the other on the fingerboard rather than in combination, and then adjust the other fingers and hand around that. Structuring the hand around the third finger is a way to compensate for a particularly short fourth finger while retaining good access to the string for the remaining fingers.

To effectively distribute weight to the fingertips, imagine that the hand in playing position is hollow; then envision four metal balls, one inside each fingertip. Glide your fingertips along the E string and experience the smooth connection. This time shift your hand from fourth position to first while allowing the weights to slip out of the fingers and into the palm. Notice how the palm feels excessively burdened with that weight while the fingers have lost their solidified contact with the string. To avoid this imbalance, maintain the sensation of the metal balls inside the fingertips, whatever the rotational flux of the hand.

Like the axis of a gyroscope, the hand's position is perpetually adjusting and rebalancing as a function of its location on the fingerboard. Lift the arm from the presentation and directing points and then rotate it into a position that minimizes its tension and maximizes the hand's many rotational possibilities.

When you leave the place of center balance, the hand's most efficient posture in a particular context, support the return of the fingers to the hand's neighborhood by imagining that your skin is made of rubber. Place your four fingers on the D string to establish the feeling of home. With the hand rubber-coated, a push in one direction creates a pull from another, owing to the rubber's restoring force. Each variation in motion is supported to return to its original position. When playing with a rubberized hand in double-stop passages, such as in the Grave of the Bach Sonata No. 2, mm.8–9 (see ex. 7.2), each variation of motion yearns to return the fingers to home position, the rubber surface exaggerating the counterbalances taking place within the hand. Likewise, if you imagine encasing your hand inside a compressed rubber ball, again the restoring force of the rubber reinforces the hand's impulse to return to its original position.

Example 7.2 Bach's Sonata No. 2, Grave in A minor, mm.8–9.

Direction of the Fingers

When the large knuckles fan open, they poise the fingers at various angles. Knowing where to aim the fingers and how they collectively operate secures accuracy in pitch. With the hand in playing position, hold a clock face up in your palm with the fingers stretched around its circumference. The first finger is at one o'clock and aiming approximately in the direction of seven o'clock; the second is at about 2:15, aiming just past eight o'clock; the third is at about 3:30, aiming at 9:30; and so forth (see fig. 7.7).

Figure 7.7 A clock face demonstrating the specificity of finger angles. *Photo credit to Gail Taibbi.*

The clock image shows the relationship of the fingers to each other as they approach the point of articulation. Aiming the outer fingers (one and four) in toward the landing locations of the second (or second and third) fingers—in other words, fanning the fingers out from the second knuckle—distributes the weight of the fingers more evenly to provide each fingertip with equal access to the string.

This time, imagine that the fingers are parallel with each other all the way to the base of the palm, and consider that in playing position, each full finger—metacarpal to fingertip—forms the shape of a bass clef. Now imagine that this whole finger leans sideways one way or another, all the way to the heel of the hand (base of metacarpal). For example, two contiguous fingers might lean away from each other from the tips all the way through the base (see fig. 7.8).

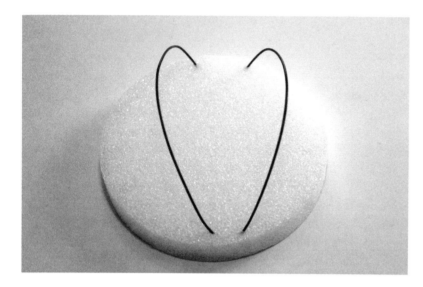

Figure 7.8 Two fingers side by side lean out from each other from the tips through the base. *Photo credit to Gail Taibbi.*

Many playing situations can be enhanced by imagining the motion taking place on a curved surface. Superimpose the thumb onto the center of the base of the palm between the first and fourth fingers. Poke your thumb through the hole in a metal washer and rest your fingertips along its circumference. The washer image encourages balance of pressure and positioning of the fingers in relation to the thumb.

Playing on the washer's edge supports an expansion of the fingers that is maximized at the second set of knuckles. To improve the rebound of the fingers, tighten the coil by aiming the fingers at the base of the thumb (or at the outer edge of the washer surrounding the thumb base). Carelessly aiming the fingertips at the thumb tip loosens the wind/curl of the fingers (similar to a lax spring that is been stretched too far) and diminishes their ability to rebound.

Imagine that the neck and body of the instrument are ghostlike, and all that exists is the string. Again, envision the washer, only this time with an edge that is grooved like a wheel on a train. Now, imagine that the washer moves along the line of the string, supporting the position and suspension of the thumb (inside the washer) and the fingers on top (see fig. 7.9). The bottom of the washer slides rather than rolls along the string to avoid disengaging the articulating fingers above. As the hand circulates the neck—for instance, when transitioning from third position to fourth, or during left-hand string crossings—the bottom of the washer engages the circumference of the string at various angles: leaning left, on top, or leaning right. If either the fingertips lose contact with the metal washer, or if the bottom of the metal washer veers away from the line of the string (the track), the hand collapses onto the neck. To boost the benefits of the washer image, play a three-octave scale focusing only on the fingertip contact to the washer; this solidifies the fingertip's relationship to the hand. Then play a three-octave scale while focusing solely on the bottom of the washer and its orbital relationship to each string.

Figure 7.9 Rest your fingertips against the edge of a washer and imagine it moving along the line of the string. *Photo credit to Gail Taibbi.*

Finger Placement

On descending scales, keep your fingertips over the string as you lift them away from an articulation; otherwise, you spend time having to retrieve them. If you allow your fingers to fly back—or be dragged by the knuckles—away from the string, they have farther to return to play the next note, especially when reaching for the next lower-pitched string. In Schumann's Scherzo at m.9 (see ex. 7.3), if after playing the fourth-finger B-flat on the E string (the first sixteenth note) the finger flies away from the string, not only do you have to retrieve it, but also you have to reach farther to place it above the A string to play the E-flat (the third sixteenth note). Pressing a pencil against the back of the four fingers imposes restraint, minimizing motion, part

Example 7.3 Scherzo from the Schumann Symphony No. 2, m.9.

Figure 7.10 Pressing a pencil against the back of the four fingers minimizes motion. *Photo credit to Gail Taibbi.*

of which is preventing the large knuckles from elevating with the fingertips, which would compromise the speed and efficiency of the fingers (see fig. 7.10).

On descending shifts, be especially careful not to pull the lower outside corner of the hand out and away from the instrument, requiring the fingers to fly back in. Imagine dropping a weight down inside the palm on the wrist side corresponding to the area underneath the third and fourth fingers to lend stability to the hand. Or imagine that the palm is filled with wet sand, providing a solid pedestal for the active fingers.

The distance between the heel of the hand and the instrument should remain relatively constant whether the left hand is more underneath or above the violin. Some variation of distance is inevitable, but it should remain as consistent as possible. To secure the proximity of the fingertips to the string, conjure up an image of a clasp attached to each fingertip and fastened around the string; then articulate the fingers with the string using this guiding restriction (see fig. 7.11). As you articulate notes, shift, or change strings, the clasp allows for only minimal motion.

Figure 7.11 A clasp attached to each fingertip to help maintain proximity to the string. *Photo credit to Gail Taibbi.*

Visualize four suction cups, one attached to each fingertip; then use them to suspend the light end of the violin. As you are articulating notes, pass the fingerboard from one suction-cupped finger to the next. This secures each finger's tonal connection to the fingerboard while supporting the neck. Move the fingers as little as possible, keeping them hovered over the notes. Dragging the fingers across the fingerboard in a straight-line route also eliminates excess motion. With left-hand string crossings, it is especially important to lift the fingers minimally; picture sliding them as if on a glass surface from one string to the next.

Leading with the Pad or the Nail Side

Although the efficiency of the left hand is established primarily through a good setup from the arm, some peripheral direction by the padded and nail faces of the fingers adds an extra vector of control during rotation around the neck. If you imagine strumming the strings with the padded, fleshy side of the fingertips on G-to-E-string ascents, and on E-to-G-string descents strumming the strings using the fingernails, that light touch assists finger speed. Also, the strumming sensation helps keep the fingers simultaneously in close contact to the strings and in a healthy proximity to the palm, maintaining the integrity of form.

The following image promotes accuracy in the left hand as well as a sense of engagement with the bow by invoking the subtle feeling of resistance to the bow's pulling of the string. First, place the four fingers on any string. Then, on the downbow, consciously counter the bow—and string's—direction with the fingernail (see fig. 7.12); the padded side of the finger resists the direction of the upbow (see fig. 7.13).

Figure 7.12 On the downbow, consciously counter the bow and string direction with the fingernail. *Photo credit to Gail Taibbi.*

Figure 7.13 The padded side of the finger counters the direction of the upbow. *Photo credit to Gail Taibbi.*

Left Arm

If you lift a more open hand, its naturally expanded state can compress and release with ease. When presenting the arm to play, for instance, on the E string, imagine expanding the hand and wrapping it around the neck, equally drawing the thumb and fingers toward the palm's center and toward that string. In so doing, the hand is poised such that all the fingers have to do is to relax the degree of flexion to assist in reaching notes on the lower strings.

The Conjoining of the Fingers and Palm

The following images call on proprioceptive relationships among various parts of the hand that support effective articulations. Notice the downward pressure in the finger conjoining with the upward motion in the palm (as opposed to renegade fingers reaching across the fingerboard), with the combination supporting lively finger response. Without the twofold motion of the fingers joining the corresponding part of the palm, the fingers can weaken from a lack of connected support. Visualize four miniature Bullworkers (an exercise device where the ends are compressed inward against spring tension), one oriented between each fingertip and its corresponding part of the palm. To mimic the interactive relationship of the fingertips to the palm at the point of articulation, compress the ends of each Bullworker, one at a time. Doing so heightens awareness of natural resources built into the hand for approaching, reaching, and retreating from an articulation with the string.

Form an image of a tunnel along the width—just inside the crease—of your wrist; then run a taut string through the opening. Lifting the string drags the base of the palm upward to meet the fingers. The tightened string assists the palm in supporting the articulating fingers (see fig. 7.14). Overall, lifting the base of the palm supports the hand and relaxes it into its spherical shape, including the natural curves of the fingers. Enhancing the hand's curvature helps eliminate unwanted tension, liberating motion in the fingers. In contrast, when the palm shape is more planar (less rounded), the fingers strain by exerting unnecessary effort during their engagement with the string.

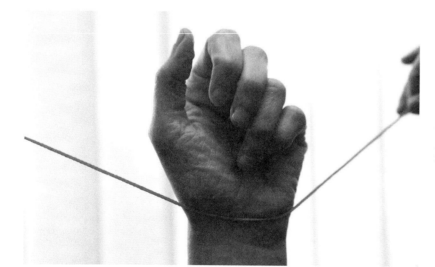

Figure 7.14 Lifting the string drags the base of the palm upward to meet the fingers. *Photo credit to Gail Taibbi.*

In general, extending fingers tends to weaken the finger-to-palm connection and the impetus of finger motion, thereby slowing speed. Maintaining a close finger-to-palm connection supports finger strength and dexterity. Think about how you access more hand strength squeezing a plum than a grapefruit. Imagine poking your thumb through the center of the neck, bringing your thumb closer to the fingertips. That close connection supports finger speed (see fig. 7.15). The fingers play to the string (and to themselves) and balance themselves around the thumb. The fingertips do not play to the tip of the thumb, however; doing that disrupts the connection between the fingertips and the palm and bogs them down.

Figure 7.15 Imagine poking your thumb through the center of the neck to bring your thumb closer to the fingertips. *Photo credit to Eva Foxon Nicholas.*

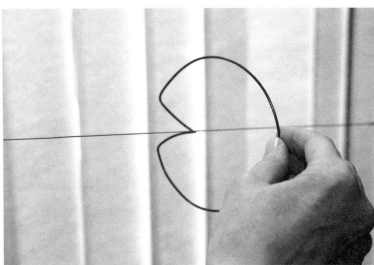

Figure 7.16 The wire represents the shape of the upright hand poised to play and the direction of the fingers. *Photo credit to Gail Taibbi.*

Imagine extending the length of both the fingers and thumb, wrapping them around the neck and looping back into the center of the palm. With the hand in playing position, keep the thumb on one side of the string barrier (underneath) and the fingers on the other (on top) as you direct the fingers toward an imaginary hole inside the palm's center. Imagine that the thumb and fingers are drawn equally into the palm's center, all the way to the large knuckles. This illustrates the ideal balance of the thumb from underneath and the fingers from above accessing equal amounts of large knuckle backup (see fig. 7.16).

Now imagine that the last segment of the thumb is wider than in actuality, with that part of the thumb providing the fingers with a steady platform on which to balance. Doing so stabilizes the relationship of the fingers both to the thumb and to the string at their articulation.

This time, call to mind the image of a vertical tube in a lobster pool designed to drain surplus water; now imagine the fingers similarly drawing into the palm's

Figure 7.17 The string coaxes the center of the palm upward while gravity encourages the outer palm downward. *Photo credit to Gail Taibbi.*

center—even down into the hollow of the forearm. Before tucking in the large knuckles, expand the hand as if wrapping it around a large ball to create a sensation of elongating the fingers, in turn allowing them to reach farther down without disrupting the overall shape of the hand.

Imagine that the hand is draped onto an apple on a stick. The elongated fingers wrap all the way around to the bottom of the apple and are drawn up through the core and into the stem. When migrating around the fingerboard, if weight in the hand is evenly distributed between the fingers and thumb, the stabilized hand is less apt to tilt out of balance, in the same way that someone on all fours and crouched close to the ground is difficult to push over. In lower positions, if you suspend from a string the center of the faceup palm, the upward pull of the string coaxes up the center of the palm while gravity encourages the frame and fingers downward (see fig. 7.17).

An image that demonstrates an exaggerated interaction between the palm and fingers on the fingerboard is a yoga position called the Crow Pose: call to mind an image of starting to crouch down, knees bent, your hands in front of you on the floor between your feet; push your hands (representing the fingers) down while lifting your whole body (representing the palm) off the ground, with your hands (fingers) now supporting your body (palm).

Now contemplate in the imagination that the faceup (supinated) left hand is suspended above the fingerboard and that the palm's center is nonmaterial, forming an opening through the middle of the hand. The fingers curl in and press downward through the opening, with the hand urged upward; turning outside in, the palm's perimeter pulls the fingers through its center with the fingers now free to navigate the strings below. The energized fingers push off the fingerboard and lift the remaining body of the hand (the palm) in the way that a yogi uses two hands to elevate the body. The ascending palm lends backup support for the fingers to increase pressure on the string. In the first movement of the Mendelssohn Violin Concerto in E minor, starting at beat three of m.27 (see ex. 7.4), imagining that the fingers move through and out the back of the hand supports the oppositional interaction of palm and fingers, creating a healthy tension that is similar to tightening a spring or cocking the hand into a position of readiness.

Example 7.4 First movement of Mendelssohn's E minor concerto, from beat 3 of m.27.

CHAPTER EIGHT

Left-Hand Finger Action

Ideally, the entire left arm with all its subdivisions—hand, wrist, forearm, elbow, upper arm, and shoulder—supports the objective of the fingers, which is to tap dance freely, unimpeded in all positions.

—Maureen Taranto-Pyatt

Finger Position

In the previous chapter, we established the balance and lateral relationships of the fingers. Their shape, suspension, and impetus of articulation influence dexterity, intonation, and clarity of tone.

To find the most direct route between the fingertip and the fingerboard, it helps to think about maintaining a gradual curve in the finger as it lifts and then snaps down. To experience that, poise your hand in playing position. Now visualize a horizontal cylinder large enough to house the hand and a violin string threaded off-center through its opening (very close to the curved wall on the left). Lean your fingernails against the constraint of that inner wall and move them up and down on that curved surface, toward and away from the string; the wall guides the small segment on an efficient trajectory toward the string.

There is substantial musculature that flexes the thumb toward various parts of the hand and fingers, all together providing oppositional strength for the fingers that therefore biases somewhat to their radial (thumb) side. Even though the impetus of the flexing and extending motion of the fingers is in the forearm, and with a properly positioned hand we look for the fingers to drop down easily without preconceptions, when certain articulations require some muscularity, feel the finger guiding its route to the string from its radial (thumb) side (see fig. 8.1). To get a feel for this, envision the radial side of each finger leaning against a vertical wall, a prop that enables the finger to draw strength from the thumb while it supports the strength and verticality of each finger in challenging positions.

Keep fingertips close to the fingerboard because extraneous motion inhibits speed. Fingers remain curved and close to the palm so they can motor up and down

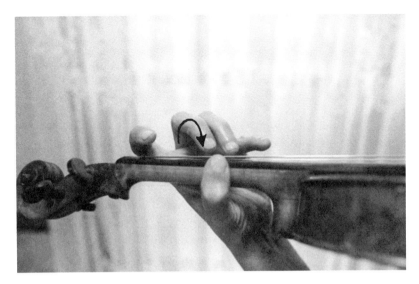

Figure 8.1 Guide the finger from its radial side to draw strength from the thumb. *Photo credit to Eva Foxon Nicholas.*

with foundational support. To optimize the fingers' ability to articulate easily, it helps to keep them parallel with each other and the tips of the fingers in a nice alignment with the string; then strike the string with the middle of the fingertip in such a way that the padding is equally apportioned on both sides of the string. The tendencies to either flatten too much onto the pads or overly lean toward the fingernail are detrimental.

Holding on to or clutching the neck sideways by squeezing together the first joint of the thumb and the first-finger large knuckle does disrupt form. When you soften the touch of the fingertips on the string, you want to proportionately lighten the contact point of the thumb to the neck.

Support for Finger Action

Because of the varying length of each finger, it is easy for the hand to fall out of balance during a mix of challenging articulations. In general, be sure to exert relatively equal effort from similar musculature underneath each finger. Otherwise, if each finger solicits support from an arbitrary place within the hand, the fingers end up articulating with the string the way that someone walks with varying leg lengths. As a result, the hand tends to rock in and out of balance from finger to finger (see fig. 8.2).

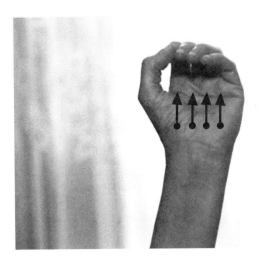

Figure 8.2 Exert relatively equal effort from the same degree of musculature directly underneath each finger. *Photo credit to Eva Foxon Nicholas.*

Weakness is the other result of neglecting the supportive connection deep in the hand. If, for example, you articulate the fourth finger, drawing strength only from the finger itself while backing up the other fingers from deep in the palm, the fourth finger will function relatively weakly. A way to ensure solid support for each finger is to aim the last segment of the finger at the corresponding metacarpal, firing each finger toward a point slightly below the large knuckle. You can also access backup support either from the big adductor muscles of the thumb or from the substantial musculature under the fourth finger.

Arbitrarily varying the choice of knuckle that supports the follow-through of the finger also knocks the hand in and out of balance. Observe each set of similar knuckles, one row at a time: the large, middle, and small. The knuckle choice varies from person to person, but in general, think of employing the heavy base knuckles to support the fingers during G-string articulation, the middle knuckles for D-string articulation, the first set of knuckles for the A string, and at cuticle level, a virtual joint near the end of the small segment to articulate with the E string. Propel each finger through the same knuckle before moving to a different string. If, for example, the momentum for the first finger runs through the small knuckle on the A string and for the fourth finger at the large knuckle, an imbalance of the hand results.

Pick a set of knuckles (the same one from each finger) and imagine that the fingers are powered by them. Picture that the rest of the finger extending beyond the knuckle used is nonexistent, leaving the full knuckle on the end of the finger. Then use the nicely rounded and weighted knuckle that is now at the end of the finger to easily articulate notes by hammering the string. This has the added benefit of reinforcing the proper relationship of the hand to the neck by positioning the neck more deeply in the hand. The weight and momentum of each knuckle pushes down the string while the corresponding thumb knuckle pushes upward.

The fingers need to move with a direct and uncomplicated motion to strike the string dead-on. Imagine that your left palm is rubber and filled with helium and that the fingers are floating above the string at the proper angle, poised and ready to strike. More or less out of gravity and with no burden of weight, the fingers find their impetus of motion very easily. Imagine a similar easy feeling with the first or second set of joints being struck from behind with a plastic hammer in the direction the fingertips are traveling. The action of the articulating fingers is a hammer and release (relaxation); it is a snapping motion as opposed to pressing and holding the finger down. Each finger builds momentum and then strikes and releases energy as others prepare to strike. Lift each finger and snap it down; when the finger hits the string, continue the motion as if it can move beyond the fingerboard barrier; it will begin the rebound on its own.

Visualize four strings running up along the back of the hand, one affixed to each of the four large knuckles, and four strings attached to the top of the second set of knuckles. To assist finger action, with the hand in playing position, envision someone simultaneously pulling one of the large-knuckle strings downward and one attached to the related second knuckle upward, and then releasing (see fig. 8.3). Alternating the pulling of the strings with the influence of gravity on the release allows weight of the first segment to flex and extend more vigorously, in that way sending more power and precision to the point of articulation.

Figure 8.3 Feel the large knuckle string pulled downward and the second knuckle pulled upward. *Photo credit to Gail Taibbi.*

To shoot fingers to a clean articulation, it is helpful to visualize the tendon running through the front of the palm and into the finger as a rope. Then snap the rope as if cracking a whip. Even though the reaction at the end of the line feels simultaneous, there is a delay as with a whip crack, the response delayed progressively out into the finger. It also helps to imagine that the finger stretches like an elastic during articulation and retracts on completion of the note.

This time imagine that the bones of each finger, starting from the base of the palm to the fingertip, form a complex set of seesaws: the entire finger is a seesaw, and then within it are seesaw microcosms, examples of which are the metacarpal (bone inside palm) and the first segment of the finger. Awareness of each seesaw length (within the hand) and its alternating motion maximizes the ability to articulate the finger.

During chord passages where all the fingers are stationary except for one, as in the Fuga of the Bach Sonata No. 2 in A minor, m.40, beat 1 (see ex. 8.1), mentally poise the bottom of the hand to the left of the string with the chord's base note; then plant a seesaw from the base knuckle to the middle joint of the finger that is leaving the pack (in this instance, the fourth finger to C-sharp); flip the ends of the seesaw / lower third of the finger contrary to each other (the large knuckle ending up higher and the second knuckle ending farther down), in that way snapping the fourth finger to the fingerboard. If two notes are stationary and two fingers leave the pack together, as in the final measure of Urstudien (Basic Studies) by Carl Flesch, exercise 1C (see ex. 8.2), poise the bottom of the hand to the left of the lowest pitched string and then pull the imaginary strings attached to the ends of each seesaw / proximal phalanx (large finger segment). Once again, the large knuckle ends higher, and the

Example 8.1 Bach's Sonata No. 2, Fuga, m.40.

Example 8.2 Urstudien by Carl Flesch, exercise 1C, final measure.

second knuckle ends lower to direct the rogue fingers away from where the rest of the hand is established.

Envision an S-shaped bar roughly the length of the hand. Now with the left hand poised to play, imagine threading that S-bar into the natural shape of the hand, with the fingers blended into the top of the S and the opposite half of the bar threaded through the bones in the palm and curling into the wrist; as the top of the S-bar rotates down when you drop the finger on the string, envision the bottom part kicking up and out the back of the hand, in that way lending a strong, deliberate intention to the articulation of the finger. On the release, the finger lifts, rotating the bar back into place (see fig. 8.4). This image supports an awareness of the wavelike, contrary motion throughout the whole hand during left-hand passage work.

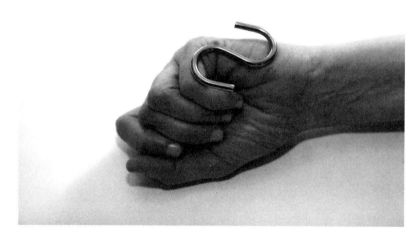

Figure 8.4 Thread an S-bar into the natural shape of the hand. *Photo credit to Gail Taibbi.*

After solidifying the left-hand mechanics surrounding the points of articulation, we back up a bit. Envision a horizontal cylinder somewhat to the right and above the line of the string. Thrust each finger around (over the top of) the cylinder, snapping the fingertip onto the string. The cylinder supports the destinations of the fingers across the width of the fingerboard (just as the creation of arcing paths supports the migrations of the fingers along the length of the fingerboard) while also providing the large knuckles with a retaining barrier. Now envision four cylinders, each one replacing the last segment of each finger. This is especially helpful for playing chords. The diameter of the cylinder is dependent on the fingertip's straight-line distance from the palm at the point of articulation as well as on the particular string articulated. Place the four fingers in first position on the E string; then use the fourth finger to articulate the note B-natural, followed by a fourth-finger articulation of the D-natural on the G string. The cylinder used when articulating the fourth finger on the E string is smaller in diameter than when transitioning the fourth finger from the E string to the G. You can also envision the fingers aiming for the inner edge of the somewhat cylindrical thumb. The cylinder image is particularly helpful during passages where the fingers walk back and forth across the fingerboard, such as in the second movement of the Beethoven Symphony No. 9, mm.906–910, all in first position (see ex. 8.3).

Example 8.3 Second movement of the Beethoven Symphony No. 9 in D minor, mm.906–910.

A Dream

I dreamed that a hand slipped itself inside the hollow of mine and executed every note with incredible speed, ascending and descending three-octave scales. An inner pulsation of those fingers drilled the feeling of clean, strong articulations into my fingers. Moments later, my fingers pounded into the neck, the fingers and thumb working together this time as though the fingerboard had the consistency of clay.

Imagine that the neck of the violin is round and sculpted with indentations—pathways for the fingers to travel. Then during slower passages that involve more muscularity, dig your fingertips into the fingerboard the way a rock climber scales a rock, dragging your hand up and down the fingerboard ledge using those indentations. At the point of articulation, drive the bone of the fingertip into the fingerboard, or picture spikes permanently attached to the center of the fingertips—projectiles—and fire them into the fingerboard to secure good contact with the neck, especially in chord configurations.

Poised Fingers

There is a tendency to overextend the fingers when crossing the fingerboard, disrupting the overall shape of the hand in the process. To maintain consistency of hand position while contending with the neck's being in the way, bring the hand in slightly closer to the neck on the E string so that with a slight rotation, all the fingers have to do is relax to drop to play on the G string (rather than exerting or overextending). If you unwind and open the fingers too much to play on the E string, you end up having to extend them more haphazardly to reach the G string, working too hard for accuracy of placement and dissipating their strength and efficiency. Taken together, there is a more cooperative motion of the fingers if you engage them all—used and unused—with an extra degree of active flexion to be ready for this lateral move.

To maintain a healthy fingers-to-palm distance in relation to the fingerboard, imagine that the neck does not exist, only the fingerboard; think of the thumb as situated directly underneath the fingerboard (not the neck) with the fingertips above (see fig. 8.5). Eliminating the neck and energetically playing to a thinner wedge brings the fingers and thumb as close together as possible and supports the fingers moving more vigorously. Angle the neck such that the thin side slips easily into the hand opening, with the hand engaging in communion with the instrument; the neck feels sandwiched between the base of the thumb and the fingers, with similar pressure from both sides. This elegant compression creates a solid foundation for the articulating fingers.

Figure 8.5 Think of the thumb situated underneath and the fingertips above the fingerboard alone. *Photo credit to Eva Foxon Nicholas.*

Feel a continual sensation of the heel of the hand wrapping around the neck, snuggling in and around it without actual contact. This enlivens the playing. To keep this energized feeling, stay aware of the constant flux of position to maintain a balanced format of the hand with the fingers, maintaining the even opposition of the thumb and fingers from their respective sides. If you feel tension, ease or soften the thumb's contact with the neck to relax the fingers. In higher positions, imagine that the body and neck of the violin are chimerical, with the fingers and thumb connecting only to the solid top and undersides of the fingerboard.

Imagery That Supports Finger Rebound

Because the up motion after articulations counters gravity, to create an environment that supports a natural rebound, form a picture of a circular wire running inside the flexed hand, just above the large knuckles (an equator for the rounded hand). Wrap your upright thumb and the crease formed above the large knuckles around the circular wire; then lasso a string around the hand and underneath the large knuckles and tighten it (see fig. 8.6). The wire holds the round form inside the hand and, together with the lasso, creates an environment where the natural state of the fingers is off the string. Then after the fingers articulate with the string, they eagerly release upward, returning to a state of active flexion. For quicker reactions, shrink the size of the round wire and tighten the lasso. Along with the strength of the flexor muscles in a primarily flexed hand, gravitational pull adds to the downward motion to finger articulation, so the lasso image helps to counter those natural forces by supporting the upward motion.

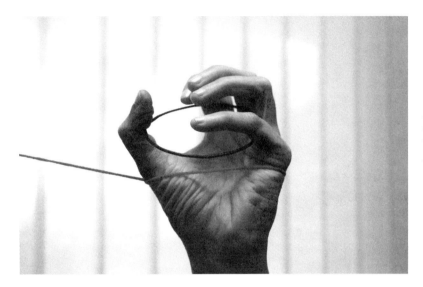

Figure 8.6 Hold a circular wire midthumb and at the base of the fingers; then tie it with a string. *Photo credit to Gail Taibbi.*

Picture the circular wire as the rim of a drum shell that is covered with animal skin. After wrapping the first joint of the thumb and the large knuckles of the fingers around its circular frame, feel the fingers rebound off the head/skin. The drum skin offers the fingertips a level platform on which to balance.

Envision four rubber bands, with one end of each attached to a fingertip and then running along the back of the hand and down to a corresponding part of the wrist (see fig. 8.7). After the finger articulates with the string, the stretched rubber band lifts the finger to support its rebound.

Imagine an open space between the forearm and hand; insert a platform underneath the bottom of the hand and then let it elevate. Lifting the hand upward to the neck, rather than drawing the neck down into the hand by default, intensifies compression between the bottom of the hand and the collective fingers without bogging down the fingers, as a result fueling the acceleration of the freely flexing fingers. The finger rebounds the moment note contact is made due to the slight release of hand compression. Imagining the thumb encompassing not only its meaty first segment but also the base of the palm can lend strength to the flexing motions of the fingers.

Envision a toothpick-sized pogo stick projecting out of the fingerboard. When articulating the fingers, feel the downward pressure and release of each fingertip on the pogo stick. Similarly, visualize that the bone inside the fingertip is a pogo stick that compresses and decompresses, in that way assisting each finger's rebound.

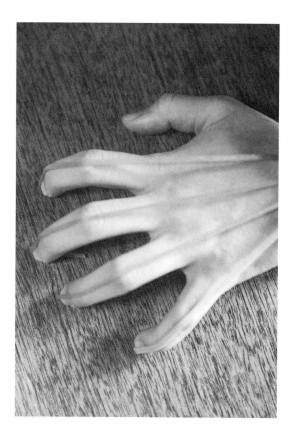

Figure 8.7 Four rubber bands support the rebound of the articulating fingers. *Photo credit to Eva Foxon Nicholas.*

Imagine that inside each fingertip is a hollow cylindrical compartment. Picture a metal ball contained inside each compartment. Hit the ball with the small knuckle, with the ball rebounding off the inside floor at the fingertip. Bouncing the metal ball inside the fingertip assists the finger's articulation, with the weight of the metal ball intensifying the motion while adding snap. During same position E-to-G-string transitions, thrust the weighted fingertips from one string to the next; the additional weight adds momentum to the finger motion, which in turn assists the hand's rotation.

Picture the neck of the instrument as a cylindrically shaped water balloon. Now rest the four fingers on the balloon as you would on the string. As each finger drops, it displaces enough fluid to slightly elevate the remaining fingers. At times you may prefer keeping the fingers as close to the string as possible, feeling the horizontal wave of fluctuation, whereas at other times you may exult in the upward motion of each finger following its drop. Either way, the articulating fingers reliably discharge the others from the string, and the continual pulsation, each new note freeing the previous one, allows the fingers to navigate passages with energy, organization, and forward momentum.

To add dimension to the sound, feel that you are plucking the string with the left-hand fingers with each finger's upward release. To strengthen the relationship of the finger to itself, visualize a miniature C-bar made from springlike material. Insert it inside the square of the flexed finger and then compress the C-bar to implement a plucking articulation; the C-bar supports the pluck, and then its decompression encourages the return to a more relaxed, extended position. Insert a C-bar in the square of each of the four fingers to effectively support the plucking of notes in rapid succession.

To maximize tone in all passage work, form a picture of the countermotion of the left-hand fingers bending the string into varying shapes (landscapes) to produce elegant and imaginative contours in the three-dimensional realm of sound. Just as raindrops displace molecules on a pond's surface, the fingers displace the string barrier as you articulate notes. During rapid passages, visualize your articulating fingers as the patter of a rainstorm. Envision manipulating the string with the fingers along with the feeling of sculpting each note with the bow to create expressive designs that transmute simple pitch into beauty of tone.

CHAPTER NINE

Left Thumb

Finding the right balance between continuous communication and functional independence of the thumb and the fingers is essential. Though the thumb does not directly engage with the fingertips as they articulate, the upward thrust of the thumb assists the downward motion of the fingers. Focusing on the thumb to guide hand rotation and steer the fingers to their destinations leaves the rest of the hand relaxed and malleable. If the thumb either strays from a connection with the finger pack or gets overly involved, then its autonomy—or its dependency—compromises the hand's infrastructure.

Balance of the Hand and Thumb

Visualize holding a ball in your left hand in playing position, with your fingers on one side of it and your thumb on the other. Generate the same feeling with the fingers on one side of the neck and the thumb on the other side, with the hand blossoming by way of the fingers and thumb in counterbalance. The outnumbering fingers tend to dominate, overpowering the thumb's integral involvement with the hand's strength, mobility, and rotational position. To retain the strength and facility that good balance promotes, bend the thumb and the fingers into similar curves and draw in the base knuckles of both to provide equal backup. If you extend your thumb instead of flexing it to mirror your flexing fingers, you'll start to notice a spreading tension that eventually hampers movements and destabilizes the overall balance of the hand.

No matter what position the hand is in—whether palm up or in higher positions upside down, whether expanded or contracted, maintain an image of the full thumb superimposed in the middle of the base of the palm with the thumb tip centered on the line of the fingertips. When playing chords (or thinking groups of consecutive notes organized as chords), center the thumb between the two framing fingers. When playing an octave, for example, functionally center between fingers one and four. Playing thirds, the thumb moves between each pair of involved fingers. For a continuum of passage work, again the default position is with the thumb centered between fingers one and four to secure the frame of the hand, but it shifts to adjust to the note clusters in chord formations within the structure of the passage. In each

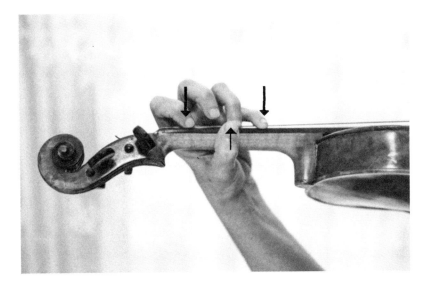

Figure 9.1 Aim the fingers through the string while the thumb pushes upward on its own vector. *Photo credit to Eva Foxon Nicholas.*

instance, aim the fingers down through the string at angles determined by the articulation while pushing the thumb upward and against the side of the neck to counter a variety of forces. Though counterbalancing each other, neither directly aims at or specifically plays to the other (see fig. 9.1). That said, when the thumb fails to engage with the fingers at all—in other words, when it does its own thing, oblivious to the fingers—the hand falls out of balance.

Whether it is relatively stationary or in flux, creative deconstructing of the hand intensifies an awareness of the hand's center balance, its naturally efficient posture in repose. Hold a circular wire that runs vertically on a path along the artificially centered thumb and over to the middle finger, bisecting the middle finger and thumb lengthwise. Then double the wire (see fig. 9.2). Let the hand bloom on both sides of the wire, toward the scroll and the bridge, also flowering across the neck from thumb to fingers to create a four-way divide and balance of this new expansion, a four-leaf clover poised crisscross on the fingerboard.

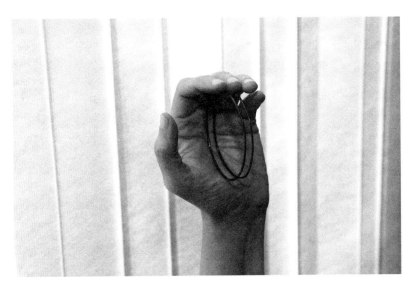

Figure 9.2 A doubled circular wire creates and supports a bilateral sense of the hand. *Photo credit to Gail Taibbi.*

Left Arm

Maintain both the circularity of the hand and the sovereignty of its divisions as it leans, whether leading or following up and down the fingerboard. If that mutual independence is lost—for example, if the left side of the thumb engages with the right side of the hand—the distribution of weight is altered, and the integrity of the system is compromised.

Because of the thumb's distance from the fingers and its separation across the neck, it is easy to miss or forget the importance of their connection. As a result, the thumb tends to disengage, usually overextending toward the scroll. A curved thumb supports curved fingers, so when you collapse the curve by bending the thumb back, you lose both muscle strength and nervous system efficiency.

Picture the thumb and middle finger wrapped around a miniature tire rim. In lower positions, the rim is small with the thumb closer to the fingers. In higher positions, where the thumb is easily left behind, they can still be in good communication thanks to an expanded rim. In the opening of the Ballade in the Ysaÿe Sonata No. 3 (see ex. 9.1), the fingers are closer to the thumb in the beginning of the phrase; then as the hand ascends the A and E strings (on the double stops), they maintain their circular connection via the tire rim that expands to accommodate the second finger's distance from the thumb.

Example 9.1 Opening of the Ysaÿe Sonata No. 3, Ballade

Imagine separating the thumb from the hand as you would a piece from a puzzle (include the important first segment within the palm). Then take a short elastic string (maybe an eighth of an inch long) and connect it again, affixing one end of the string to the thumb's metacarpal and the other end to the center of the base of the palm (see fig. 9.3). Doing so gives the thumb a sense of additional freedom to expand as the hand ascends into a higher position, and to easily retract (due to the elastic's restoring force) on the return, all the while maintaining its connection and communication with the rest of the hand. This image encourages pliability at the base of the hand, where tension is commonly held.

A secondary benefit from this image is experiencing the thumb in its entirety, directed from an area deeper in the wrist. Thumb movements ideally are initiated by way of that first meaty segment, with the portion from the large knuckle out staying relaxed and responsive. Powering the thumb primarily beyond the large knuckle ignores the essential foundation of the thumb, leaving it to congeal and ultimately transferring its tension to other areas of the hand and wrist.

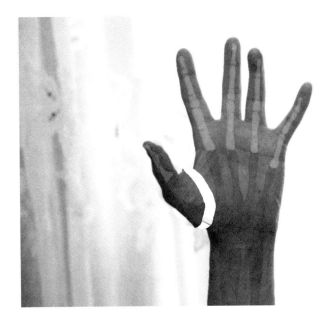

Figure 9.3 Imagine separating the thumb from the hand and reconnecting it with a short elastic string. *Photo credit to Eva Foxon Nicholas.*

Because finger lengths and palm sizes vary from person to person, the distribution of weight inside the hand is also somewhat individual. To sort that out, it is helpful to picture a track along the wrist (similar to one that suspends a pocket door; in this case, the thumb suspends somewhat sideways). Affix the base of the thumb to the track and then slide it along, correspondingly positioning it underneath each finger one at a time or in between any two fingers (see fig. 9.4).

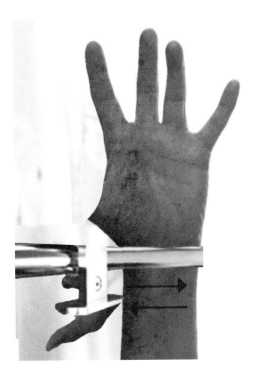

Figure 9.4 Affix the thumb base to a track along the wrist, similar to one that suspends a pocket door. *Photo credit to Eva Foxon Nicholas.*

Notice how repositioning the thumb affects the distribution of hand weight and finger balance. With a long fourth finger, suspending the thumb (from the track) either between the first and second fingers or directly underneath the second finger supports good balance for that hand; suspending the thumb somewhere from the second to the fourth compensates for a shorter fourth finger by tilting the hand such that it brings the fourth finger closer to the string. Choose whichever supports equal fingertip access to the string. Once the thumb position relative to the fingers is decided on—in other words, once you find your personal point of balance—permanently affixing the thumb base in that location will help you maintain continued access to the fingerboard by all four fingers.

Thumb Contact with the Neck

A distinction between using the stabilized neck as a prop that supports the motions of the hand and the thumb's requirement to be one of the stabilizing forces further elucidates the thumb's delicate balancing act. Because what happens on one side of the hand affects the other, when you press the neck with the thumb, the tendency is to counterpress from the first-finger large knuckle, constricting the hand and impeding its ability to orbit the neck (see appendix H). And if the area between the fingers and thumb collapses, the neck intrudes and impedes the firing speed of the fingers. Instead of holding on, picture the thumb's connection to the neck as a safety belt that secures the rest of the hand. Although the hand rotates, the thumb travels against the neck with a feeling of frictionless contact as it loops around and slides up the neck into higher positions. Compatible with the shape of the neck, the thumb's curvature and its rotation support the shape and direction of the fingers. Feel the thumb swinging under and over the top of the fingerboard with the ease of an acrobatic, assisting the direction of the hand's rotation around the neck.

Securing the Hand's Tunnel

When rotating the hand around the axle of the neck, if any part of the hand is stuck supporting the neck, its rotation is impeded. For instance, if you lean or hold the neck on the edge of the first-finger large knuckle, that makes it difficult to elevate the fingers such that they clear the fingerboard and drop down without distortion of shape. To maintain the circular shape of the hand, insert an imaginary cylinder inside the hand's opening/tunnel; then rotate the hand around the cylinder.

To support the curvature of the thumb (and hand) during its revolution of the neck, imagine that the neck is cylindrically shaped and that a second, larger cylinder encases the hand and the first cylinder—a cylinder inside a cylinder (see fig. 9.5). The fingers and thumb orbit the neck-cylinder, with the whole hand guided by the inside wall of the larger cylinder.

Figure 9.5 A larger cylinder encases the hand and the neck reshaped cylindrically. *Photo credit to Gail Taibbi.*

Thumb-to-Fingertip Rotation

Besides its cooperative relationship with the fingers (shape and support), the thumb participates actively in rotating the hand; otherwise, with a passive thumb, the hand's tunnel can deteriorate, hindering movement around the neck in the way that a warped wheel impedes a smooth rotation around its axle. The following image illuminates the mechanics of steering the hand around the neck. Form a C shape with the thumb and middle finger. While maintaining this shape in playing position, feel a push down on the tip of the thumb (or thumb pad) that rotates the hand up and over, with the fingertips now dropping down more easily on top of the fingerboard. Releasing the rotation restores the thumb to an upright position. The curved shape of the thumb reinforces the curved orbit of the fingers crossing the fingerboard in position in the way the stones of an arch cooperate in shape and strength. A loss of that dynamic strength while directing the hand around the neck is similar to pushing a boat offshore with a long pole that either collapses into itself or folds in the middle.

If the thumb joints fold instead of maintaining extension (active flexion) vis-à-vis the palm, the infrastructure of the hand collapses, and the fingers collide with the fingerboard as a result. When the thumb maintains its integrity, it is able to engage the components of the palm. Because it is easier to push an object with a shorter reach than one that is longer and likely more flexible, imagining that the thumb as a stump provides a solid base from which to rotate the hand (see fig. 9.6).

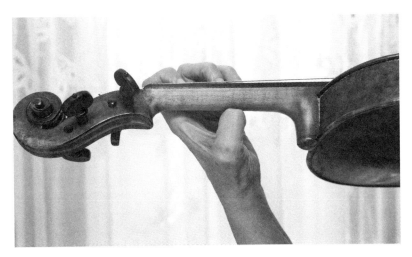

Figure 9.6 Imagining that the thumb is a stump. *Photo credit to Eva Foxon Nicholas.*

To explore this in the fourth movement of the Mozart Symphony No. 35, mm.131–139 (see ex. 9.2), rotate the hand by pressing and releasing either the tip of the thumb or the top of the thumb stump (the base knuckle) to steer the fingers back and forth from one string to another while maintaining the hand's round shape. The press-and-release sensation of the thumb feels like submerging a bobber underwater and allowing its return to the water's surface. In m.131 (first position) the thumb is upright for the E-string eighth notes; on the last eighth (on the A string), press the tip of the thumb (or stump) down slightly, rotating the hand to take the fingers to the A string position; continue playing in m.132 (eighth notes all in first position). In m.133 continue on the A string. In the last eighth note of the measure (the F-sharp on the D string), press the tip of the thumb down more, again rotating the hand counterclockwise, spilling the fingers onto the D string for mm.134–35, transitioning first to half position and then back to first. Finally, in the last eighth note of the measure (the B-natural on the G string), press down the tip of the thumb even more until the hand's rotation places the fingertips above the G string in mm.136–137. Releasing pressure off the thumb tip reverses the hand's orbit, with the fingers having access to the D-string notes in the remaining measure as well as the first eight notes in m.138. In m.139 releasing more pressure from the thumb tip allows further clockwise rotation of the hand, placing the fingers above the A string for the remainder of the passage. When shifting into higher positions, pressing down the tip of the thumb directs the frame of the hand diagonally, in that way steering the fingers up the fingerboard while promoting an overall expansion of the hand.

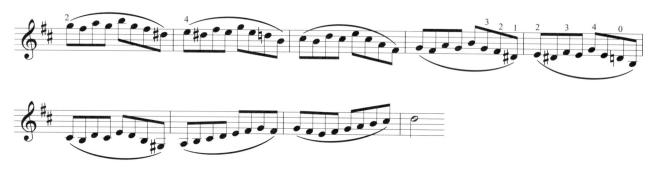

Example 9.2 Fourth movement of the Mozart Symphony No. 35 in D Major, mm.131–139

The use of visual aids is particularly helpful with the complex challenge of suspending and directing the fingers, the failure of which carries with it myriad obstacles to efficient and beautiful playing. Tilt the left hand clockwise onto its lower outside corner to shift its point of balance, and divide the hand in half with a line that we'll call the "spine," extending from the first-finger large knuckle to the lower outside corner (see fig. 9.7). Separate one-half of the hand from the other using this line and picture the spine as a dowel with some substance. Balance the base of the thumb against the opposite side of the palm. When you rotate the hand counterclockwise underneath the neck, think of the thumb half lifting the dowel/spine and corresponding finger half to a position more on top; in reverse, the finger side rotates the hand clockwise, lifting the thumb side and restoring it to the left of the neck (see fig. 9.8). Imagining each half of the hand volleying the dowel back and forth energetically assists rotation of the hand around the neck, especially during E-to-G-string or G-to-E-string passages (or incremental rotations), creating a feeling of interplay within the hand.

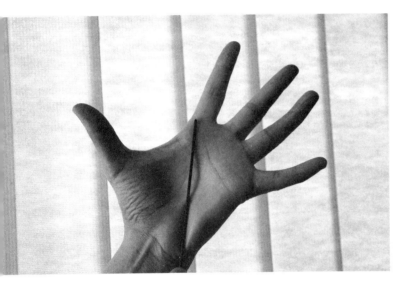

Figure 9.7 Defining a new axis of rotation for the hand. *Photo credit to Gail Taibbi.*

Figure 9.8 Each side pushes through the imaginary dowel/spine, lifting and rotating the other around the neck. *Photo credit to Gail Taibbi.*

Whether the transition is gradual, as in the first movement of the Mendelssohn, pickup to m.35 (see ex. 9.3), or immediate, such as in the first movement of the Lalo *Symphonie Espagnole* in D minor, m.41 (see ex. 9.4), on the transition from beats 2 to 3 (E string to G), the action of pressing the thumb tip underneath the neck is the same both times. During same position G-to-E-string passages, releasing the hand's/thumb's rotation restores the thumb to an upright position. Suspend the thumb either upright to the left of the neck or upside down to the right. Aim for either one thumb suspension (upright) or the other (upside down). Stay in transition; motion disallows stasis.

Example 9.3 First movement of the Mendelssohn, pickup to m.35.

Example 9.4 First movement of the Lalo *Symphonie Espagnole*, m.41.

Invisible Props for Thumb Support

When playing on the same string for an extended stay, lean the thumb against an imaginary string as a barrier so the hand does not rotate prematurely into its comfort zone (see fig. 9.9). Envision four strings (which we'll call G^1, D^1, A^1, and E^1) underneath the neck, spaced farther apart than the actual strings (see fig. 9.10); lean the tip of the thumb on the imaginary string that is diagonally underneath the positioned fingers on the string played. Analogous to a gymnast on uneven parallel bars, the thumb accesses support from the offset strings.

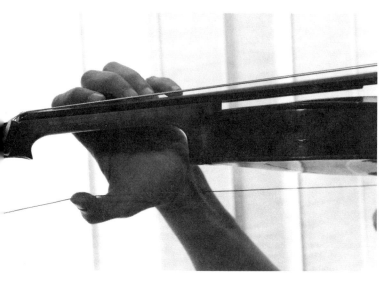

Figure 9.9 Lean the thumb against an imaginary barrier/string to hold steady. *Photo credit to Gail Taibbi.*

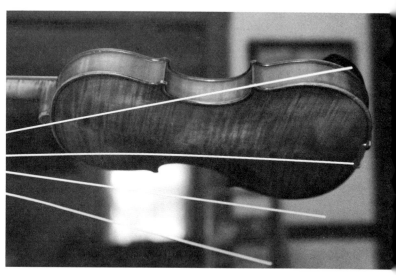

Figure 9.10 Envision four strings underneath the neck, spaced farther apart than the actual strings. *Photo credit to Eva Foxon Nicholas.*

When the fingers play on the G string, the tip of the thumb energetically rests against the right side of the E^1 string, in that way unburdening the hand. When descending from a higher position to a lower one—say, seventh position to fifth or fourth—the tip of the inverted thumb slides along that supportive string to the right of the neck to avoid rotating prematurely (clockwise) and placing the fingertips out of reach. In lower positions, especially when playing on the E string, to prevent the thumb from its natural tendency to rotate clockwise over the top of the fingerboard, place an imaginary G^1 string parallel and to the left of the neck (above the thumb tip) at a height that supports the thumb's positioning of the fingers.

Support of imaginary strings that either buttresses the ascending thumb or bolsters the inverted thumb ensures that the fingers will retain their shape during prolonged passages. They also prevent the fingers from falling away from the actual strings. For instance, in the first movement of Mozart's D major concerto, 32 measures after the solo entrance (see ex. 9.5), the hand starts off in the E-string comfort zone. In beat 4 of m.32, the notes are all on the A string, and a slight extension of the fingers is not noticeably detrimental. In m.33 the notes are now on the D string, however, and if the hand and fingers are still positioned on the E string, the fingers need to extend farther, losing speed and pulling the hand out of balance. Besides distracting them from their support in the palm, unnecessary reaching slows the response of the fingers by not only the extra time it takes to reach farther but also the added time it takes for them to retract. Adjusting the thumb's position from one imaginary string to the next is a reliable way to secure the proper placement of the fingertips to avoid the unnecessary extending of the fingers.

Example 9.5 Mozart's D Major concerto, 32 measures after the solo entrance.

The Thumb's Role in Hand Compression

In a balanced hand, the awareness and use of compressions promote speed by adding strength and shrinking the range of motion. Consider the compression between the upward motion of the thumb and the downward motion of the articulating fingers, especially at the corner posts of the first and fourth fingers. What you do on the finger side has consequences for the thumb side. If motion happens on the right side of the neck and the thumb is passive (or immobilized by tension), the fingers become strained; but as soon as the fingers and thumb work together, compressing and releasing in coordination, the fingers gesticulate naturally.

To secure the hand's frame without producing tension, raise the first joint of the thumb until it lines up with the base knuckles of the fingers (see fig. 9.11). Extended upward, the thumb can now suspend the fingers, allowing them to relax and curl, sinking deeper into themselves. When the thumb tip is lowered, the hand extends, and the fingers unfurl, enabling G-string finger access. Experiment with varying the focus of the finger-to-thumb compression; for example, urge the thumb tip upward and the fingertips down, or urge the thumb's small knuckle upward while lowering the fingers' first or second set of knuckles, and so on.

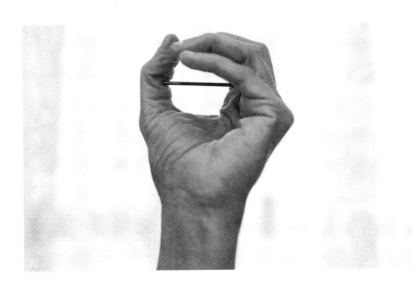

Figure 9.11 Raise the first joint of the thumb until it lines up with the base knuckles of the fingers. *Photo credit to Eva Foxon Nicholas.*

CHAPTER TEN

Finer Balances of the Left Hand

As we have now established, when the thumb is in a haphazard relationship with the fingers, the full abilities of the fingers remain unrealized. The thumb's positional relationship to the fingers supports proper balance among the fingers. Acting either as a lever or as a gymnast's hand circling a bar, the thumb also contributes to the poising of the fingers above the string and to their migration along the length and across the width of the fingerboard.

Thumb-to-Finger Balance

Just as there is a primary balance with the thumb counterbalancing the fingers on opposite sides of the neck, there are secondary balances that, when factored in effectively, can reinforce the small motor functions of the fingers. Imagine taking a horizontal Popsicle stick and centering the thumbnail underneath with the fingertips balancing on top to create a seesawing of the stick. Then similarly sensory-project the fingers and thumb so configured above and underneath a string played, with the thumb as a fulcrum centered underneath the fingers that are playing on top. Recreate the seesawing motion of the stick as the balance of weight moves among the fingers, with the thumb continually adjusting to stay centered (see fig. 10.1).

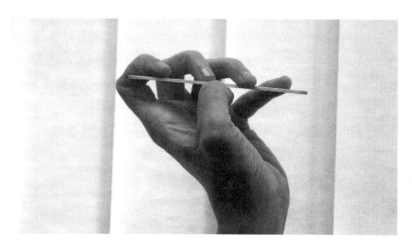

Figure 10.1 Center the thumbnail vertically underneath the stick and balance the fingertips on top. *Photo credit to Gail Taibbi.*

Thumb-to-Finger and Thumb-to-Palm Rotational Relationships

The next motion is similar to the seesawing of the Popsicle stick with the thumb as fulcrum, except that the rotation takes place deeper within the hand. Superimpose the thumb onto the center of the base of the palm. Then picture a solid, round cookie cutter, and imagine punching out a circle that allows the insertion of the thumb; the peripheral hand rotates around the perimeter of the cookie cutter. The thumb rotates with the hand, but not in a one-to-one correspondence; the rest of the hand moves semi-independently, conforming to the musical task while continuing to harmonize with the adapting thumb, which is continually shifting weight underneath any finger eager to act.

Conjure up an image of a ball inside a hooded caster turned upside down. In higher positions, visualize that the thumb is parallel to the floor (horizontal) and stationary. Place the hood part of the caster against the thumb and the large knuckles on top of the ball, which is cradled in the hood (see fig. 10.2). While staying in the same position on the same string, rotate the ball with the palm to transfer weight from one large knuckle to the next, in that way lending backup support to the articulation of each finger around the thumb. By rolling the palm against the ball, the fingers are assisted in sequential finger strikes—one, two, three, four, three, two, and one—with minimal thumb motion. In lower positions, imagine that because the thumb is upright and stationary, the caster is rotated ninety degrees (see fig. 10.3).

Figure 10.2 The palm manipulates a ball cradled in the hood of the caster, transferring weight among the knuckles. *Photo credit to Gail Taibbi.*

Figure 10.3 Turn the hooded caster ninety degrees for a hand in first position. *Photo credit to Gail Taibbi.*

This image invites us to explore, appreciate, and employ the small motor functions from the palm that control the fingers. These micromotions are used when navigating same-position passages, as in Schumann's Scherzo, pickup to m.1 (see ex. 10.1).

Example 10.1 Opening of the Scherzo from the Schumann Symphony No. 2 in C Major.

This time, poise your hand to play and then roll the thumb pad against the stationary back of the caster. Notice how this motion directs or steers the fingers. It is especially helpful during intricate passages involving left-hand string crossings.

The Left-Hand Bow Hold

There are various ways that the fingers can interact with the thumb to assist the hand's migration along the line of the string. Imagine that the neck and body of the violin are phantom; then play only to the string (see fig. 10.4).

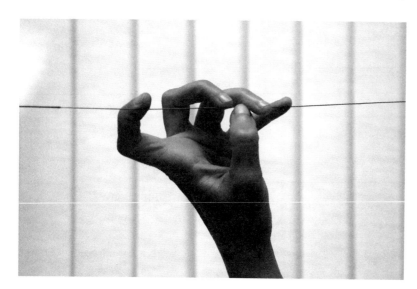

Figure 10.4 Imagine that the neck and body of the violin are phantom and play only to the string. *Photo credit to Gail Taibbi.*

Now imagine that a particular string magically transforms into a bow, staying on the fingerboard. Center the left-hand fingers with a good bow hold, aiming the thumb between the first and second fingers; then mentally project the tip of the thumb through to the side of the small knuckle of the second finger. Holding the string as you would hold a bow intensifies the awareness of the line of the string while securing left-hand formation. The impetus of the shift is similar to the initiation of the bow stroke, even though the fingertips slide back and forth on the string. During large shifts, lead from the mid-forearm, thrusting the left wrist as you would fire your hand and bow with the right arm, with the fingers relocating on the string without losing their shape. When you reach the destination, the fingers and thumb release the bow and articulate their notes. Another similarity to bowing is finding in the left-hand thumb and fingertips a buoyancy similar to when bowing spiccato. As with the bow hand, the left hand continually reestablishes balance.

This time flex the thumb into the palm and rest the four fingers on the edge of the thumb's last segment (see fig. 10.5). Now slip the neck of the violin into the hand while remembering this feel. The fingers aim for both the string played and the inner edge of the thumb. Although separated by the neck, imagine the string somewhat sandwiched between the fingertips and the thumb. Doing so helps to ground the hand by inhibiting excess motion of the thumb during the lifting and dropping of each finger while supporting an overall balance of the fingers.

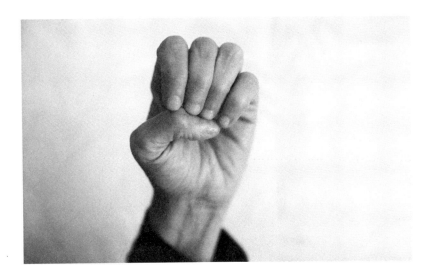

Figure 10.5 Resting the four fingers on the edge of the thumb's last segment grounds the hand. *Photo credit to Eva Foxon Nicholas.*

With ascending or descending passages on one string, such as in the first few measures of the Paganini Caprice No. 24, Variation 3 (see ex. 10.2), both the row of fingers and the inner edge of the thumb can migrate as a unit, with the thumb driving with the same kind of energy from underneath the neck as the fingers from above. Especially when crossing the fingerboard, the thumb can be both a force that anticipates and a rudder that steers the fingers to each destination as in Variation 5 (see ex. 10.3).

Example 10.2 Opening four measures of Variation 3 of the Paganini Caprice No. 24

Example 10.3 Paganini Caprice No. 24, Variation 5, 1–3 measures after the repeat.

Now tilt the left hand counterclockwise onto its lower inside corner, just under the base of the thumb, and imagine it resting on the fingerboard. This has a relaxing effect on the thumb from its very root, which in turn helps to release unhealthy tension throughout the rest of the hand. Once it fully relaxes, visualize the base of the thumb moving as a hull of a sailing vessel on top of the string. That secure foundation for the fingers stabilizes any errant motion.

Or imagine leaning the lower outside corner of the hand into the base of the thumb while the fingers play to the thumb's inner edge. This supports a lovely open hand formation that is especially helpful during E-to-G-string descents, a setting where the tunnel of the hand tends to collapse.

Look for the subtle motion where the thumb anticipates its next position, setting up a platform for the fingers to land on. The fingers arrange themselves en route between shifts or string changes and then land with full weight on the inner edge of the thumb-platform. The fingers play to the thumb; the fingerboard happens to be there. It is grounding for the fingers to imagine that the thumb is round and sculpted with indentations, pathways for the fingers to travel. Once one sequence of articulations is complete, the thumb can anticipate the next one. When aiming for the string without backup support, the fingers tend to land prematurely, requiring an adjustment that creates a delay, an imbalanced hand, and a subsequent unevenness of notes.

The flexed thumb can use both the curvature and the straight lines of the neck to guide the fingers along the line of the string. Experiment with each one and then both together. When playing on the G string, feel the fingers crashing as a wave over the fingerboard onto the edge of the thumb. This image supports a feeling of spaciousness inside the tunnel of the hand while unburdening the fingerboard.

The Thumb Lever

The thumb can act as a lever to help propel the fingers shorter distances. Whether in lower positions with the fingers dangling to the left of the upright thumb or in higher positions with the fingers articulating to the right of the thumb, the thumb engages with the fingers by defining a pivot point for, and adding energy to, the various rotations involved in setting up for the new position. Without the thumb's assistance to keep a relaxed rotation in the hand, the forearm steps in and impedes the facility of the fingers because of the forearm's inability to handle the smaller increments of motion.

A good place to see this is at the pickup to m.276 in the first movement of the Tchaikovsky Symphony No. 4 in F minor (see ex. 10.4) where the upside-down thumb lever and the right-side-up fingers swing opposite each other along the fingerboard: as the thumb shifts its position toward the scroll (on the fourth sixteenth note of the pickup, for example), the fingers move toward the bridge, and then they reverse on the ascent. The thumb lever moves contrary to the fingers *during shifts*, as in the previous example, but it remains stationary (relative to the fingers) on passages *in between shifts*, as in the scale passages between shifts in the first movement of the Mozart Concerto No. 4, 11–12 measures after the solo entrance (see ex. 10.5).

Example 10.4 Pickup to m.276 in the first movement of the Tchaikovsky Symphony No. 4 in F minor.

Example 10.5 Mozart's Concerto No. 4 in D Major, 11 measures into the first movement solo.

An example in higher positions is in mm.189–192 of the second movement of the Mahler Symphony No. 4 in G Major, in the bottom line (see ex. 10.6), where the fingertips are to the right of the thumb. In the four-note sequences that follow, the thumb lever ratchets up each time as it propels the fingers farther down, with weight centered in either fingers two and three or one and four.

Example 10.6 Pickup to m.189 in the second movement of the Mahler Symphony No. 4.

The Thumb's Suspension of the Fingers

It is ideal to operate the fingers from a suspended position that is enabled by ensuring the thumb has a solid, albeit gentle and nongrasping, connection to the neck. Sustaining thumb contact with the neck enables the palm to reliably extend above the fingerboard and steady the fingers as they reach down from above. In so doing, the fingers are also able to clear the fingerboard when shifting. Without good contact with the neck, there is no steady resistance away from which the fingers can rebound.

While staying in the same position on the same string, imagine a sudden magnetism pulling your thumbnail toward the neck, holding the pad of the thumb in place. This supports suspension in the fingers that allows them to drop in a healthy fashion from an above-the-fingerboard position.

When orbiting around or migrating along the neck, the thumb communes with the neck from various parts of itself during its movements. For instance, notice that the neck is in more contact with the last joint of the thumb while playing in the first position on the G string, but more with the pad of the last segment in fourth position and higher.

This time, imagine attaching a string to the inside of the elbow and pulling it to the right in a horizontal plane (not in an upward curve), locking the last joint of the thumb into the neck. The forearm and hand stand like a young tree supported by a wire (see fig. 10.6). This firm connection of the thumb to the neck secures the hand both during running passages and for enhanced vibrato. The wrist has a kind of sturdiness with resilience that is also similar to an immature tree. Maintaining a degree of firmness in the wrist allows the forearm and hand to tilt without the hand collapsing against the neck, either from the wrist or the thumb-first finger opening of the hand.

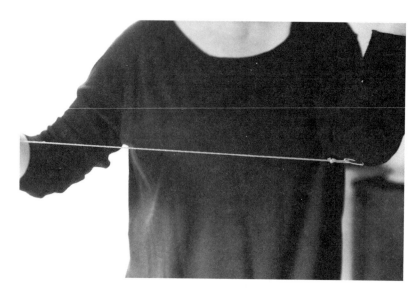

Figure 10.6 Pull the elbow to the right in a horizontal plane. *Photo credit to Eva Foxon Nicholas.*

In passages with a lot of shifting, as well as with scales and arpeggios, a relaxed thumb that maintains contact with the neck thwarts the tendency to lean the base of the first finger against the neck. Imagine a sensation of the back of the thumb leaning, rolling against, or pivoting off the right side of the neck to support that healthy connection at the thumb's actual point of contact.

If you envision holding a baseball in your left hand, part of the ball's surface is exposed. If you now imagine holding the ball while navigating passages, retaining a sensation not only of the hand but also of the ball's contact with the neck, both the hand's infrastructure and its ability to migrate will be assisted.

Again, picture holding the baseball, this time while imagining the hand-as-ball rolling inside the pocket of the wrist. Feel the perimeter of the wrist expanding, in that way supporting either the bottom of the hand or the fingers during the hand's rotation, especially during third-to-fourth-position changeovers. An expanded wrist rallies around the hand during its varying rotations, catching the bottom of the hand, the lower outside corner, the base of the thumb, or the fingers, with its flexibility encouraging the hand to center-balance in any position.

Imagine that the thumb is like the trunk of a tree and the line of large knuckles comprise a limb that is either centered or to the left of the thumb in lower positions or to the right of the thumb in higher positions. Weighted like four apples in a row, the fingertips dangle from the branch.

Envision a small, upright tire. Align the tire with the fingerboard, positioning it such that the tire can roll along the length of the fingerboard. Place the fingertips inside the bottom curve of the hollow tire—the top is ghostlike and does not impede the motion of the fingers (see fig. 10.7). Holding the same position, perform consecutive one, two, three, four, three, two, one drops of the fingers, the fingertips rotating the tire slightly, back and forth between the bridge and scroll. Specifically, when pressing the first finger inside the tire, the tire rotates scroll direction, and when pressing the fourth finger, the tire rotates toward the bridge. Doing so supports a healthy musculality of the fingers, also reinforcing their position and alignment with the string.

Figure 10.7 The fingertips placed inside the bottom curve of the hollow tire. *Photo credit to Eva Foxon Nicholas.*

The Thumb Axle

This time picture that the first thumb joint is against the neck and the palm and fingers are free to rotate around the thumb, similar to a person grabbing onto a flagpole with their toes against the bottom of the pole, leaning back and swinging around it. In passage segments (running notes between shifts), the fingers can rotate around a stationary thumb, as in the first movement of the Mendelssohn, mm.29–31 (see ex. 10.7).

Example 10.7 First movement of the Mendelssohn, starting in beat 3 of m.29.

When orbiting the neck in shifting passages, especially when the hand transitions from underneath to above the instrument, or the reverse, the fingers loosen their orientation to the thumb and then refocus postshift. To get a feeling for that relaxed connection, call to mind the image of a (horizontal) wheel frame; then lean the large knuckles against the outside of the frame with the thumb centered inside, akin to an axle inside a wheel (see fig. 10.8). The large knuckle crease lines on one side of the wheel line up with the crease line of the first joint of the thumb. The thumb is now centered among the large knuckles of the four fingers, each staying in contact as it rotates one way or the other around the vertical axle of the thumb.

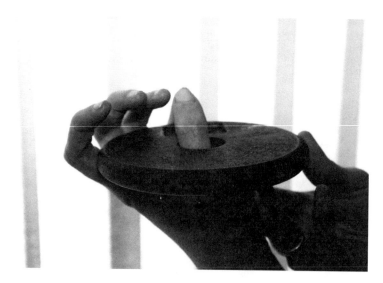

Figure 10.8 Lean the large knuckles against the outside of the iron frame with the thumb centered inside. *Photo credit to Gail Taibbi.*

If a planet were to rotate without a relatively stable axis, because of being untethered to other bodies, the destabilizing of its rotation would not alter its orbit. Unlike a free-floating planet, however, the hand's rotations are influenced by—and in turn influence—the larger motions of the arm. It is important, therefore, to keep the hand motions elegant (simple, efficient, graceful) to avoid migrating into unwanted orbits. Try creating a well-defined axis for each rotation to keep random influence—entropy—to a minimum.

Imagine that the hand is a planet, and picture the bottom of it resting on a horizontal platform. Visualize that the thumb is a vertical axis on which the planet/hand rotates. Envision a materialized ring bordering and hovering around the hand's large knuckles that is similar to the rings surrounding the planet Saturn's equator, only closer and with more influence. Then imagine the materialized ring coated in rubber. This ring surrounding the large knuckles helps keep the hand center balanced, like a gyroscope for the articulating fingers (see fig. 10.9).

Figure 10.9 The ring surrounding the large knuckles helps keep the hand center balanced. *Photo credit to Eva Foxon Nicholas.*

Figure 10.10 The position of the hand/ring bouncing off the bridge end of the fingerboard. *Photo credit to Eva Foxon Nicholas.*

Figure 10.11 The position of the hand and ring bouncing off the scroll end of the fingerboard. *Photo credit to Eva Foxon Nicholas.*

The planet/hand (at various angles, but always with the large knuckles and the rings in the same plane) can also lean on the imaginary ring, so its second function is unburdening either side of the hand while lending buoyancy to the hand's motion. During same position E-to-G-string passages, the thumb side of the ring bounces off the ring to the left of the neck, with its rebound propelling the hand to the right (or up the scale), and the finger side rebounds off the ring to the right, with the hand bouncing to the left and assisting the scale's descent. The conjoined hand and ring can also bounce off the bridge and scroll at each end of the fingerboard (see fig. 10.10 and fig. 10.11). Whichever direction the hand/planet tilts, the solid ring / bumper prevents the planet/hand from tipping over by providing a buffer on which to lean.

Thumb and Fingerboard Usage and Imagery

When playing a rapid passage with back-and-forth ascending and descending shifts, visualize the upright thumb placement midway between the ends of the passage. Akin to the pole used in pole vaulting (a lever), the thumb can then launch the fingers from a lower beginning position over the top of the thumb/pole into a higher end position. Then imagine the reverse on the scale's descent, with the thumb/pole hurling the fingers from a higher to a lower position. Picture the fingers traveling on these arcing paths from one destination to the next.

During rapid ascending and descending scales, when the thumb/pole vaults the rest of the hand to its right or left, the pole length varies depending on hand destination: visualize a short thumb when vaulting the hand shorter distances and a longer thumb when carrying the hand further. In actuality, the whole hand extends, which invites the illusion of a highly expandable thumb. When using the pole-vaulting concept, do not allow the palm to break the line of the arc by leaning on the violin in fourth position. Rather, allow it to lean only when the fingers land on the fingerboard at the bottom and top of the scale. While the fingers hop from one location to another without fully touching down, the palm remains suspended. In higher positions, the heel of the hand touches the violin but does not rest until the passage is complete. Allowing the palm to land prematurely interferes with the ability of the fingers to reach their destination easily and on time, and it results in the fingers having to drag the palm along with the palm weight distorting the finger shape.

When the fingers settle into a higher position, as in the Mendelssohn, 37 bars after the second solo entrance—all in fifth position (see ex. 10.8), then the palm can rest against the shoulder. In the first movement of the Tchaikovsky Symphony No. 6 in B minor, mm.70–72 (see ex. 10.9), in beat 3 of m.70, the hand is established in eighth position; on the descending shift (first two sixteenth notes) in beat 1 of m.71, the thumb/pole thrusts the fingers from eighth position over the pole into fifth position to complete the passage. In beat 3, the thumb/pole then hurls the fingers back over the top (toward the bridge) into eighth position to repeat the sequence a second time.

Imagine the fingertips pushing down on an actual string while the thumb (tip or small knuckle) pushes upward against an imaginary string that is parallel and to its left (see fig. 10.12). This image reinforces the compression between the thumb and fingertips and strengthens the ability of the fingers to rebound while maintaining the independence of the thumb and fingers.

Example 10.8 Mendelssohn, 37–38 measures after second solo entrance.

Example 10.9 Movement I of the Tchaikovsky Symphony No. 6, mm.70–72.

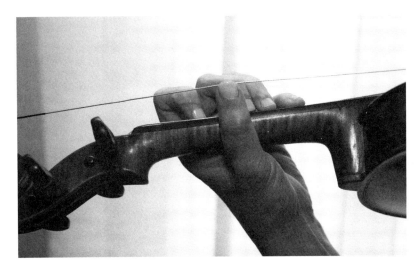

Figure 10.12 While the fingertips push down an actual string, the thumb pushes upward against an imaginary string. *Photo credit to Gail Taibbi.*

There is a certain amount of letting go necessary to achieve a rapid finger response, and the wrist is a crucial area to consider. Zero in on the relationship between the fingers on the string and the disposition of the wrist. Rather than consciously bending the wrist to position the fingers, place a relaxed wrist above the elbow. With the left hand in playing position, envision a vertical string connected to the inside bump of the elbow; then gently lift the elbow string (swinging the elbow underneath the instrument), in that way elevating the hand such that the heel of the palm feels energetically higher than the fingers, resulting in the weight of the hand migrating into the fingers. Whether lifting or lowering the elbow, position the heel of the hand such that weight travels to the fingers.

Try experiencing the elbow as the point from which the hand is suspended, a sensation of being functionally or energetically higher, allowing weight to travel easily into a relaxed hand to give the fingers the best opportunity for an unimpeded articulation with the string. Overly arching the wrist impedes the process of weight traveling to the fingers, both because of the likelihood of increased tension and also because weight will find any excuse not to travel uphill. Similarly, if the forearm rotates too much one way or the other on its long axis (as in the bow arm; refer to chapter 18, "Stabilization of the Wrist"), the weight will disburse by falling off to the side before reaching its destination, destabilizing the balance of the fingers.

CHAPTER ELEVEN

Left Hand Formation

We have developed a good awareness of the motions and balances of the thumb as it relates to the rest of the hand. So now we concentrate on the formation of the full left hand, first in conjunction with the right hand.

Symmetry

There is a strong positive correlation, often a symmetry, between the right- and left-hand formations. To experience that, drop your arms to your sides and then lift your right and left hands with palms facing up. Slip the bow into one hand and the violin into the other (see fig. 11.1).

Figure 11.1 Slip the bow into one hand and the violin into the other. *Photo credit to Gail Taibbi.*

As with the right hand, good left-hand function necessitates a roundedness of form. Balance the left hand around the neck, with the fingers on one side and the thumb on the other. Drop the violin into your hand as if the hand were a sling shot; the weight of the neck favors the thumb. The thumb, now independently in contact with the neck, is able to liberate the rest of the hand. It allows the fingers to suspend from the supported palm and therefore articulate more easily, analogous to the right thumb enabling the opposing fingers to exert fine-motor control of the bow. Maintain curved fingers and thumb (both portions of hand) at all times; otherwise, tension creeps in, just as it does with the right hand that slips into a flat-fingered ("bird's beak") bow hold.

The Home Position

Effective playing requires that the hand rotate around the neck such that the fingers poise above the string tension-free. Setting up a home position for the left hand benefits from an awareness of three component rotations that make up the position of the hand on the wrist. The first is a flexing forward and back of the palm on the long crease of the wrist. The second is a sideways waving in the plane of the palm. The third is a turning on the long axis of the forearm. Continuous adjustments in each of these rotations set up the hand for its optimal position as it crisscrosses the fingerboard. That said, the initial migration of the hand into playing position is easier to conceive by combining the complex combination of rotations into a simpler conception. As the left hand rotates clockwise (from an aerial view) approaching the violin, picture a line segment from the large knuckle of the middle finger to the hand's lower outside corner becoming more vertical until it is aligned with the pinky side of the forearm, the ulna. Now the hand is in position to play (see fig. 11.2).

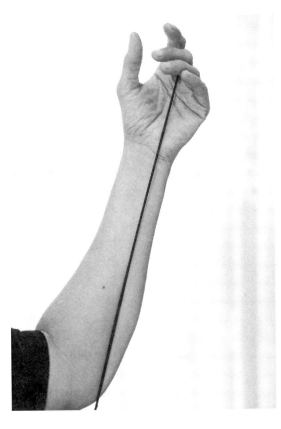

Figure 11.2 A line from the middle finger large knuckle to the hand's lower outside corner is aligned with the ulna. *Photo credit to Eva Foxon Nicholas.*

Left Arm

Our home position has the hand slightly supinated from its natural extension on the forearm, in contrast to the bow hand, which is slightly pronated from the otherwise horizontal arm. Think of the rotation as distributed between the hand and the whole arm and combined into one flowing gesture of presentation. Unless there is a sensitive consideration of this complex rotation, the hand, on the losing end of the computation, tends to fly away from the neck whenever lifting the fingers from the string.

Rotation of the forearm is a pivoting of the radial (thumb) edge around the stationary ulnar (pinkie) edge. There is no longitudinal line in the forearm around which everything rotates evenly; forcing a centralized rotation robs freedom of motion from the wrist and stresses the soft tissue in the elbow. Again, comparing the two arms, a good suspension of the bow arm sets up the ulna to do most of the work via its hinge at the elbow, with the roll of the radius adjusting the position of—and adding power to—the hand as needed. Similarly, full left-arm rotation at the shoulder helps set up the elbow point on through the lower outside corner of the hand (the ulna), leaving the rest of the adjustment to the radial/thumb sector. If you still have difficulty with the fingers engaging the string, position the fourth finger above the string and build a left-hand form around it to provide all four fingers with easier access.

That said, an image that helps create a natural, relaxed left arm is to picture elevating the arm by lifting the radius via the back of the arm. Lift all the way through the thumb and then suspend the other (ulnar) side. This establishes the operation of the fingers and the thumb as integrated but separate, with neither encumbering the other.

To lend a feeling of muscularity to the hand while stabilizing its rotation, picture a vertical pencil stub, point down and affixed to the bottom of the hand underneath the fourth finger. While bearing down on the pencil, imagine drawing a line on the fingerboard from the E string to the G, ultimately directing the fourth finger above each of the four strings. Or imagine the fourth-finger edge of the upright hand pushing through clay to create a feeling of resistance during the hand's rotation from one string to the next.

Balance the hand in playing position by bringing the palm under the fingers and then play fingers one, two, three, four, three, two, one, adjusting the position of the hand until all four fingers articulate with ease. Do not stretch the fourth finger; find the position where you can just place it down; then adjust the other fingers and hand around that.

Zero in on your middle-finger large knuckle and your elbow point. Think of each one advancing and retreating, representing its own independent microcosm of rotational possibilities, but each in subtle ways also responding to the other, though one more fundamental and the other more dependent: a relationship of the highest order (see fig. 11.3).

Specifically considering the arm's support of the hand, think of the elbow point rallying around underneath the middle-finger large knuckle, reminding it not to overextend, or when transitioning from a higher position to one lower (e.g., fourth position to first), supporting the wrist as it morphs from a flexed position to one that is ultimately more upright or slightly extended.

Figure 11.3 The elbow point supporting the large knuckle of the middle finger from underneath. *Photo credit to Gail Taibbi.*

Hand Angle Relative to the String

Monitoring the placement of the wrist relative to the string is a way to set up hand placement for optimal finger facility. Attach two imaginary loops, one to each lower corner of the left hand. Clasp both loops around each string as it is played (see fig. 11.4). Because all four strings—most prominently the G and E—are slightly fanned out rather than parallel to one another, the loop image enforces the hand's precise position relative to each string. Especially when ascending on the G string, as in the first movement of the Mendelssohn concerto, pickup to m.37 (see ex. 11.1), without consciously accounting for the outward fanning of the G string, therefore failing to adjust the hand, the tendency in the ascending hand is for the corner of the hand underneath the fourth finger to distance itself from the string.

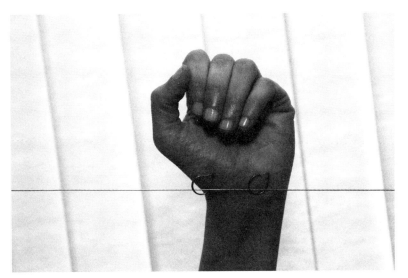

Figure 11.4 Imaginary loops attached to the lower corners of the left hand to keep it well positioned. *Photo credit to Gail Taibbi.*

Left Arm

Example 11.1 First movement of the Mendelssohn Violin Concerto in E minor, pickup to m.37.

During scale ascents from first to fourth position, there is a tendency for the left hand to track the line of the neck, rather than a better, diagonal line extending from the scroll to the outer shoulder of the violin (see fig. 11.5). Without tracking wider, the hand collides with the shoulder during the changeover from third to fourth position. Picture the rim and tire of a bicycle wheel positioned horizontally (floating like a halo), and then insert the violin inside the rim, securing the scroll and button to the rim's inner surface (see fig. 11.6). Acting as an invisible guide, the rim redirects the hand, preventing a collision with the shoulder.

Figure 11.5 Following a diagonal line extending from the scroll to the outer shoulder of the violin. *Photo credit to Eva Foxon Nicholas.*

Figure 11.6 Violin inserted inside the rim and tire of a horizontally positioned bicycle wheel. *Photo credit to Eva Foxon Nicholas.*

Building Left-Hand Forms

There are core formations that can support the hand's shape and balance. To maintain the circular formation of the hand's tunnel, formed by the curved fingers and thumb in playing position, interpose a triangle in the shaped left hand in playing position: it extends from the last joint of the thumb to the base knuckle of the first finger, from there to the fourth-finger large knuckle, and then back to the thumb, completing the third side of an equilateral triangle. The poles secure the hand's circular shape by way of reinforcing the hand's tunnel (see fig. 11.7). The triangle prevents two types of collapse: First, it blocks the thumb from any tendency to fold in on the palm. And second, because squeezing the first joint of the thumb and the first-finger large knuckle together collapses a healthy hand formation, the triangle also prevents the thumb from leaning or swinging toward the first-finger large knuckle, itself blocked by the neck from similarly surrendering its stability. The sides or poles lengthen or shorten in proportion to the hand's degree of expansion and contraction.

Figure 11.7 Interpose a triangle in the shaped left hand in playing position. *Photo credit to Gail Taibbi.*

The triangle can be either suspended from or supported by one of its angle points. When the first-finger large knuckle is the suspending apex, the structure in the hand is similar to a percussionist holding a triangle—the base of the triangle formed by the base of the thumb and the fourth-finger. Or the hand can be balanced on the lower outside corner, in which case the pole extending from the small joint of the thumb to the base knuckle of the fourth finger remains level—parallel to the floor—as a way to monitor the hand's balance.

The framework of a kite is a useful image in considering the structural support for left-hand form. Superimpose the wooden slats that hold the diamond shape of the kite onto the palm; the base knuckle of the first finger secures the peak while the other end of the vertical slat connects to the lower outside corner of the hand: the thumb base and base knuckle of the fourth finger grab the ends of the horizontal slat (see fig. 11.8).

Left Arm

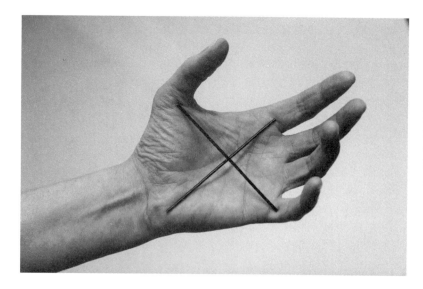

Figure 11.8 Superimpose the wooden slats that hold the diamond shape of the kite on the inside hand. *Photo credit to Gail Taibbi.*

Inside this new structure, the fingers and thumb play into the hand with an interaction similar to the oppositional pull of the straps of a straitjacket. With the hand balanced on its lower outside corner, the slat extending from the first-finger large knuckle to the lower outside corner is vertical (refer to fig. 9.7).

While imagining a hole in the lower outside corner of the hand/kite, loop a string through it with a small weight that is heavy enough to stand the long slat of the kite (extending from the first-finger large knuckle to the lower outside corner) straight up and down. By positioning the palm's spine, the hand's balance on its lower outside corner is reinforced (see fig. 11.9).

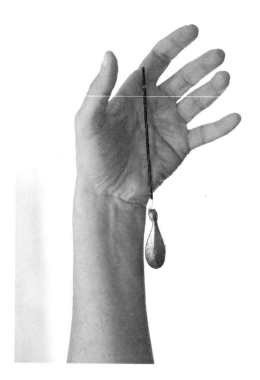

Figure 11.9 A weight hanging from the lower outside corner stands up the long slat of the kite. *Photo credit to Eva Foxon Nicholas.*

Now drag the hand/kite by an imaginary string and feel the adjustments in the wrist. Responding to the tension from the string, the wrist acts as a release valve to allow the hand to rotate slightly, letting go to accommodate the imposition of weight that each new finger action precipitates. Just as a change in breeze is about the only thing that affects the kite's changes of direction, surrounded by a feeling of space (especially inside the wrist), the hand can operate similarly relatively autonomously with respect to its ground.

The Equator

Either sinking the hand below the neck or submerging the neck too deeply into the hand upsets the relationship of the fingers to the fingerboard. Divide the upright hand horizontally in half and then imagine that the palm half is a bowl with a lid at the level of the large knuckles—a slice that could be thought of as the equator of the hand. The string played cuts through the diameter of the bowl just underneath the cover, suspending the hand/bowl (see fig. 11.10).

Figure 11.10 The string played cuts through the diameter of the bowl just underneath the cover. *Photo credit to Gail Taibbi.*

The neck stays below the lid of the bowl/palm. If the hand sinks too low with the equator line below the neck, the neck will impede the shape of the fingers, consequently affecting articulation. The bowl image supports the shape of the palm while sustaining its autonomy by drawing attention to the left-hand equator's position relative to the fingerboard.

The Sphere of the Left Hand and Its Axes of Rotation

The mold of the hand morphs continuously while in transit, so it is valuable to use imagery that supports maintaining its essentially-circular shape, especially during left-hand string crossings; otherwise, the frame alters too much to accommodate each new string position and becomes unsteady. For the following exercises, form a picture by working partly with the realistic image of a hand and partly with phantom material, the combination creating the shape of a ball.

Thinking of your hand now as an orb, use a circular wire to reinforce the structure of its global shape. Place the wire horizontally, distributing the contact points of the hand around it, with the second joint of the thumb opposing the base knuckles of the fingers. The wire creates a circular cross-section of the spherical hand, reinforcing the equator that divides the hand's globe in half. The wire balances and restrains the large knuckles and thumb, supporting a healthy dynamic among these knuckles, particularly between the thumb and first finger, an area prone to constriction or collapse. As always, the goal is a relaxed aliveness since unnecessary tension in one area restricts pliability in another (see fig. 11.11).

Figure 11.11 A circular wire acts as an equator and reinforces the global shape of the hand. *Photo credit to Gail Taibbi.*

Now superimpose two strings in a V shape in the same plane cutting through the circular wire. Tie the end of one string to the base of the first finger and the other end to the thumb. Then tie the other string from the base of the fourth finger to the thumb. Like a person dangling from a parachute, the thumb pulls fingers one and four (horizontally) around the circular wire (see fig. 11.12).

The concept of the parachute is particularly useful in lower positions while changing strings, where the intrusion of the neck tends to pop the first-finger knuckle away, disrupting the large knuckle distribution. The parachute strings coax the first- and fourth-finger knuckles to fan open evenly, challenging the forearm to maintain its rotation. Keeping the large knuckles in a circular formation (with the thumb opposed) is essential to playing passages effectively.

When preparing to play, it is helpful to balance the hand from its bottom center and then to feel a sensation of proportional weight distribution within the continually adjusting hand. Imagine that the hand situated in an upright playing position is a ball. Join the tip of the thumb to the tip of the middle finger to complete a circle that defines a vertical slice of the ball. Divide the thumb and middle finger longitudinally into halves, with half of the thumb and the middle finger on each side of the

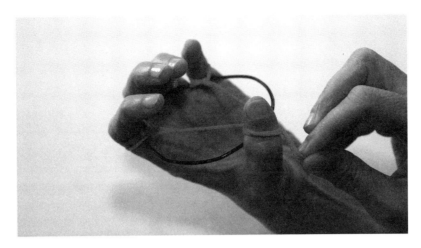

Figure 11.12 The thumb pulls the fingers against the wire, similar to a person dangling from a parachute. *Photo credit to Gail Taibbi.*

ball. Then divide the hand again, with the second cut running horizontally along the second set of knuckles. The imaginary quartering of the ball/hand encourages a uniform flowering of the hand, especially as it perches on its south pole at the balance point formed by the two longitudinal lines.

Center the bottom of the hand on a spring as if the hand were a bobblehead. Without its natural vertical buoyancy, the hand can get stuck leaning too much to the right or to the left, impeding articulating fingers. When leaning sideways too far to the right to articulate a passage, the thumb tightens; when leaning your hand too far to the left, the third and fourth fingers constrict. Experimenting with the range of palmar rotation, pushing your hand a little too far to the left and right, awakens an awareness of the exact spots where the fingers and thumb start to lose their freedom, establishing where they are most liberated.

If during transition the hand topples toward its heavier first-finger side, the fourth fingertip loses access to the string. Creating a feeling of weight in the lower outside corner of the hand and fourth-finger large knuckle compensates for the heavier thumb side. Or imagine that the fourth finger (digit and metacarpal) is made of heavy metal to offset the hand's tendency to roll in the thumb direction.

A ball rolls easily and equally in all directions, but the hand needs to arrive at certain specific rotational positions to sustain finger balance. The following demonstration conveys an efficient approximation of the rotational properties of the hand: impose an axis in the hand on which the hand's tunnel rotates; the axis cuts through the center of the circle formed by the fingers and thumb like a rod inside a rolling pin (see fig. 11.13). The axis allows the hand to rotate without spinning out of control while it maximizes the follow-through motion of its rotation.

Figure 11.13 The axis cuts through the center of the circle formed by the fingers and thumb. *Photo credit to Eva Foxon Nicholas.*

Left Arm

Visualize that the hand is a ball suspended on a rotisserie and that the spit runs through the center of the tunnel formed by the fingers and opposing thumb; then affix a string to the bottom center of the hand (see fig. 11.14). During lower-position, E-to-G-string rotations or when transitioning from third position to fourth, when you pull the string (out the back of the hand) toward the ceiling, the hand flips around the neck to a position above the instrument with the fingers dangling down; then when you pull the string toward the floor, the hand flips back underneath, with the fingers now upright.

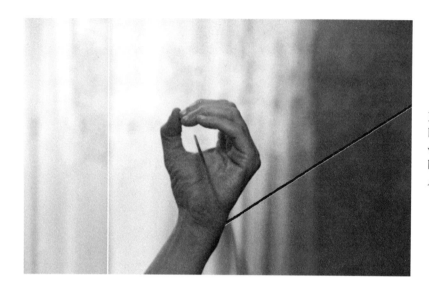

Figure 11.14 The hand is a ball suspended on a rotisserie with a string affixed to the bottom center. *Photo credit to Eva Foxon Nicholas.*

Suspend a bead on an imaginary taut wire (travel line), nut to fingerboard end, and imagine that the bead is your hand, coasting effortlessly to any destination (see fig. 11.15). With the help of this image, the hand suspends high enough above the actual string to fully clear the fingerboard. Then try attaching one end of the wire to the top of an imaginary vertical pole at the scroll end, suspending the hand several inches above the instrument. Drag the bridge end of the wire to the left or right of the body of the violin to assist placement of the hand/bead above the string. Running through the hand's tunnel, the wire gives the hand a direct route on its ascent and descent of the fingerboard while facilitating its clockwise and counterclockwise rotations. Like the bead, the hand slides easily back and forth on the imaginary line while rotating one way or the other. Placement of the fingers and notes determines the direction of the wire and the hand rotation.

Again, suspend the bead (symbolizing the hand) on an imaginary taut wire. See in your mind's eye two strings: attach the end of one to the center bottom of the hand with the other end exiting out the back of the hand; then affix one end of the other string to the peak of the large knuckle of the middle finger, with the other end dangling in front of the palm. Pull that string down and the other back to rotate the hand/bead ninety degrees, maximizing the speed and efficiency of the hand's revolution.

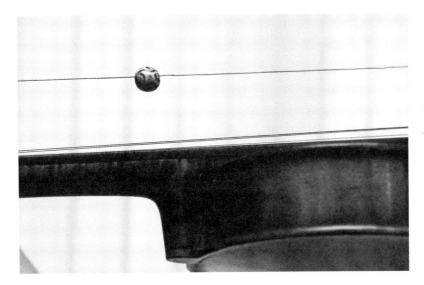

Figure 11.15 Suspend a bead on an imaginary taut wire for a sense of coasting effortlessly along the fingerboard. *Photo credit to Gail Taibbi.*

Maybe when you were a child, you and your friends alternated turns with a game where one curled up in a large barrel (or a large tire) and the other rolled it. The idea was to brace yourself against the inner surface of the barrel or tire so when it rolled, you rolled as one with it to avoid getting bumped around. It was easier to hold yourself when the barrel stopped rolling if you were either on your back or on your hands and feet. Similarly, to maintain form as the hand rotates in between two contrasting destinations (one higher with the palm on top of the fingers and the other lower with the hand leaning away and the fingers dropping into the palm), either push outward against an outer mold or pull inward against a ball. If the in-between places need special support, employ the barrel image as needed to avoid getting bounced around.

Imagine suspending a smaller barrel partially filled with sand inside a larger barrel (both on their sides) with a rotisserie spit running through the center of both barrels, such that when you roll the larger barrel, the inside smaller barrel remains stabilized (does not roll with it). Similarly, amid the left-hand journey up, over, and around the fingerboard, feel a continuous, inner-balance restabilization of the hand's tunnel on a rotational axis.

Combining Weight Imagery with Hand Pressures

It is important for the left-hand fingers to be able to feel the weight of their component parts and to use that weighted feeling to relax with gravity in any position. To experiment with two positions, when the palm is facedown, the fingers can drape down (see fig. 11.16), and when the palm is faceup, the fingertips can fall into the palm (see fig. 11.17).

In conjunction with an awareness of opposing pressures within the hand, using weight imagery is grounding for the hand and fingers, especially during transitions. The hand is stable enough staying either in the lower positions or in higher positions. The changeover from third to fourth position is challenging, however. By

Left Arm

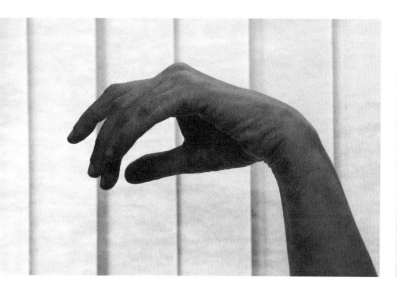
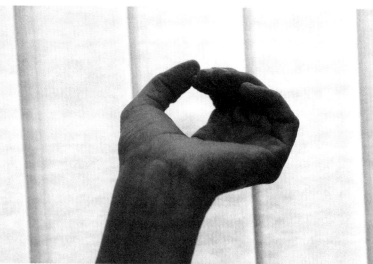

Figure 11.16 When the palm is facedown, the fingers drape down. *Photo credit to Gail Taibbi.*

Figure 11.17 When the palm is faceup, the fingertips fall into the palm. *Photo credit to Gail Taibbi.*

strategically adding weight, you can push through the changeover more smoothly and in the process augment speed. Imagine superimposing your hand onto a medium-sized rubber ball that has extra weight added to the two poles, north and south. Picture that the fingers cover the north pole and that the base of the hand sits at the south pole. When the hand is shifting above the instrument or back into first position, as it approaches its new position, it flips over somewhat quickly due to the placement of the weight. The weight distribution plus the acceleration of that weight increases the momentum at the end of the move that helps finish the shift more definitively. The motion of the hand follows through more with less actual effort. Imagining that the palm is filled with wet sand provides a solid pedestal for the active fingers. Or add wet sand to the fingers, making them into little sandbags.

Call to mind an image of holding a smooth, round metal ball inside your left hand—baseball size or smaller, something that fits most comfortably. Rest your hand on the fingerboard and then envision the ball trying to levitate to the ceiling. As the metal ball pushes upward against the underside of the hand, with a force equal to the downward gravitational force of the hand, it reinforces the hand's round shape and prevents it from crashing onto the neck. The elevating ball image helps to develop a good feel for the use of weight in navigating the fingerboard, and it enables the fingers to exert muscularity without undue tension and without collapsing onto the fingerboard.

Now imagine that the metal ball glues itself to the center of the upside-down palm and suspends itself from that point, pulling the apex of the flexed palm downward. The assistance of the weight encourages a deeper connection to the fingerboard (as in slower passages and vibrato) while it prompts a conscious effort to maintain the palm's proper elevation.

To apply left-hand weight without creating tension, tie a noose around the wrist/bottom of the hand and suspend the hand; then imagine affixing a weight to the elbow to create a dynamic extension of that continuum.

Left-Hand Suspension

It is easy to look at the hand from one side only, a point of view, in this way limiting a fuller awareness. The hand can be experienced from many angles, including from the inside out, as a way to build that awareness. The story of the blind men and the elephant teaches us that we may never really understand a particular perspective or know the whole of anything. Removing the active hand from the fingerboard frame of reference while maintaining a sense of what it feels like to play can help to deepen our awareness of the hand and its potential to connect to the instrument.

Considering the fingerboard as a floor on which the fingers operate can distort the fingers and slow articulation. Just as it is easier to jump down from above rather than leap upward from below, likewise, reaching down with the left hand from a position above the fingerboard enhances mobility of the fingers. Imagine that you are dangling over the side of a cliff with one end of a rope tied around your waist and the other tied to a tree branch above you. As you bump into a wall of slate, you have to kick yourself away. That dangling and kicking feeling is similar to the feel of the finger reacting against the fingerboard from the suspended hand. Wrap a bungee cord around your wrist, suspending both your arm and hand from the loop; then experiment with touching down and running your fingers. The suspended hand tips weight toward the fingertips, providing greater facility (see fig. 11.18). Use the up motion of the finger push-off to guide the hand's weight toward the next finger articulated. During rapid articulation, the motion is not preconceived; the fingers simply run.

Figure 11.18 Wrap a bungee cord around your wrist and suspend both your arm and hand from the loop. *Photo credit to Gail Taibbi.*

Expansion and Contraction of the Hand

As the hand rotates and orbits the neck, an easy lateral expansion and contraction of the hand assists finger placement relative to interval size. Work on maintaining the flexibility of your palm. If forced to expand from a chronically constricted palm, the fingers lose their relaxed rhythm, and eventually they lose range. If you lift a more open hand, its naturally expanded state can compress and release with ease.

Imagine encasing the fingerboard inside a horizontal cone, with the narrow end pointing toward the scroll. Then wrap your left hand around the cone. The cone shape accommodates the expansion and contraction of the hand's frame among different positions. In the first movement of the Mozart concerto, 11 measures after the solo entrance (see ex. 11.2), during the shifts in beats 2 and 4, the distance between the thumb and fingers expands while the distance between the large knuckles shrinks because of closer intervallic spacing in higher positions. When descending, as in seven measures after the solo entrance (see ex. 11.3), the palm contracts while the large knuckles expand laterally to accommodate the wider spacing of intervals in the lower positions. The surface of the cone accommodates the shape, balance, and rotation of the hand.

Example 11.2 First movement of the Mozart Concerto in D Major, 11 measures after the solo entrance.

Example 11.3 Mozart's concerto, 7 measures after the solo entrance.

Imagine that the flexed hand is a cone-shaped coil with each finger's loop completed by the thumb when engaged. When ascending the fingerboard, push the smaller thumb and first finger end through the larger coil end formed by the thumb and fourth finger. When descending the scale, reverse the direction of the coil with the thumb and fourth finger now forming its narrower end; then push the smaller fourth finger end through the now larger thumb and first-finger end (see fig. 11.19). Whether ascending or descending a scale, pushing the narrow end of the coil/fingers through its wider end propels the fingers to their new location without disrupting the fundamental shape of the hand. During running passages, slightly tightening or compressing the thumb and fourth finger coil can serve to increase speed.

Figure 11.19 Picture the hand as a cone-shaped coil: when shifting, push the smaller end through the larger end. *Photo credit to Gail Taibbi.*

Optimizing Hand Flexibility

Because flexibility serves the hand in maneuvering passages, imagine a division among the large knuckles with a spring inserted sideways between each pair, fanning them open. The springs support a lateral buoyancy and the rebound of the large knuckles (see fig. 11.20).

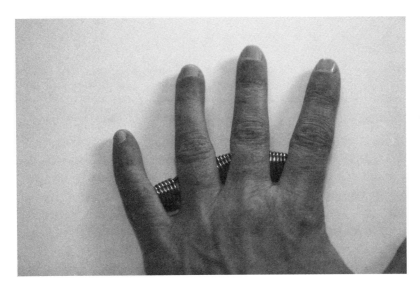

Figure 11.20 Imagine a Slinky or spring, inserted sideways, between each pair of large knuckles. *Photo credit to Gail Taibbi.*

Similarly, think of the left-hand large knuckles as bellows, with the handles opening or closing depending on intervallic spacing, the direction of the hand in relation to gravity, or the type of shift. To address the irregular expansion of half- and whole-step intervals in hand formation, with the hand poised to play, imagine inserting wedges between the large knuckle pairs to sustain the whole step spacing of the fingers.

CHAPTER TWELVE

Lower Outside Corner

We have now developed the left hand and configured the intricacies of its suspension, rotation, and balance. In this chapter, we shift awareness to the lower outside corner and draw attention to the hand's internal transfer of balance.

Hand Balance

Consider the hand's position on the wrist to be in a state of flux, often balancing on its bottom center, sometimes on its lower outside corner, or somewhere in between, such as when transferring vibrato from one finger to the next in a stable landscape. The hand's progression starts in its fundamental *home position*, a place of maximum range of motion for the hand but restricted reach: some lateral rotation of the arm plus a bit of clockwise rotation in the plane of the palm. To this, now add a small amount of rotation in all three planes with the hand until it is sitting on its lower outside corner, with the "spine" continuous with the line of the ulna (see appendix diagram A.3). This is a position of less freedom at the wrist but maximal reach, especially for the fourth finger. Besides perching the hand up on its toes for an easier reach across the fingerboard in all positions, balancing on the lower outside corner is also a way of miniaturizing the healthy motions of the hand for the efficacy of the fingers as they travel further from home.

With this clockwise rotation of the hand (in all three planes), look for a sensation of the lower outside corner and the top of the ulna sinking or locking into its shared joints in the wrist, in that way solidifying a stable posture of the hand on the platform of the wrist. If the hand loses its point of reference or experiences a sense of disconnection from its staging, it is apt to flounder. Especially in rapid passages, picture the hand tilted onto the lower outside corner whisking around like a top, spinning from its single point to transport the fingers across the fingerboard (see fig. 12.1).

When playing chords such as octaves, rock the hand back toward a flatter orientation with the forearm and fingerboard, with the bottom of the hand acting as a platform, supporting and balancing the multiple fingers from underneath (see fig. 12.2). With the octaves in the first movement of the Mendelssohn concerto, from the pickup to m.41 (see ex. 12.1), despite the challenging reach, balance the hand on its bottom center; then in mm.33–36 (see ex. 12.2), shift to its lower outside corner to support overall balance with the rapid articulations in that musical framework.

Lower Outside Corner

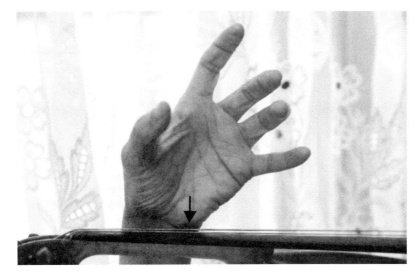

Figure 12.1 Tilting the hand onto the lower outside corner. *Photo credit to Eva Foxon Nicholas.*

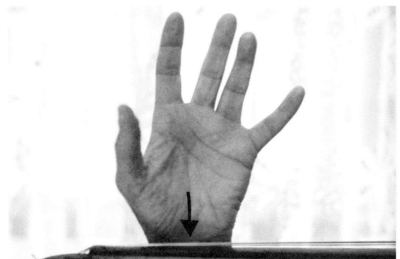

Figure 12.2 The bottom of the hand acts as a platform. *Photo credit to Eva Foxon Nicholas.*

Example 12.1 Octaves in the first movement of the Mendelssohn from the pickup to m.41.

Example 12.2 First movement of the Mendelssohn, in mm.33–36.

133

Whether easing off the axial rotation, going into a bit more extension, or rotating back toward the bottom center, any of these individually or together create more latitude in the hand. Subtract some torque when playing slower passages where you want to exaggerate the subtle motions of the hand, intentionally carving out each and every note, in that way transmuting sound into shape and form. Ultimately, because hand shapes and collaborative finger lengths vary from person to person, so too will the areas of balance fluctuate slightly within each person's hand, always in service of the fingers relating to the strings.

As suggested earlier, when balancing the hand on the lower outside corner, observe two perpendicular, intersecting lines on the palm that are similar to the slats on a kite as they divide the hand as follows: a *vertical line* that runs from the large knuckle on the first finger to the center of the lower outside corner that we call the *spine*, and a *horizontal line* that extends from the large knuckle of the thumb to the large knuckle of the fourth finger, with the two lines forming a cross (refer to fig. 11.8). This crosscut acts as a useful division, quartering the hand by way of its new axis of rotation, perched on the lower outside corner.

Imagine that this spine of the hand is hollow; then thread a wire through it, corner to corner, first-finger large knuckle to lower outside corner (see fig. 12.3). Then pull the ends of the wire tight to reinforce a new upright position, balancing the hand via the lower outside corner. The upright hand has the ability to rotate clockwise and counter, spinning on its axis or spine, which also leans to best position the hand for its journeys across the fingerboard and up into higher positions, all now with a greater sense of control. Think of that leaning, an angular revolution also based on the lower outside corner, for the moment as being more like the boom of a sail that circles the mast of a sailboat, with the palm then responding as if captured by a breeze, directing the hand across the waters of the fingerboard, the lower outside corner spinning and steering the hand toward the next string played. Another helpful image is the lower outside corner of the hand as the bottom tip of a spinning top, that simultaneous feeling of quicker rotations on the axis and slower angular revolutions of the axis steering the hand and fingers up, down, and across the fingerboard.

Figure 12.3 Imagining that the spine of the hand is hollow, thread a string or wire through, corner to corner. *Photo credit to Gail Taibbi.*

Picture a metal ball inside the lower outside corner of the hand, with the weighted ball supporting the hand's upright position.

During same-position, E-to-G-string descents, a strong fourth finger is essential in negotiating the descending scale pattern. Balancing the hand on the lower outside corner above the string enhances fourth-finger access, especially to the lower strings. During left-hand string changes, if the lower corner is inactive, the fourth finger gets left behind. With a lower-outside-corner orientation, the fingers whisk from one destination to the next, as in two measures of the first movement of the Mendelssohn, starting at the pickup to m.35 (see ex. 12.3).

Example 12.3
First movement of the Mendelssohn, starting at the pickup to m.35.

To secure the hand's structure when balanced on the lower outside corner, visualize that the upright hand's spine (the vertical axis rising from the lower outside corner up to the index finger's large knuckle) is a backbone and that the fingers and thumb are the ribs (picture the thumb spliced into four ribs to counterbalance the four fingers). Envision a string tied to the lower outside corner and running through the circular opening, a tunnel formed by the curved fingers and thumb (parallel to the spine). Pull straight up on the string attached to the corner of the hand so the fingers, suspended like ribs that are articulating with the spine in the center of hand, can relax downward (see fig. 12.4). Drawing the corner upward against the gravitational pull of the fingers (including the thumb) adds potential energy that

Figure 12.4 A string lifts the corner of the hand straight up while the fingers, suspended like ribs, relax downward. *Photo credit to Gail Taibbi.*

Left Arm

strengthens and supports the fingers' rebound while setting up the hand in a perfect formation, one that steadies it while allowing all four fingers easy access to the line of the string. It is also another way to think of suspending the left hand for crossing the fingerboard to lower strings.

The Lower Outside Corner's Relationship to the Wrist

When the hand is directed from the lower outside corner, the lower outside corner balances itself by way of the wrist's center. The chain of support begins in the torso and moves out through the elbow; elbow position supports the neutral hand. Then the corner of the hand balances itself with the whole wrist around the wrist's center point, in that way promoting strength and communication between the fingers and the string played.

On E-to-G-string descents, a hand balanced on the lower outside corner rolls over on the (flat) fingerboard to its left, akin to vaulting from a kneeling position on one knee to all fours. Picture the hand playing an imaginary violin to the left of the actual one, thereby securing the hand's position in relation to the actual instrument. The forearm might feel as if it too can roll onto its anterior side on top of the fingerboard along with the hand (see fig. 12.5).

Figure 12.5 The hand can play an imaginary violin to the left of the actual one. *Photo credit to Gail Taibbi.*

Again, in the two measures of the Mendelssohn at the pickup to m.35 (see ex. 12.3), on the E-string pickup, the hand is positioned on one knee. As the passage descends from the E string to the A and D en route to the G, the "spine" swiftly dives across the fingerboard. Or by projecting the hand's position to the left of the fingerboard, the fingers easily situate above the G string, securing their position within its most challenging territory.

Imagine that the hand is a duck: the thumb is one wing, the fingers are the other, and the lower outside corner its tail. In a first-position two-octave G major scale descent, the duck descends as if landing on a pond, leading with the tail.

Lateral Hand Balance

Finding a sense of equipoise with the hand that is at times suspended from and other times balanced on the wrist involves numerous complex interactions. Each specific configuration has its opportunities that are paired with some vulnerabilities. For example, when the hand is balanced on the lower outside corner, range is increased, but because of its precarious balancing, the "spine" needs to be stabilized by the rest of the hand. Again, draw a diagonal line from the large knuckle of the first finger to the lower outside corner of the hand (refer to fig. 9.7). Superimpose the shape of a dog on your facedown palm, with the diagonal line being the dog's spine; the first-finger large knuckle is the neck end, and the lower outside corner is the tail. If you then lift the dog up by the tail, it balances evenly on its front paws (the tip of the thumb counterbalancing the fingertips). Similarly, as a child, you may have had someone lift you by the ankles so you could walk on your hands. These images help maintain a feeling of equal balance between the thumb and finger portions defined by the spine regardless of the hand's rotational or orbital position.

Maintain an awareness of weight distribution to create a consistent balance of strength and motion. Imagine that the hand's spine is a seesaw on a fulcrum. Rest a specific amount of weight on one end at the lower corner (in the wrist), holding it down to lift the other end (the fingers). No matter where the point of balance is established along the hand's spine/seesaw, whichever end is weighted, suspended, or neutral, the rest of the hand rallies around that point of balance.

Transporting the Hand via the Lower Corners

To transport the balanced hand without disrupting its frame, think of a string lassoed around the wrist, with the lasso pulling it diagonally across the fingerboard. For example, on a G-string ascent, with the hand superimposed to the left of the string, pull the lower inside corner with the lasso toward the right side of the bridge, which in turn drags the hand against the left side of the string and up the fingerboard (see fig. 12.6). For a G-string descent, pull the lower outside corner with the string toward the right side of the scroll. The G string acts as a wall of resistance to the hand.

Left Arm

Figure 12.6 Pulling the hand superimposed to the left of the string toward the right side of the bridge. *Photo credit to Gail Taibbi.*

On an E-string ascent, with the hand to the right of the string, pull the lasso to the left of the bridge, which in turn drags the hand against the right side of the string (see fig. 12.7). For an E string descent, pull the string lasso to the left of the scroll. The string creates a barrier (but with little friction) for the hand to lean against and travel as it is towed by the lasso. The string lends direction to the hand while reinforcing its structural relationships and their related strengths. During shifts, the hand's navigational relationship to the string is similar to a person leaning against a stair rail while ascending or descending steps in the dark, with the rail/string steadying the legs/hand.

Figure 12.7 On an E-string ascent, with the hand to the right of the string, pull the lasso to the left of the bridge. *Photo credit to Gail Taibbi.*

On E-to-G-string descents, visualize a string attached to the lower outside corner, with its other end tied to a fishing weight. Throw the weight overboard to the left of the neck. When the hand descends the scale, especially from the E string to the G, the fishing weight sinks, assisting the hand. As the hand ascends the scale, the lower outside corner lifts and drags the attached weight, the weight all the while encouraging the hand's upright balance on its lower outside corner.

Envision a tunnel formed by the flexed thumb and fingers. When descending positions, chuck the lower outside corner of the hand through the tunnel scroll direction; when ascending a string, pitch the inside corner of the hand up the string through the tunnel and away from the thumb. Doing so propels the full mass of the hand in a balanced format. For incremental shifts, back and forth, you can push and pull from either corner. When crossing strings from the E string to the G, lob the outside corner of the hand through the tunnel G-string direction. Pick a well-chosen line with consideration for the specific direction the hand is travelling, either along the straight line of the fingerboard or diagonally toward the bridge or scroll.

As in all activities of life, balance in the left hand is a moment-to-moment adjustment and readjustment. Wherever or however your hand is situated on the instrument, play with gravity by manipulating both actual or artificially created mass. Operate as if the weight is either in constant flux (the intentionally moving hand influenced by the direction of the gravitational pull) or, when advantageous, nonexistent.

Structure and Rotational Pathways of the Hand

Like reinforcement used to shore up the infrastructure of buildings, imaginary circular wires can support the hand's structure from within the molded hand's primarily circular shape. Insert a circular wire horizontally along the palmar surface of the flexed hand, running from the second joint of the thumb along to the large knuckles and around to the starting point (an inside equator); this wire maintains the hand's circular structure while dividing it in half horizontally (refer to fig. 11.11). To further secure the hand, also wrap the thumb and middle finger around an imaginary vertical wire or rim. Where they cross at their poles, the two wires form four ninety-degree angles. Once the inner hand structure has been secured, place three circular wires around the hand to illustrate the pathways of the hand's three primary rotations (see fig. 12.8).

Figure 12.8 Place three circular wires around the hand. *Photo credit to Gail Taibbi.*

Left Arm

The first wire runs horizontally around the hand's equator to map out the hand's rotation around a vertical axis. A second wire encloses the hand along the midline of the thumb and middle finger to demonstrate the track of the hand in a waving motion. The third circular wire tunnels through the long dimension of the wrist and circles the outer edges of the playing hand (encasing the second set of knuckles), showing the path of rotation in the plane of the palm, from bridge to scroll. The circular wires reinforce the roundedness of the hand's structure while providing reminders of both the fundamental dimensions of movement and the hand's natural inclination to move in circular (nonlinear) motions. Think of the three wires as being symbolic of virtues that represent balance, love, and light, moving from a more cerebral awareness to one that fosters soulful, musical expression.

CHAPTER THIRTEEN

Shifts

After having systematized the formation and movement of the left hand, as well as examining hand rotations that facilitate orbiting the neck, we now explore fully the process of making longitudinal positional adjustments of the hand on the fingerboard—the shift. Shifts are footsteps on a set of stones in a pond, each destination determining the shape, length, and rhythm of the stride and the nature of your footfall. Approaching each landing point, the hand morphs from its prior shape into a form that quickly finds balance, serving both this moment and an anticipation of what follows. The hand's continuous transformation supports continuity in the playing.

Finger Shape and Hand Positioning

It may seem that they simply go along for the ride, but it is essential to carefully consider the participation of the fingers in shifting. Dragging the shift finger along the string with any appreciable weight impedes the shift two ways: slowing its pace and distorting the finger (correcting takes additional time; failing to correct compromises accuracy). This is especially important with downward shifts, whereas lightening the touch of the finger without leaving the string (as the hand ascends and descends on an arc) before solidly landing imposes less resistance. Also, avoid losing the active flexion of your hand during the shift. In the first movement of Mozart's D major concerto, 19 measures after the solo entrance (see ex. 13.1), do not allow the square of the second finger to collapse (flatten) on the descending shift from D-natural to C-sharp; otherwise, you have to reposition the hand between the shifts, with that extra motion hindering speed.

Example 13.1 First movement of the Mozart Concerto in D Major 19 measures after the solo entrance.

For neighboring shifts, thrust the shift-finger large knuckle above the others in the direction of the shift to propel the hand up and down the string. For larger shifts, use a twofold motion of leading the hand with the heel followed by a firing of the large knuckles in the direction of the shift. For ascending shifts, extend the hand early so that all the fingers have to do when they arrive is drop down to articulate with the string. Do not reach for the note with your fingers. With the first finger ascending shift starting on beat 2 of the Mozart, 11 measures after the solo entrance (see ex. 13.2), there is a tendency to overextend the fingers; do not elongate the fingers in anticipation of the shift. When a finger breaks out of the pack, it disturbs the finger-to-palm connection by leaving the palm behind, forcing the hand to readjust to renew its interactive relationship. This creates extraneous motion that takes time, impeding the fingers. If, in this example, the first finger extends, then to restore its shape and reunite with the palm, it has to drag the palm forward (toward the bridge) in a caterpillar crawl. When the finger maintains its shape (does not extend), the finger and hand move as a unit without the finger having to backtrack. The heel of the hand leads the way. When shifting upward from a low position to high, especially on lower strings, as in this first-movement passage of the Mendelssohn concerto from the pickup to m.37 through m.40 (see ex. 13.3), the hand ascends between shifts while the thumb secures the proper rotation of the hand around the neck. Cradle the neck in the relaxed curvature of the thumb. It helps to think of the strings as guiding cables using a twofold awareness, with the fingernail half of the fingertip in light contact with the fingerboard and the other half running alongside the string/cable. Ultimately, the aim is to arrive at each shift destination with the hand balanced around the second finger, or the second and third fingers. During large interval stretches, because your range is better from a relaxed suspension rather than from reaching up, position the left hand higher than it otherwise wants to be. From a higher-note position, the hand relaxes back to the lower note, maintaining its position. For example, be closer to third position when playing in second. If you imagine that the thumb and each finger form a series of coils—as on a Slinky—resting in third position, allow the third-, second-, and first-finger coils to relax back scroll direction via the large knuckles, in that way allowing the fingers to gain access to second position.

Example 13.2 First movement of the Mozart Concerto in D, 11–12 measures after the solo entrance.

Example 13.3 First movement of the Mendelssohn Violin Concerto in E minor, pickup to m.37.

Strategies between Shifts

To ground passages between shifts, give special consideration to the notes just before the shift, as with the first five notes 11 measures after the solo entrance in the Mozart, (see ex. 13.4); sit on the last note before the shift and then scoot; widen the window of time between shifts to help you relax into the note before the shift while anticipating your next position. Or when you see a measure of music, think of groups of notes as chords to avoid scrambling to get through them. For example, in beat 1 of m.99 in the Preludio from the Bach Partita No. 3 (see ex. 13.5), the second, third, fourth, and fifth sixteenth notes form a four-note chord. Whether the note clusters take the shape of two-, three- or four-finger chord formations, identifying them and synchronizing the fingers is far more efficient than focusing on one note at a time. Keeping the fingers down in a chord formation also supports the necessary continuance of weight transference to the fingertips, rather than the default tendency to transfer the weight of uninvolved fingers to the base of the palm.

Example 13.4 First movement of the Mozart Concerto in D, 11 measures after the solo entrance.

Example 13.5 Bach's Partita No. 3, Preludio in E Major, m.99.

Lateral Movement

The chord-formation strategy for melodic passages can also work well for the initial notes after a shift. It is common to focus mostly on the last finger in the previous position and the first finger to be articulated after the shift, with the rest of the notes following the shift left unaccounted for. Instead, preconceive the pattern of the first set of notes in the new location to fully realize the repositioning. For example, in the second sequence of the cadenza in the Paganini Caprice No. 5 (see ex. 13.6), form a picture of each group of notes in the descending scale as a four-three-two-one chord *on the single string* (instead of each note individually); factor in the E-natural and then shift down and capture another finger chord, four-three-two-one; shift again, and so on. To achieve smooth transit of the fingers during shifts, keep them in good

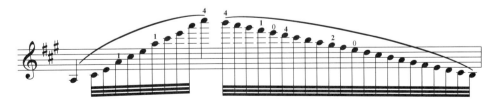

Example 13.6 Second cadenza sequence in the Paganini Caprice No. 5.

side-by-side alignment. Imagine that the large knuckles are four large, unsecured beads on a horizontal string (with the spacing relative to the note intervals); then propel the knuckles remaining in front of each shift finger toward either the bridge or the scroll (with the domino effect). Notice whether any of the knuckles pop out of alignment during transport, disrupting the continuity. Similarly, let the shift finger steer and propel the other fingertips up and down the fingerboard.

To reinforce the hand's lateral movement, place each finger, large knuckle to fingertip, next to one another on top of the fingerboard the way children pack themselves tightly, side-to-side, in a wagon. The first finger pushes the second, which bumps the third, pushing the fourth, in this way propelling the wagon toward the bridge. The reverse, starting with the fourth finger pushing the third and so on, rolls the wagon toward the scroll. Besides building momentum from their proximity, placing the fingers in an imaginary miniature wagon keeps them level with each other while maintaining the suspension of the fingertips above the fingerboard.

During shifts in rapid passages, urge the hand to feel full of exuberance, like a child who with abandon jumps into the wagon standing up, riding and directing. While holding the image of the wagon, the fingertips lightly ride the string's surface. Heavy fingertip pressure in the moving hand misaligns the large knuckles, compromising speed and accuracy. For another light-touch image, conceive of a groove (indentation) on the pad of the finger at the tip, like the one on a train's wheel, and imagine that the string is the rail; the fingertips slide back and forth on top of the decompressed string. As a variation, envision someone taking their fingers and gently pulling the large knuckle of the shift finger toward the bridge or the scroll. To further support the domino effect of the fingers, imagine one edge of the somewhat vertically positioned forearm leading the other, with either the radius pushing the ulna on an ascending shift (see fig. 13.1), or the ulna bumping against or directing the radius on the shift's descent (see fig. 13.2). The ulna can also pull the radius and vice versa. To add momentum to the migrating hand, envision an outside force tapping the thumb side of the forearm on the scale ascent and the fourth-finger side on the descent.

Figure 13.1 The radius pushing the ulna on an ascending shift. *Photo credit to Eva Foxon Nicholas.*

Figure 13.2 The ulna directing the radius on the shift's descent. *Photo credit to Eva Foxon Nicholas.*

During double-stop shifts, say with thirds, the first finger can push the third while the second bumps the fourth to ascend; the reverse takes place with the fourth finger propelling the second and the third finger pushing the first. The articulating fingers propel the unused fingers up and down the fingerboard along the line of each finger's respective string. As with single-line passages, ascend and descend on arcing paths when executing double-stop shifts.

The Third-to-Fourth-Position Changeover

As suggested earlier, try affixing a string to the bottom center of the hand (refer to fig. 11.14). During third-to-fourth-position transitions, when you pull the string (out the back of the hand) toward the ceiling, the hand rotates around a horizontal axis to a position on top of the instrument, with the fingers dangling. When the hand is above the instrument in higher positions, with the balanced fingers relaxing down, the thumb and fingers approach the neck with equal distribution of weight. During fourth-to-third-position changeovers, when you pull the string toward the floor, the hand flips back underneath the now-upright fingers.

Again, attach a string to the bottom of the hand. To access third-to-fourth-position transitions on the lower pitched strings, this time imagine placing the bottom of the hand to the left of the neck; snap the attached string ceiling direction, flipping the hand upside down and onto the fingertips during the third-to-fourth-position transition. Imagining the wrist to the left of the neck positions the fingers for an easy drop.

Descending Shifts

Using proper sideways motion of the wrist repositions the hand without disrupting its balance, allowing optimal articulation of the fingers with the string. When calling on the third or fourth finger, if the hand is rotated toward the scroll rather than the bridge, then those fingers have to extend to reach the string; if the hand is rotated toward the bridge when articulating the first finger, then that finger similarly has to overextend. Anticipate the need and rotate ahead of it.

In the three-octave E major scale descent (see ex. 13.7), as the bottom of the hand coasts down the string, replace the resting point of the bottom of the hand underneath the first finger with the bottom of the hand underneath the third. Then the three, two, one fingering within the tier is implemented with the hand rotating back toward the first finger, righting the ship. Then once more, the bottom of the hand underneath the first finger shifts its weight underneath the third finger, with the third finger then firing from its supported position. Rocking the bottom of hand from bridge to scroll direction assists in raising the first finger and dropping the third, whereas rocking the hand in a scroll-to-bridge direction helps lift the third finger and drop the first. Combine the motions of coasting and rocking to transport the hand while properly positioning the fingers.

Example 13.7 Three-octave E major scale.

With scale descents on one string, for instance from seventh position to fourth, as the bottom of the hand rotates clockwise to engage the third finger while it coasts toward the next descending position, imagine that a weight inside the first fingertip does not allow it to lift fully off the string. On downward shifts that use fingers in a three, two, one, shift, three, two, one pattern, as the third finger replaces the first, the weighted (not pressed) first finger slides down and out of the way *without* releasing the string as the third finger snaps down (see fig. 13.3). The hand continues to rock in

Figure 13.3 As the third finger replaces the first, the first finger slides down without releasing the string. *Photo credit to Gail Taibbi.*

the direction of (rotates toward) each finger as it fires, keeping its cohesion with itself and the string in anticipation of the next shift.

As the arm extends during a scale descent on one string, a situation where the fourth finger is prone to fly away from the neck, it is helpful to imagine an impulse of lateral rotation (turning the palm up) coming from the shoulder, with the follow-through into the forearm and fourth-finger corner of the wrist constituting a hugging of the fingerboard throughout the descending motion. You can also imagine that the fourth-finger edge of the palm is dragging a cloth along the fingerboard the way an ice resurfacer (Zamboni) drags a towel across the ice. Besides keeping the fourth finger close to the fingerboard, the dragging motion creates a feeling of resistance that helps to stabilize the fourth-finger side of the hand, in that way deepening the connection of the fingers to the fingerboard. Whether ascending or descending, the ultimate aim is to arrive at each shift destination with the hand balanced around the second finger or the second and third.

Stretching the Limits

With momentary large shifts, expand your comfortable shifting range by visualizing that the palm stretches like a bungee cord. On the ascent, the fingers expand quickly to the right of the thumb and then close back to the left on the descent, traveling on an arc that stretches from the original note to the shift destination. For example, at m.14 in the Tuileries movement of Mussorgsky's *Pictures at an Exhibition*, played on one string (see ex. 13.8), the wrist snaps the hand forward, with the palm stretching to a length the fingers need to easily articulate with the string; then the wrist rebounds, whisking the hand back to its original shape. Now with plenty of range, form a picture of what the hand looks like in third position, hold that thought, and then snap the hand forward to and back from that remembered place.

Example 13.8 Mussorgsky's *Pictures at an Exhibition* in B Major, Tuileries m.14.

To compensate for a fourth finger that feels too short (as in higher positions or on the G string), imagine stretching the area of palm underneath that finger to assist in balancing the fourth finger's reach with the remaining fingers on the string. Use the imagination to have a real effect on the tissue and its movement capabilities, whether lengthening or otherwise bolstering the full limbs or any subset of them to serve playing facility.

In another classic passage, starting at the pickup to eight measures before the end of the Finale in Saint-Saëns's *Carnival of the Animals* (see ex. 13.9), even though this passage is light and humorous and you might be tempted to toss it off, playing it well necessitates a skill set that is also integral to performing passages that are more serious in tone and technically more challenging. With the violin in performance position, picture putting the left elbow on a table or platform while the forearm implements a windshield wiper motion, with the forearm oscillating effortlessly up and down the fingerboard. To enhance the image, imagine the wiper blade / forearm moving against glass, brushing along a wet pane that extends from the scroll to the outer shoulder of the violin.

Example 13.9 Another example of sudden large shifts, this time from the Finale of the Saint-Saëns *Carnival of the Animals*.

Think of the hand as a ball; then bounce the hand/ball on the fingerboard. The rebound effect creates momentum and supports continuity of motion. If you allow the palm to rest against the body of the violin while the third finger is sliding into the harmonic E, or to rest on top of the fingers in first position (or against the neck), you interfere with the finger's ability to reach its destination easily, cleanly, and in time. In the eight-note pickup, the hand is set up in third position, making it easier to slide the third finger into the double E harmonic. When sliding along the line of the E string, aim the fingertip in the direction of the A string to circumvent that finger's tendency to slip off the string. To expand shifting range, visualize that the palm stretches like a bungee cord; on the ascent, the fingers swing to the right of the thumb (with the weight of the hand centered in fingers two and three), rebound, and then swing to the left of the thumb, completing the descent (still with the weight centered in fingers two and three). In the two measures starting six before the end, consciously aiming for the lower notes makes the E-string harmonics less threatening.

Ultimately, the nature of the hand's transitions is a function of speed, and they are synchronized with the tempo of the composition of the moment. The hand performs its many rotations as the fingers cross strings, shift, and find their various tonal destinations at speeds that are proportional to the tempo of the piece. Whether the motion is bowing, shifting, or articulating with the string, adjusts the pace of everything to correspond to a common tempo. For maximum effect, no one motion is disproportionally faster or slower than any other. Feel that each finger and bow change is deliberate and even (notes should sound equally precise, clean, and articulated). When you play slowly, you should shift slowly; when playing fast, all parts of the shifts are faster.

Guiding Imagery Using the Violin String

Imagine tucking the shift finger underneath the string, latching on and lifting upward to secure the form of the moving hand and to support the articulating fingers.

The interplay involved with the motion of lifting and handing the string over to various fingers while the hand ascends or descends adds stability to the shift by providing the finger with a guideline and keeping it active midflight (between tiers).

During an ascending scale on the E string, for instance, play the notes inside the tier and then lift the E string up (energetically) with your first finger, pulling the finger (still underneath the lifted string) up to the next position, once more articulating within that note tier. On the turnaround, lift the string higher (with your first finger), making it more accessible to the fourth finger (and third) during the scale descent; then fire the fingers in reverse, dragging your first finger down the scale (still held underneath the string) until you reach the A string. At this point, stretch the E string, energetically bending it sideways (to the right), using it as leverage to assist the fourth, third, and second fingers (in intervallic position) over and onto the A string, then onto the D, and finally onto the G, assisting the fingers (especially the fourth) in their descent (see fig. 13.4).

Figure 13.4 Energetically bend the A string to leverage other fingers over and onto the D string. *Photo credit to Gail Taibbi.*

During a descending arpeggio or other passage, whichever finger is last to leave the string lifts and bends the string sideways to launch the rest of the fingers to the next lower-pitched string. In the third note of m.32 in the Bach Preludio (see ex. 13.10), bend the E string with the second finger (G-natural) to move the fourth finger from the E onto the A string; then for the second note of beat two, bend the first finger (B-natural) on the A string to assist the third finger (G-natural) onto the D string.

Example 13.10 Bach's Preludio in E Major, m.32.

CHAPTER FOURTEEN

Scales

We have demonstrated through imagery the micromotions involved in effective shifting. So we now combine the shifts into sweeping gestures that exhibit larger left-hand applications implemented for the ascent and descent of a multi-octave scale.

Combining Imagery for Left-Hand Support

Playing a scale provides opportunities to experience the fully expanded and contracted hand as well to use the full span of the fingerboard. Imagine that the left hand in home position is rolled up like a shade around the vertical thumb. As the hand ascends the scale, it begins to open, with the shade unrolling and stretching out until it is fully expanded; then it slowly retracts to its home position, with the thumb once more wrapped in the palm. Once the shade is pulled close to the bridge, the roller (thumb) is fully rotated; on the roll-up, it reverses fully. Maintain a continuous interplay between the thumb and the fingers as the expansion takes the hand into higher positions, with the retracting pull reuniting the fingers with the thumb for a progressively more natural interplay on the descent. Keep the hand malleable in its unfolding.

The opening two measures of the Rondo of Beethoven's violin concerto provides a good example (see ex. 14.1). First, imagine what the beginning (home) position feels like in the hand in first position. Then venture into the higher position and snap the hand back to that remembered place of balance around the thumb. On the top note, the A, exert equal pressure of the thumb and fourth fingertips on the same platform, like a person starting to do a split. Think of the elbow point, the thumb, and the fourth finger all together forming a *V*, and then push the elbow point in the

Example 14.1 Opening two measures of the Rondo movement of Beethoven's violin concerto.

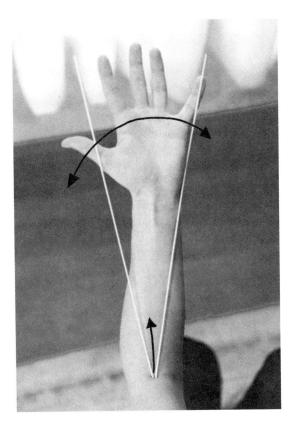

Figure 14.1 Push the elbow toward the hand for a feeling of expansion and overall cohesion. *Photo credit to Eva Foxon Nicholas.*

direction of the thumb and fourth finger. This creates an overall feeling of cohesion, with the elbow (forearm) assisting in the necessary expansion of the hand (see fig. 14.1). Ideally, the large knuckles are elevated enough above the fingerboard to allow them to bloom laterally so the fingers drop with ease onto the string.

Arcing Paths above the Fingerboard

The left-hand fingers tend to bog down after a prolonged period of playing. By ascending and descending on arcing paths, rather than traveling on flat lines, the hand is liberated, the motion becomes more eloquent, and its energy is more robust and unflagging.

Catapulting the Hand from the Bottom Center

To relocate the hand across the fingerboard without disrupting its shape, catapult the hand from its bottom center. Form a picture of the path the hand travels; carve out your exact path as if you are a bobsledder on a track and then follow that path, leading with the bottom of the hand. The following model uses a three-octave E major scale passage to demonstrate the hand's process: on the ascent (see ex. 14.2),

Example 14.2 Three-octave E major scale.

first the bottom of the hand on the lowest string aims for the E string, latches on, and then catapults the hand (clockwise) to an upright position. When you ascend the E string to fourth position, it is not that you consciously think of going over the top of the violin, but rather project the bottom of the hand on top of the E string and then simply rotate the hand into the correct position for the fingers to drop easily.

Once you reach the top of the scale, the bottom of the hand begins its descent, staying to the left of the E-string barrier; then as the hand approaches first position, it rotates to the right of the string, aims for the D, and coasts to its destination, bumping and skipping over the string in between. Once there, the bottom of the hand pivots over the top of the D, leading the fingers to their D-string destinations before repositioning itself once more to begin the ascent of the next scale. The curvature of the fingerboard encourages a gradual transition of wrist rotation.

Improperly projecting bottom-of-hand position (for instance, if when playing on the G string, projecting the wrist to the A string rather than a location to the left of the G) creates the feeling that the fourth finger is too short or that the neck too large for the hand. To place more of the hand above the fingerboard, visualize a fifth string to the left of the G; then imagine clasping the bottom of the hand to that fifth string. With that feeling, the hand is positioned better to play on the G string. And it can lean back to play a higher string without losing that orientation. Then it can simply straighten up again to play on the G, using that fifth string for leverage.

In higher positions, where passages cross the fingerboard (E string to G direction), the bottom of the hand still initiates the motion, but then the large knuckles take over, leading the rotation as the fingers find their points of articulation. For instance, after the solo entrance in the first movement of the Brahms concerto, m.19 (see ex. 14.3), when moving the fingers back and forth between the E string and the A, aim the wrist to the left of the A string and then lead the fingers via the knuckles to articulate with the E and back again to the A.

Example 14.3 First movement of the Brahms, 19 measures after the solo entrance.

When you catapult the wrist across the width of the fingerboard, to stay relaxed and keep their momentum, the fingers can sweep across in response, such as with the previous three-octave E major scale (see ex. 14.2). As the bottom of the hand aims for the E string, catapulting the hand to the right, the fingers can sweep the D and A strings en route to the E.

Escalating the Left Hand

To facilitate ascending from the G string to the E, picture an upside-down, L-shaped bar attached to the scroll; the bar starts at the scroll and extends vertically and then bends at a ninety-degree angle, heading horizontally toward the bridge. The bar rotates on its vertical segment, the horizontal piece swinging to the right or left of the violin. When ascending from the G string to the E, visualize pushing the horizontal part of the bar to the right of the neck with the back of the large knuckles; when descending from the E string to the G, imagine driving the bar to the left of the fingerboard with the front of the large knuckles, aligning the large knuckles and the fingertips to the string played (see fig. 14.2). Directing the horizontal bar with the large knuckles supports the back-and-forth transfer of weight, facilitating a controlled rotation of the hand. To amplify speed, especially with long descents on one string, let the unified arm lead the way with the fingers scrambling to catch up or to keep up.

Figure 14.2 Visualize pushing a horizontal bar to the right or left of the neck with the large knuckles. *Photo credit to Gail Taibbi.*

Hand Mobility without Disruption of Form

The hand is most apt to fall out of form when migrating from one longitudinal position to another. Imagine that the bottom of the hand is suspended above the fingerboard; then envision attaching two bungee cords, one to each lower corner of the hand. Before ascending scales, pull down the inside corner cord (thumb side) while raising the lower outside corner cord (fourth-finger side) toward the ceiling; then shift (see fig. 14.3). Before descending scales, weigh down the lower outside corner while lifting the heavier thumb side of the wrist (see fig. 14.4).

Place an imaginary (vertical) tire tube to the left of the hand on the fingerboard and lean the curved thumb and first finger—one end of the hand's tunnel—against it (see fig. 14.5). Pushing (or pulling with rope) the upright tire tube against the C-shaped thumb and first finger carries the relaxed hand easily and quickly anywhere on the fingerboard. The tube image is particularly effective when the hand is shifting to a radically different location, as in the Paganini Caprice No. 24, Variation 7, mm.3–4 (see ex. 14.4), because as previously mentioned, implementing hand

Left Arm

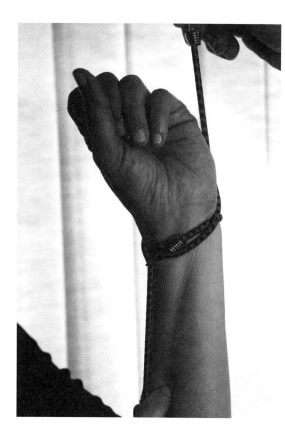

Figure 14.3 Before ascending scales, pull the inside corner down while raising the lower outside corner. *Photo credit to Gail Taibbi.*

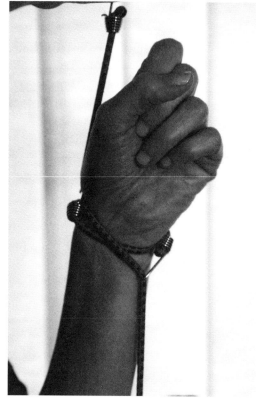

Figure 14.4 For descending scales, weigh down the lower outside corner while lifting the heavier thumb. *Photo credit to Gail Taibbi.*

Figure 14.5 Using a vertical tire tube to move a relaxed hand. *Photo credit to Eva Foxon Nicholas.*

Example 14.4 Paganini's Caprice No. 24 in A minor, Variation 7, mm.3–4.

motion by activating the feeling of an outside force releases tension and promotes greater dexterity.

Form a loop with the thumb and each shift finger, and then steer a small ball in your hand up or down the fingerboard with the shift. During an ascending scale, imagine pushing the ball along the fingerboard with a thumb-to-first-finger loop. On a scale descent, direct the ball toward the scroll with a thumb-to-fourth-finger loop.

Alternatively, on a scale descent, instead of holding the ball, picture pushing it toward the scroll with the thumb-to-first-finger loop. As you do that, drag or pull the shift finger—the second, third, or fourth finger. On the scale ascent, envision pushing the ball toward the bridge with the thumb-to-fourth-finger loop, again dragging the shift finger—the first, second, or third.

When descending from a higher position to a lower one—say, fourth position to first—there is a negative tendency to rotate the first finger counterclockwise in the plane of the palm, making it more difficult for the fourth finger to articulate with the string. When transitioning from a higher to a lower position, maintaining a palm position that is either level or even somewhat more clockwise in that plane supports a more vertically positioned first finger, at the same time allowing all four fingers easier access to the string.

Attach an imaginary string to the end of the scroll; then run it the length of the violin and beyond, through a track that takes it toward and across the top center of your head before descending down your back. Imagine someone standing behind you pulling the string, in that way lifting the scroll level higher, the way a drawbridge

Figure 14.6 Run a string from the scroll across the top of your head and down your back. *Photo credit to Gail Taibbi.*

is raised over a waterway (see fig. 14.6). The pulling or releasing of the string is a way to monitor the height of the fingerboard. When you imagine someone else doing the monitoring, the hand unwittingly participates without becoming overly involved. This is particularly effective for those not wearing a shoulder pad.

Chords and Double Stops

When playing a progression of chords, feel the dance of the hand as it leaps from posture to posture on the fingerboard. Each chord calls for a pattern of articulating fingers in concert with the corresponding foundations of those fingers and the thumb in the palm. As the mix of chords progresses, the hand dances this way and that, with the solid footfall of each configuration securing the balance of the hand during the navigation of multiple strings. The dance continues even with parallel motions, such as octave shifts, where the corners of the hand lift and lower along with the first and fourth fingers. Each stance is slightly different as the hand continually adjusts with microrotations along its sequence of placements. The unused fingers lift in reaction to the fingers articulated, the combined motion of the firing and nonfiring fingers adding to the picture of a complex, contrary-motion choreography.

When implementing thirds, sixths, octaves, or any simultaneous combination of notes, think of the alternating movement of the fingers as pistons firing, feeling the upward motions to be nearly as vigorous as the downward motion. The pistonlike motion of the fingers and their corresponding areas inside the wrist propel the chord progressions with energy and continuity.

CHAPTER FIFTEEN

Trills

A pastel body suspended, its cone penetrating sweet nectar; I hear the hum, or is it the wing-flap of angels?

—Maureen Taranto-Pyatt

Because the trill combines rapid articulation with reciprocal responses, the left-hand balances and applications previously described are crucial to its development. When trilling, the whole arm needs to be in balance, with the hand suspended at a suitable height and properly configured. The fingers flutter, and that activity helps sustain the hand above the fingerboard.

Hand Position

Place the back of your hand on a table and then make a fist, touching each of the four fingertips to its foundational support in the palm. Practice the connection of playing the fingers to the palm without involving the thumb. The farther away the articulating fingers are from the center of the hand, the more important—and challenging—it is to keep this connection. Again, all else being equal, strength and control come more easily squeezing a plum than a grapefruit.

The trill is optimized when the well-balanced hand is totally relaxed, especially around the large knuckles. A more relaxed hand can be experienced with one of several simple exercises: (a) lean the back of the hand against a table with the fingers falling into the palm; (b) place the closed hand on a table with the palm facing down, the first (largest) segment resting on top of the third segment (the distal phalanx); (c) lean the front or back of the large knuckles against an imaginary barrier/bar; or (d) place the hand on its side on a table and vertically stack the large knuckles.

Because wrist tension slows the trill, imagine resting the bottom of the hand on a platform. Or conjure up the image of the hand floating slightly beyond and above the wrist—with space in between. When you trill in lower positions, imagine placing the back of the hand against the left side of the neck of the violin as a way to relax the whole hand (see fig. 15.1).

Figure 15.1 Placing the back of the hand against the left side of the neck to feel a relaxed wrist. *Photo credit to Gail Taibbi.*

To steady the trill in the first three positions, call to mind the image of the palm leaning against the shoulder of the violin in each of those positions, with the projected shoulder providing the hand with the same sense of stability that materially exists in fourth position. For trills that are higher than fourth position, again lean the palm against an imaginary platform. When trilling the first finger, lean the thumb-to-first-finger loop against an imaginary wall toward the scroll. And when trilling the fourth finger, lean that edge of the hand against an imaginary wall on the bridge side. Find a way to support the hand; then begin to trill.

Hand-Arm Balance

When the fingers are properly balanced in the hand, they flex and extend more efficiently, approaching and departing their articulations with the string quickly and cleanly. To find good balance in the fingers, start by relaxing your whole arm from the shoulder through the hand. Feel the thumb relaxing into a natural curve as a result, and then balance the hand around it as you place the trill finger down. By itself, the relatively vertical positioning of the last segment of the finger in the well-balanced hand improves your accuracy because it is poised for the simplest drop down.

Presenting the Finger

The metacarpals are the bones inside the palm that are the foundations of the fingers. When you are looking at your palm, they run from about a half inch below the top to about an inch up from the bottom. The fingers each rotate on a mutual joint when they flex into the hand. For the greatest strength and comfort in the closing hand, feel the metacarpals rotate up to meet them, both from their common joint at the large knuckle and from the wrist as the hand extends (rotates posteriorly). Then consider the rotating metacarpal actually empowering the first segment of the related finger (the proximal phalanx); with support from the metacarpal, the finger snaps down with ease. To visualize opening the hand in between articulations, picture stepping on a pedal that opens and closes the lid on a trash can, where the pedal is the heel of the hand flexing forward and down and the fingers constitute the lid extending up. In between them are the metacarpals emerging from the now-expanding hand that is gathering potential energy to spend on the actions of the trill.

Finger Shape and Articulation

Given that the bones inside the palm are angled (fanned) out from the wrist in a relaxed hand, imagine expanding outward the wrist ends of the metacarpal bones of the base-trill and trill finger such that they line up parallel to each other. Or form a picture of stalls inside the hand, a wall separating each full finger from the other. Use either of these images to encourage the fingers to stand up straight, allowing the tip of the finger to drop solidly onto the string with full weight and backup support of its palmar partner.

Imagine attaching a string to the tip of the trill finger and then running it through an imaginary opening in the neck of the violin, with the string dangling underneath. Then call to mind an image of a church bell ringer pulling and releasing a rope. That pull adds momentum to the up-and-down motion of the finger.

To access speed in the trill, initiate motion from the first segment, the most proximal (closest to the body) third of the finger. To add buoyancy to the trill finger, insert an imaginary miniature ball inside the square-shaped room of the finger, with the ball reinforcing the connections of the finger to itself (refer to fig. 16.4). Wrapping a rubber band around the square-shaped finger secures the finger's shape.

For rapid passages, set the angle of the fingers to the fingerboard as perpendicularly as possible, especially in lower positions. When the fingers are rotated too far toward the scroll or when they relax too far back into extension, they can lose momentum. If you notice a leftward lean or a southward slip, reorient the fingers more squarely to the string and then fire down and release up with intention. Similarly, if the hand position is too low or too high relative to the fingerboard, the fingers work too hard and get bogged down.

To reinforce the fingertip's efficient articulation, think of the fingertip as the bottom of a square box; lift the box, keeping it relatively level, and then land it flat. To minimize the hand's involvement in holding the instrument when practicing trills, rest the scroll on a platform somewhat level with the top of the collarbone. Or imagine suspending the scroll from a string affixed to the ceiling that maintains a level positioning of the violin table.

With the left hand poised to play in third position, balance the heel of the hand on a post (refer to fig. 5.9). Because the placement of the post is south of the hand's center of gravity, weight shifts toward the fingertips in support of more possibilities with the trill. That extra weight lends both robustness and control, and the relaxed fingertips are positioned such that they more easily rebound off the fingerboard. As it is in all finger action, but especially important with trills, the touch of the finger is a press and release against the fingerboard, not a pressing and holding down. Forcing the trill causes the fingers to become muscle-bound, impeding the motion.

Left Arm

It is helpful if you lower the base-trill fingertip into the string by experiencing a sinking of the corresponding metacarpal into the wrist. The sensation is one of driving a stake into the earth. Like the previous description of the metacarpal cooperating with the first segment of the finger, you can feel it lean as it plants itself. And on the other end, it locks into its common joint at the large knuckle with the base-trill finger (see fig. 15.2). The grounding of the stationary finger has a stabilizing effect on the neighboring metacarpals during the potentially destabilizing motion of the trill finger. To assist continuity of the trill, gradually elevate the palm, particularly the planted metacarpal of the base-trill finger. For trills that begin with a base-trill finger, generate a sensation of rolling uphill the bottom of the hand underneath the trill finger onto a smooth, rounded rock or onto a wedge, in that way elevating both the base-trill and trill fingers (see fig. 15.3).

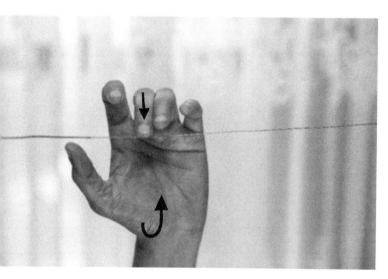

Figure 15.2 Lower the base-trill fingertip while syncing its corresponding metacarpal into their common joint. *Photo credit to Eva Foxon Nicholas.*

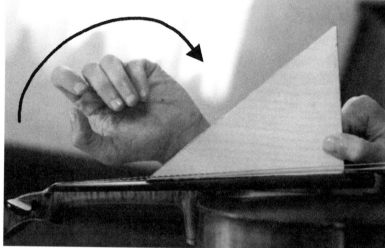

Figure 15.3 Roll the bottom of the hand underneath the trill finger uphill onto a wedge. *Photo credit to Eva Foxon Nicholas.*

Imagine inserting a wedge into the wrist along the crease line; the wedge gets thicker as it approaches the area underneath the fourth finger. Then roll the hand up the wedge in varying degrees depending on the trill finger. To jump-start trills that begin from above, experience a sensation of bouncing the bottom of the trill finger's metacarpal off a trampoline.

Contrary Motion of the Base-Trill and Trill Fingers

It is important to consider that the contrary motion between the base and trill finger involves the full length of each finger, including the corresponding metacarpal. To explore this alternating motion, envision two people controlling puppet strings: one is assigned always to rotate the base-trill finger by pulling in opposite directions a fingertip string and a string at the base of its metacarpal; the other has the same assignment with the trill finger, always moving opposite the base-trill puppeteer, with the combination supporting the crisscross motion of the two fingers.

Affix two strings, one to the tip of the base-trill finger and one to the metacarpal base of the trill finger (see fig. 15.4); dangling the hand from those two points prevents the transfer of extraneous motion from the hand to the trill finger while allowing it (without impediment) to reach down from a place of suspension. The two-point suspension creates a healthy tension, feeding energy to the trill while reinforcing the vertical direction of the articulating finger.

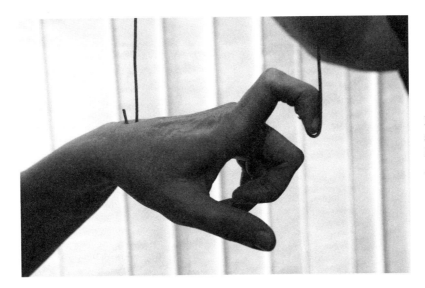

Figure 15.4 Affix two strings to relax and focus the hand for effective trilling. *Photo credit to Gail Taibbi.*

Countermotions and Pressures within the Hand

Keep the trill and base-trill fingers in continuous communication with each other. Walking with alternating leg strides is far more natural and efficient than hopping on one leg; similarly, the base-trill and trill fingers can collaborate with a motion like the cross-crawl coordination of walking, providing the trill with more speed and better balance and buoyancy than motion relegated to the trill finger only.

Countermotions and pressures sustain trill continuity, and the following explorations demonstrate the interrelations of base-trill and trill fingers within this context. If the thumb moves upward toward the ceiling, the fingers can sink deeper into the palm in response. Now picture the fingertips—base-trill and trill—pushing down on an actual string while the thumb tip pushes upward against an imaginary string that is parallel and to its left (refer to fig. 10.12). This creates a vertical buoyancy of the fingers, with the upward thrust of the thumb supporting the alternating motion of the fingers (the base trill finger subtly moving sympathetically once the trill finger is set into motion). As mentioned in chapter 7, because overextending fingers impedes speed and power by weakening the finger-to-palm connection and consequently the impetus of finger motion, maintain a close finger-to-palm correspondence to promote strength and dexterity. Conversely, you can monitor the spring tension in the hand by noticing how close or far away the base-trill finger is to the palm.

This time, visualize two children on a trampoline, one standing firm (base-trill finger) and the other jumping (trill finger). Though maintaining contact with the trampoline, the first child is also bobbing up and down in response to its active playmate. This image helps heighten awareness of a subtle interplay that takes place within the hand: the palm elevating by flexing the trill finger and lifting the base-trill finger as a consequence.

Similarly, imagine that the string is a seesaw with a fulcrum centered underneath and between the base-trill and trill fingers (see fig. 15.5). Though the base-trill finger keeps contact with the fingerboard, the action of both fingers—base and trill—alternates, shifting weight, rocking back and forth, up and down, as two people on a seesaw (though the trill finger more actively pushes one end of the seesaw down and allows its release). Maintain the finger shape, and then flex the finger and let it bounce back; drop the finger and do not think every note. The touch of both fingers—the base and trill—is light. Avoid digging the base-trill finger into the fingerboard, which causes the trill finger, its seesawing partner, to over-exert.

Figure 15.5 Envision the string as a seesaw with a fulcrum centered between the base-trill and trill fingers. *Photo credit to Gail Taibbi.*

There is a negative tendency when trilling to compress the large knuckles and constrict the trill. As a rule, keep the compressions of the hand more vertical with trills. Just as well-coordinated countermotions and pressures sustain trill continuity, so too does the well-considered lateral expansion of the hand. With whole-step trills, for example, the large knuckles have a tendency to return to their unexpanded state prematurely. To thwart this tendency, again picture the large knuckles as a string of four pearls; when you pull the ends of the string, the knuckles expand as the fingers are also suspended on the line.

Imagine that the large knuckles are four plastic balls connected to a fishing line and floating in water (with the hand luxuriating in a state of relaxation). If you submerge one of the bobbers (representing either the second- or third-finger large knuckle), the surrounding bobbers cave in around—or join together above—the one that is submerged. If you then release the submerged one and allow it to resurface, it comes up underneath the surrounding bobbers, pushing them to the side. Now allow it to emerge and submerge only to the point where it can tap the underside of its two neighbors without displacing them. Likewise, think of pressing down on the large knuckle of the trill finger and in so doing allowing the adjacent large knuckles (like the surrounding bobbers) to cave in on top. When you release pressure, the trill-finger large knuckle rises, displacing the neighboring knuckles. If you then submerge it but do not release it all the way, it can tap or bounce off the undersides of the conjoining knuckles. Doing so minimizes the knuckle's motion, supporting a rapid trill. You can also bounce the large knuckle of the trill finger off the top of its two neighbors, in that way effecting a rebound.

Compressions That Support Trill Finger Rebound

Compressions are oppositional pressures exerted from the periphery of a system, naturally or deliberately, that can be consciously manipulated. As in chapter 13, envision a C-bar made of spring-like metal material, and then align the C-bar with your finger and corresponding part of the palm. As you compress the ends inward, the energy for rebound builds due to the C-bar's restoring force. The compression and return to normalcy of the C-bar exaggerates the feel of palm and fingertips conjoining and releasing at the moment of articulation for simple note production and especially for trills. Or as in chapter 8, try holding a circular wire between the first joint of the thumb and the large knuckles; then lasso a string underneath the large knuckles before tightening it (refer to fig. 8.6). The wire maintains a round hand formation and supports the upward motion of the fingers, with the trill fingers now automatically rebounding after each articulation.

The feeling of bouncing the palm is a beneficial way to jump-start the trill. Picture a rubber ball resting on the fingerboard; then bounce the center of your palm off the ball. The compression of the ball and its return to form support the bouncing/rebounding motion of the large knuckles, which enhances the effectiveness of the trill. In fact, this image can be used to release extraneous tension and restore balance of the hand ahead of any technically challenging sequence.

Support for the Trill Finger

It is psychologically freeing to imagine lifting and suspending the strings or even the fingerboard with the tips of the fingers, and that sensation serves the trill. Envision a special glue on the base-trill finger that also sticks to the string but stretches enough to allow the finger to separate from the string while lifting it. Or think of the base-trill finger suspending the platform of the fingerboard and presenting it to the trill finger, which is then better supported for more rapid articulations. Use the special glue or substitute suction cups (previously described in chapter 7), each with the ability to lift the fingerboard without fully adhering.

Left Arm

Extra support for the trill finger is especially important when crossing the fingerboard. With your hand palm up and fingers extended, superimpose the four strings across the pads of your fingers in a fan shape that is similar to the way strings are distributed on the fingerboard (see fig. 15.6). If the string closest to the fingertips is the E string, note how the increasing angle of the other strings to the E increases their distance to the fingertip. Because the hand needs to extend progressively farther over the top of the fingerboard for the fingers to gain access to the next farthest string, form a picture of tucking more of the finger (proportionally informed by the fanning image) underneath each string relative to the distance from the E, in that way coaxing the hand into a position where the fingers can relax rather than (over)extend to play on strings farther from the E, all the way to G. So for E-string trills, feel that you are burrowing underneath the string and then lifting the string with the tip of the base-trill finger; on the A string and D, lift from an area deeper into the finger (the finger tucks under the string); and on the G string, picture lifting the string from the first joint.

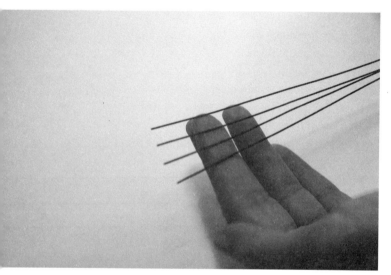 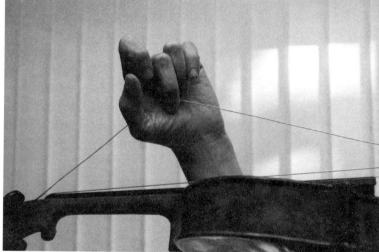

Figure 15.6 Superimpose four strings like they normally distribute on the fingerboard. *Photo credit to Gail Taibbi.*

Figure 15.7 Visualize the base-trill finger tucked underneath the left side of the string and lifting off. *Photo credit to Gail Taibbi.*

The trill mimics the motion of a bird with one wing flapping. The base-trill finger tucks under the string and tries to lift off while the trill finger, like the flapping wing, manages to push off the string, sustaining the body of the bird (base-trill finger) above the fingerboard (see fig. 15.7). Like a stork carrying a bundle, the effort of the base-trill finger lifts the violin while the trill finger articulates with the string. When the base-trill finger presents the string to the trill finger, it furnishes the trill finger with something taut off which to bounce. Elevating the string with this image decreases the distance the finger needs to travel to articulate. Visualizing the base-finger holding the string also reinforces its curved shape while it counters the hand's tendency to weigh down the scroll end.

To prevent the hand from rocking excessively during trills, weigh down the large knuckles to the right of the trill finger, or imagine attaching a string to the outer edge of the fourth-finger large knuckle and then fastening it to the fingerboard as when tying a corner rope around a stake hammered into the ground while pitching a tent (see fig. 15.8). The idea is to evenly distribute the weight across the large knuckles on each side of the trill finger like two pillars. When trilling the fourth finger, imagine an additional large knuckle to its right, or tilt the hand in the fourth-finger direction. The thumb contributes stabilizing weight to the left of the trilling first finger.

Figure 15.8 Attach a string from the outer edge of the fourth-finger large knuckle to the fingerboard. *Photo credit to Gail Taibbi.*

Coordinated Compressions within the Hand

Through a sense of coordinated compressions, we can create an environment in the hand in which the fingers rediscover their natural rebound. Envision separating the palm between the base and trill fingers, right down into the base of the palm (like a parting of the sea). Picture that the base of the palm and the rest of the wrist is the body of a bird and that the two fingers, base and trill, are its wings. Find the interactive motion in the hand between the bottom of the hand (representing the bird's body) and the two fingers, base and trill (the wings). When the body of the bird/hand drops, the wings / two fingers elevate it. This deep separation amplifies the awareness of weight and wingspan.

To get a feeling of elevating the palm against the downward press of the trill and base-trill fingers, take three strings: attach one to the body of the bird (center of the base of the palm) and then tie one around each wing—the second knuckle of the base and trill fingers. Pull open and downward the two strings attached to the base and trill finger knuckles / wings (the base finger pulled scroll direction, the trill finger toward the bridge), and simultaneously pull the string that lifts the body/base palm up through the middle of the two fingers; this induces compression, enhancing the rebound of the fingers (see fig. 15.9).

Left Arm

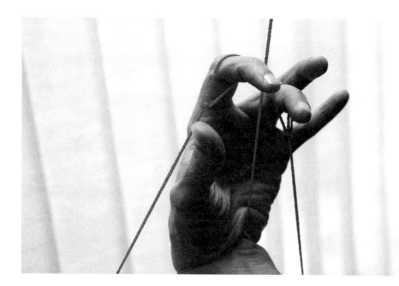

Figure 15.9 Pull open and downward the base and trill fingers while pulling up the other string. *Photo credit to Gail Taibbi.*

Visualize the hand on the fingerboard in the shape of a ball; then press the fingers open and downward against the resistance of the hand/ball. Similarly, the upward pressure of the base of the palm against the downward pressure of the two fingers—base and trill—creates a dynamic of buoyancy and rebound while feeding continuity to the trill. Without adequate compression, the hand is like a ball that has lost air.

Again, visualize that the hand on the fingerboard is in the shape of a ball. Affix a string to the bottom center of the hand/ball, threading it up through the hand between the second and third (base and trill) fingers. Then experience the sensation of someone lifting the string to elevate the hand/ball, with the weight of the fingers succumbing to gravity as they accumulate the relaxed energy to trill effectively. Horizontally adjust the placement of the suspending string to support the finger-pair being used.

This time, spread the middle two fingers as base and trill, holding them apart as a butterfly would flatten its upright wings; then elevate the lower outside corner of the hand in the direction of the flexing fingers. This compression adds speed to the trill. The upward motion of the trill finger allows the springlike feel of the hand to momentarily decompress.

For each set of trilling fingers, it is helpful to configure the rest of the hand to best support the strength and freedom of those fingers. It may mean engaging a corresponding area underneath those fingers: if the wing spread is between the index finger and second fingers, for example, flex up the lower left corner of the hand. Or a diagonal support might sometimes work better: when trilling the first finger on an open string, you may decide that flexing the lower outside corner diagonally toward the middle of the tunnel formed by the thumb and first finger is most effective. When trilling with the fourth finger, you might flex the meat of the thumb either straight up or diagonally toward the third- and fourth-finger wing spread, or you can also urge the heel area underneath the base-trill finger upward, whichever exerts more effective compression.

To use some real-world examples, when trilling with the third finger, as in the Kreutzer Caprice 15, the pickup to three measures before the end (see ex. 15.1), the center of the bottom of the hand (the area underneath the base trill finger) ascends (or flexes up) in between the second- and third-finger wing spread; when trilling the second finger, the base of the thumb at the lower left corner of the thumb flexes up through the middle of the first- and second-finger wing spread (base-trill and trill fingers); and when trilling with the fourth finger, the fourth and last eighth notes, flex the base of the thumb either straight up or diagonally toward the third- and fourth-finger wing spread, or engage the palm area directly underneath the base-trill finger. Pick the one that channels more energy to the trill.

Example 15.1 Kreutzer's Caprice 15, the pickup to 3 measures before the end.

When trilling while balancing the hand on the lower outside corner, imagine that the lower outside corner is a ball with a string attached. Separate the area between the two fingers, base-trill and trill, and hold them apart. Pull the string attached to the lower outside corner / ball through the palm and between the metacarpals of the base-trill and trill fingers; the corner of the hand rises up and tucks in between, forcing the base of the metacarpals to expand. When the hand is balanced on the bottom center, visualize that the base of the palm directly corresponding to the area between the base and trill fingers rises up, forcing its way through the metacarpal bases and out the back of the hand, once more holding apart the bones inside the palm. Similarly, envision tucking a ball in between the metacarpals of the base-trill and trill fingers at the heel of the hand, laterally expanding the foundation for the trilling fingers. Or contemplate in the mind's eye the base of the metacarpals as four pearls on an elastic string; when you pull the ends of the string, the base of the palm expands, in that way supporting the straight-up-and-down orientation of the trill finger. The idea of all of these is to create a system of balanced pressures that supports the trill and then sets it into motion.

Taking into account individual differences in anatomical structure and tension patterns affecting the functional unit in question, the exact configurations of hand balances and applied compressions will vary from player to player, but the principles should be widely applicable. How small we are, and yet from minuteness, the lark ascends.

CHAPTER SIXTEEN

Vibrato

A bumblebee, on a morning stem graced with lavender bells, knocks a drop of light into the pond; the circle grows till it is no more.

—Maureen Taranto-Pyatt

Balancing the Hand

Before generating the motion of vibrato, it is essential to understand a new balance with respect to the palm and fingers. Balance of the hand for vibrato is different from the fundamental configurations for passage work. Flex the hand at the large knuckles, forming a V shape. Think of the two sides of the V as springy legs: from one large knuckle to its fingertip is one leg, and from that large knuckle to the wrist (through the metacarpals) is the other (see fig. 16.1). See the fingertip as one foot and the base of the metacarpal as the other; then balance both feet on a board (see fig. 16.2).

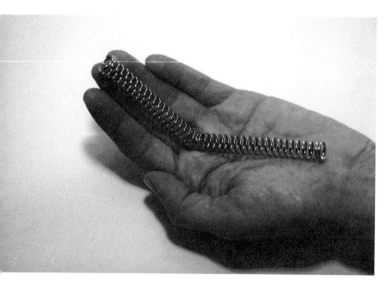

Figure 16.1 Flex the hand at the large knuckles forming a V shape, thinking of the two sides as springy legs. *Photo credit to Gail Taibbi.*

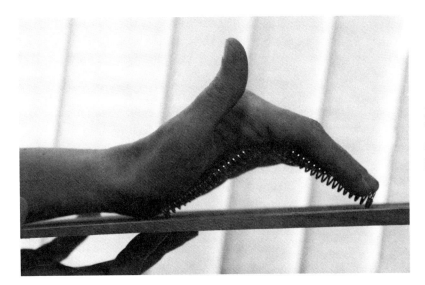

Figure 16.2 Balance both "feet," fingertip and base of metacarpal, on the same plane. *Photo credit to Gail Taibbi.*

In lower positions, choose the position (the plane) of the board to equally benefit the position of the articulating fingertips and the supportive hand. As the angle of the board to the neck (the approach of the hand to the fingerboard) varies to meet the musical need, continually reestablish balance so weight is not more prominent in one foot than the other. Lift the large knuckle and plant the fingertip and the metacarpal base equally (on both feet). Now bounce the fingertip and bottom of the hand off the imaginary board (the fingertip and base remain balanced with each other). Then vibrate the finger by propelling the joint you wish to vibrate. The knuckle motion is circular, causing a circular motion all the way into the fingertip, with the remaining fingers drawing little circles of their own. While changing from one finger to the next, spring upward or leap to jump-start vibrato.

In higher positions, as in the first movement of the Brahms Violin Concerto in D, 47 measures after the solo entrance (see ex. 16.1), when the fingertip bounces off the fingerboard, visualize that the heel of the hand rests on a post that lifts it slightly higher than the fingertip (refer to fig. 5.9). The off-center placement of the pole enables the hand to shift weight toward the fingertips, causing them to drape downward onto the fingerboard in support of a narrower oscillation, especially desirable in higher positions.

Example 16.1 First movement of the Brahms Violin Concerto in D, 47 measures after the solo entrance.

The foundation of each finger begins at the base of the metacarpals, the bones of the palm that sit on the wrist. As described earlier, the dual balancing of the ends of each full finger stabilizes the digit for effective vibrato. Divide the ends of each full finger—fingertip and corresponding metacarpal base—in half lengthwise, creating a pair of arms with hands at the tip of each finger and a pair of legs with feet at the end of each metacarpal. While the hands (on either side of a bisecting line that splits the nail face in half) are close together on the string, the feet are farther apart, counterbalancing at the heel of the hand. Or visually imagine an athlete with hands close together around a pole (as are the sides of the fingertip around the string in our previous image), but feet (the metacarpal foundation of the finger) spread apart, seeking counterbalance. For instance, when vibrating the middle finger, the feet expand out equally, balancing against the lower corners of your hand (see fig. 16.3).

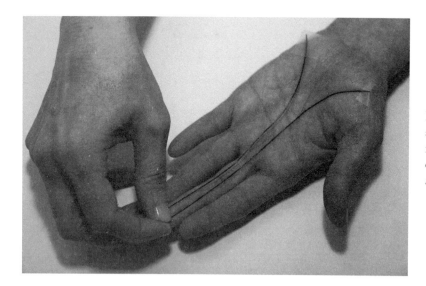

Figure 16.3 Imagine an athlete grasping a pole with feet spread apart, seeking counterbalance. *Photo credit to Gail Taibbi.*

Bottom-of-Hand Balances

To transition the motion of vibrato from one finger to the next, begin by establishing a connection between the foundations of both the thumb and the vibrated finger. Balance the base part of the thumb on an imaginary platform along with the foundation of the hand underneath the vibrated finger. Then place two vertically positioned springs, one inside the base of each metacarpal. When vibrating the first finger, balance the base of the thumb with the bottom of hand below the first finger; when vibrating the second finger, balance the thumb base with the base of the hand below the second finger; and so on. The two springs support balance and buoyancy of motion for the thumb and the vibrated finger together. Favoring one side is like jumping up and down on one foot rather than on two, with the latter lending stability, strength, and creative possibilities.

To position the hand well for the proper balance, it helps to picture a track along the wrist that is similar to one that suspends a pocket door (in this case the thumb suspends somewhat sideways). Affix the base of the thumb to the track and then slide it along the track, correspondingly positioning it underneath each finger one at a time or in between any two fingers (refer to fig. 9.4). Notice how repositioning the thumb affects the distribution of weight within the hand and among the fingers. Think of dropping weight inside the base of the palm; then sense a subtle sideways shift of weight of the hand, with the change in position of that weight effecting a slight sidewise rotation of the palm that further enables each finger to vibrate more easily in a more neutral, straight-up-and-down position. The human body—a galaxy within, spiraling from the center of origin.

Inside the Square-Shaped Finger

Imagining the calculated placement of varying sized balls in and around the hand and arm encourages a rebound effect while it suggests the easy roundedness of authentic movement. To add buoyancy to the vibrated finger, imagine flexing your index finger into a square shape around a miniature ball (see fig. 16.4); then press the proximal (closest) and distal (farthest) segments against the ball in between. Release, and the finger lengthens as it rebounds away. This awareness generates a feeling of buoyancy as it reinforces the rounded connection of the finger to itself.

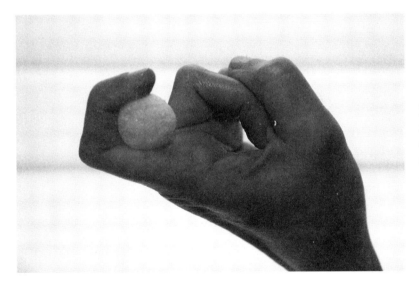

Figure 16.4 Flex your index finger (into a square shape) around an imaginary miniature ball. *Photo credit to Gail Taibbi.*

The Palm

Flexibility in the palm is a key to broadening the possibilities and range of movement underlying vibrato. To create a field of flexibility in the palm, picture the center circle inside the palm moving independently from the motion of the hand matter around it; think of this center area responding like a balloon membrane would as it is dragged to and fro underwater. This helps to loosen the vibrato.

Left Arm

Another ball image helps to maintain a supple hand. Balance a baseball in the center part of the palm. The ball, resting between the palm and the fingerboard with the large knuckles on top, provides the palm with something to bounce off as it reinforces the structural effectiveness of the rounded hand. This time roll the ball/hand slightly across the fingerboard so the large-knuckle weight shifts from on top of the ball to your left on an incline. With the large knuckles draped over the ball, weight is able to travel to the fingertips without the hand getting bogged down (see fig. 16.5).

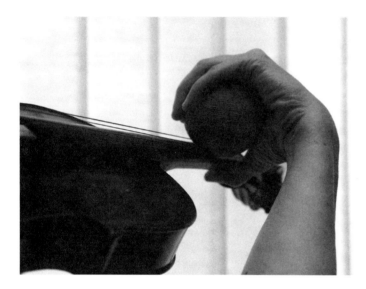

Figure 16.5 Use a ball to roll the large knuckles into a position that allows weight to fall easily into the fingers. *Photo credit to Gail Taibbi.*

The Inner Circle

Picture a beach ball held by the flexed upper and lower arms at their midpoints. When you press and release the inner (anterior) aspects of both segments of the arm against the ball, the elbow joint expands and contracts, releasing tension. Now use the beach-ball image to help the upper arm and forearm keep an active flexion through the elbow as the vibrating fingers shift into higher and lower positions. When ascending the fingerboard, the arm rotates around the ball while the medial (pinky) edges close on each other (the rotation coming ultimately from the shoulder) to accommodate the change of balance in the hand. During the descent, as the arm extends, the lateral (thumb-side) edges of the forearm and upper arm rotate the other way.

For an image that supports the expansion of the hand and a balanced transfer of weight to reinforce a solid range of oscillatory knuckle motion, imagine aiming each finger toward a point on the arc (of the cross-contour) of the biceps that varies with the choice of finger. The first finger aims at and vibrates on the left-side incline of the biceps, the second and third fingers aim more toward the top of the arc, and the fourth finger aims at the right-side incline of the cylinder. In contrast, when you are vibrating in one position on one string, the cross connections take place more within the hand with the shoulder remaining neutral.

The smaller ball in the hand affects a faster rebound than the larger beach ball, with the motion of vibrato being more dynamic in the fingers and less active in the arm. If you wish to implement a finger-arm vibrato, wrap your arm around a beach ball and then flex the upper arm and forearm, with this connectedness supporting the rebalancing with each finger change. The arm's compression creates a stable platform for the hand while averting the danger of it getting involved with holding onto the neck.

The Shoulder

Place a ball (approximately softball sized) filled with helium under the arm to both support and liberate the arm as well as achieving a more vertical forearm. The ball sustains a strong position of the upper arm relative to the torso without the muscular work that might migrate into tension. During a three-octave scale, the ball creates a healthy resistance, allowing the hand to catapult into higher positions and drop back without the upper arm collapsing against the torso. Place one under each arm; the elevating ball supports a feeling of depth and breadth, conferring the sensation of a pair of wings in flight. When vibrating, everything is supple and bouncing off each other.

Rotational Interactions of the Arm and Hand

The relationships of hand to fingerboard, lower arm to upper arm, and arm to torso can distort without a sense of how to correct them. Individually and together, the ball images support awareness and reveal guiding strategies. In service of the forearm's position for the hand, the whole arm rotates laterally as it rolls the ball leaning against the torso. The forearm is guided around the larger, stationary ball in direct service to—finding and keeping a balance among—the vibrating fingers. Think of the hand/ball's orbit in higher positions as taking in the top of the shoulder socket to complete the inter-galactic exchange. The rotation of each sphere is influenced by the other members of its celestial system. Beyond the creation of our small galaxy's positional relationships, when strategically placed, the ball images add a feeling of buoyancy to the entire arm and hand (see fig. 16.6).

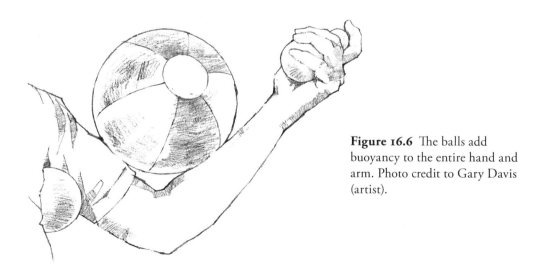

Figure 16.6 The balls add buoyancy to the entire hand and arm. Photo credit to Gary Davis (artist).

Employing the Knuckles

Once the overall limb is shored up, focus attention on the components of the hand, for instance the knuckles. Having joint flexibility and knowing how one part of the hand interacts with another are both integral to producing a good vibrato. Contemplate in the mind's eye a compass (the instrument for drawing); place the needle straight up and down and then draw a circle around that center point with the pencil. The last (small) segment of the finger is similarly poised (slightly below the pitch) when vibrating, and the knuckle travels the circular pathway of the pencil. Vibrate to the pitch. If you vibrate above the desired pitch, either the finger is placed too high or the vibrato is too wide.

Discovering the relationship of each knuckle to other parts of the hand and to the string reveals many variables with which to expand the range and types of vibrato. When vibrating, imagine that the large knuckles neighboring the oscillating finger are a pair of ascending wings. The nonvibrated fingers lift off the fingerboard, essentially moving out of the way to make room for the vibrating finger's oscillation. Otherwise, the large knuckle of the vibrating finger knocks into the adjoining large knuckles and that restricts its range of motion.

The speed of vibrato varies with both the thickness of the string and the position of the fingers. It also fluctuates with functional finger length. Circular motion becomes smaller as the length of finger use shortens; therefore, vibrating around the base joints has the largest and slowest oscillation. Middle-knuckle vibration moves more quickly. As you get closer to the base of the nail, the natural pace accelerates. Illustrating this, consider that a person standing with feet wide apart can move the upper body in a wider circle than with the feet close together. Similarly, when vibrating the large knuckles, their balance mandates a larger footing than when vibrating the small joints. When vibrating the large knuckles, your supporting feet are the bottom of the hand and fingertips (on the same plateau), and when you vibrate the middle knuckles, your balanced feet are the large knuckle and fingertip. As the distance of the footing closes, the size of the circular rotation is progressively reduced.

Speed and width of vibrato are also influenced by the involvement of the primary elbow flexor: the biceps. If you add a little more effort from the biceps in supporting the hand (see fig. 16.7), that activated muscle strengthens the arm platform and energizes the vibrato without adding tension to it.

Notice each set of knuckles (one row at a time)—the large, middle, and small, as well as an imaginary joint where the cuticles are. Bend at each knuckle to reinforce the alignment of one finger segment to another. Roughly speaking, the base knuckles are used for G-string vibrato, the middle knuckles for D-string vibrato, the first set of knuckles for the A, and the artificial joint inside the small segment at cuticle level to vibrate on the E. The same principle of proportional progression applies as you move up the string, with the oscillations graduating from the large knuckles in lower positions to smaller ones as the pitch rises in higher positions. If there is a knuckle that is stiff or limited in mobility, substitute one that is more flexible. For example, if there were a lack of flexibility in the third-finger small knuckle, normally used to vibrate a note on the A string, either substitute the third finger's middle knuckle or vibrate at cuticle level.

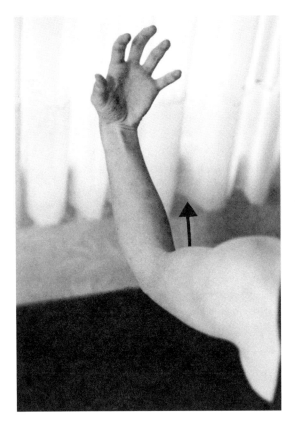

Figure 16.7 Lifting the left arm with more involvement from the biceps. *Photo credit to Eva Foxon Nicholas.*

As weight shifts among the four joints (one imaginary) of each finger, lift and lower each knuckle like a bird ascending and descending. The opening two measures of the solo in the first movement of Tchaikovsky's Violin Concerto in D use each of the four knuckle sets (see ex. 16.2). In m.1 on the G string, suspend the hand from the apex of the large knuckles and vibrate (see fig. 16.8); on the D string, suspend the apex of the middle knuckles and vibrate the downbeat of m.2 (see fig. 16.9); on the A string, suspend the apex of the first joint on the first two sixteenth notes of beat 2 in m.2 (see fig. 16.10); and on the E, suspend the cuticle from an imaginary joint for the rest of the passage (see fig. 16.11).

Example 16.2 First two measures of the opening solo in the Tchaikovsky violin concerto.

For a combination hand and arm vibrato, especially in higher positions, feel a sense of balance and cohesion along the line between the inside bump of the left elbow and the fingertips as they are articulating (see fig. 16.12). Within that larger context are subbalances: on the G string, balance the base of the hand with the fingertip (see fig. 16.13), and then vibrate around the large knuckle; on the D string, balance

Left Arm

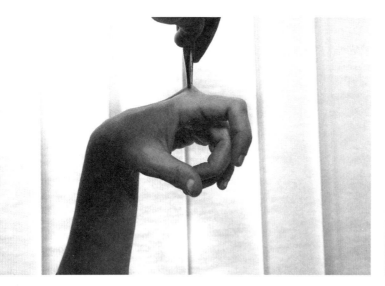

Figure 16.8 On the G string, suspend the hand from the apex of the large knuckles. *Photo credit to Gail Taibbi.*

Figure 16.9 On the D string, suspend the apex of the middle knuckles. *Photo credit to Gail Taibbi.*

Figure 16.10 On the A string, suspend the apex of the small knuckle. *Photo credit to Gail Taibbi.*

Figure 16.11 On the E, suspend the cuticle from an imaginary joint. *Photo credit to Gail Taibbi.*

Figure 16.12 Align and balance the inside bump of the left elbow and articulating fingertip. *Photo credit to Gail Taibbi.*

Figure 16.13 Align and balance the base of the hand and articulating fingertip. *Photo credit to Gail Taibbi.*

Figure 16.14 Align and balance the area under the large knuckle and articulating fingertip. *Photo credit to Gail Taibbi.*

Figure 16.15 Align and balance the midsection of the large knuckle and articulating fingertip. *Photo credit to Gail Taibbi.*

Figure 16.16 Align and balance the top of the large knuckle and articulating fingertip. *Photo credit to Gail Taibbi.*

the area under the large knuckle with the articulating fingertip (see fig 16.14), and then vibrate using the middle knuckle; on the A string, balance the midsection of the large knuckle with the fingertip (see fig. 16.15), and then vibrate the first joint; and on the E, balance the top of the large knuckle with the fingertips (see fig. 16.16), and then vibrate the cuticle (an imaginary joint).

Optimal Support for the Vibrating Finger

To achieve a full sound on a solo note, experiment with making diagonal connections in the hand. When you vibrate the first finger, point the finger toward the lower outside corner of the hand to make that connection, as in the first solo note of the Tchaikovsky concerto (see ex. 16.2). Aim the vibrating fourth finger toward the lower inside corner of the hand to secure its connection to the upper right corner (see fig. 16.22). Each of these encourages a round vibrato with full backup support of the hand, with the joint used determining the size of its oscillation.

To focus the sound, balance the square-shaped finger perpendicular to the line of the string (not leaning up or down the string) with the large knuckles hovering above the string. Within the same finger, the larger joint empowers the smaller one, which in turn rotates the surface of the fingertip. Do not allow the finger to collapse or the top of the hand to flop. To assist the vibrating finger, feel that you're bringing the thumb forward to join the rest of the fingers. The hand stays supple but firm, always including pressure from the thumb. Do not press the tip of the thumb to the fingertips; press the vibrated finger down where it contacts the fingerboard and then oppose with the thumb. Press the thumb from the fleshy part of the first segment with a vector that combines radically varying amounts of support for the neck, opposition to the fingers, and retraction of the instrument back toward the neck (see fig. 16.17). The vibrato will stiffen if you lock the thumb or use it as a rigid crutch to hold the neck. Keep the action moving with the three-way connection (upper arm flexor, thumb, and finger joint) supporting the three component vectors as needed.

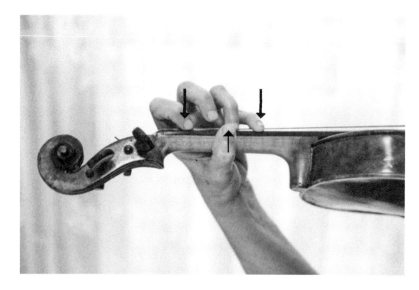

Figure 16.17 The vibrated finger and the thumb never aim at each other. *Photo credit to Eva Foxon Nicholas.*

A relaxed, curved, and responsive thumb allows the fingertips to rock. If any joint constricts, the vibrato is interrupted, so it is beneficial to keep everything fluid.

Jump-start the vibrato by thrusting the oscillating finger (along the line of the string) against the fingers in front of it. For example, when initiating vibrato using the first-finger small knuckle, that knuckle propels the second-, third- and fourth-finger small knuckles forward. When jump-starting vibrato using the second-finger middle knuckle, that knuckle propels the third- and fourth-finger middle knuckles toward the bridge, and so on. Because holding down the finger inhibits motion, use a press-release motion against the fingerboard to initiate vibrato. The touch of the vibrating finger is relatively light on the string. Do not shorten (chop off) the higher part of the circle, leaving the lower part full and making it lopsided; the motion should be round. When you vibrate one finger to the next, change to the next finger on the higher point of oscillation to provide continuity. Access motion more from the fingers than from the palm; otherwise, you will destabilize the fingers.

Concentrate on the center of the vibrato, but not for pitch; the pitch is at the top of the oscillation. Center yourself on the point where the fingertip contacts the fingerboard, sending the bone inside the first finger segment straight down; it rebounds off the fingerboard as a pogo stick bounces off pavement without the flesh of the fingertip losing contact. Maintain continuous motion, but do not force the motion throughout the sustained note. Neither should you slow down or speed up; otherwise, the sound will bend. Begin the note and then relax. If you stop at the top of the oscillation or somewhere in between—say, by retaking in the middle of a note—the motion of vibrato is interrupted, causing the tone to be erratic. If you push the circle wider than is natural, the vibrato will wobble. Push the vibrato and then allow it to take over on its own. Do not overcontrol it; let the pendulum move all the way out to complete the swing.

All parts are free to move. If there is constriction, assess whether it is in the arm or hand by creating a tension loop that extends from the shoulder to the hand (or mentally wrap your arm around the perimeter of a ball); this locates and flushes out the tension. Then relax the entire hand and arm. Form a picture of vertical springs inside the vibrated joints and horizontal springs between the large knuckles, separating one from another. To sustain the motion of the vibrato as well as keep the motion of the vibrated fingers alive and electric, imagine that the full finger is a taut spring and that your whole body is a system of springs.

The horizontal movement in vibrato is often imbalanced such that there is too little finger play in one direction and an overabundance of motion in the other, creating a warped vibratory oscillation. The oscillation of your vibrating finger tends to happen more easily in lower positions because the knuckles express a relaxed circular motion with the more horizontal fingers and wrist at the scroll end, rather than the more vertical orientation higher up. In higher positions, the lateral rotation of the arm is reaching its limit, so the oscillation tends to be lopsided, with the circle getting wider toward the scroll and being shortchanged (short cut) or flattened on the flip side. Using weight imagery will help prolong an evenly distributed oscillatory motion. Visualize that each knuckle is a hollow sphere containing a metal ball within it; spin the metal ball around the inside of the knuckle/sphere to promote the oscillatory motion. By placing a round metal ball inside the vibrated knuckle and thrusting the knuckle forward with hula-hoop motion, the amplifying weight assists the knuckle in rounding out the circular motion while adding momentum to the oscillation. Feel the rotation of the knuckle spiraling up the arm toward the shoulder with the motion broadening and lessening as it ascends while the overall energetic connections (structural and functional) at the same time support fingertip activity.

Aiming the Fingertips

Fire your fingertips through the fingerboard into the palm, wrist, or elbow with a clear sense of direction while grounding the vibrato. When vibrating the finger without consciously aiming the tip toward a destination, the structure slackens and in so doing loses its shape and effectiveness. An ambitious finger informs the shape of the hand while a sense of the finger playing into itself produces a finger vibrato naturally. But the biggest benefit of directing the fingers is to connect them with their various vibratory partners.

Imagine extending your fingertips through the phantom neck of the violin into the center of the palm to support a hand vibrato (see fig. 16.18). Similarly, aiming the fingers toward the wrist creates a wrist vibrato (see fig. 16.19). Aiming the fingertips toward the mid-forearm or elbow, forming an even larger circle of motion, generates an arm vibrato (see fig. 16.20). And aiming the fingertips toward the shoulder forms the largest circle of motion and generates an even more robust arm vibrato, (see fig. 16.21).

Deliberately pitching your fingertips through the fingerboard into the palm, wrist, or elbow also varies the circumference of vibrato. For instance, with emphasis on the same knuckle, aiming the fingers into the palm creates a smaller oscillation of the knuckle than when directing your fingertips into the wrist, elbow, or shoulder. The motif of the music and your personal interpretation presides over the combination: choose a finger, hand, wrist, or arm vibrato, or whether to energize sound with the biceps, all the while placing emphasis on a particular knuckle group.

Finger Vibrato

The scroll of the violin is wood that is carved such that it appears to curl into itself. Similarly, if you take scissors and scrape the surface of a strip of paper, the paper curls into itself. Likewise, the vibrating finger can play to itself, generating a sensation of the finger infinitely wrapping around and into itself. Comfortably flex the knuckles and then isolate motion by aiming the fingertip toward the large knuckle of that same finger to produce a finger vibrato. On a macro scale, the left arm—fingertips to shoulder—can be experienced as curling into itself, in that way securing all the connections throughout the continuum; from any disconnection in the sequence, the fingers can become destabilized.

Vibrato

Figure 16.18 For hand vibrato, the fingertips are fired in the direction of the palm. *Photo credit to Eva Foxon Nicholas.*

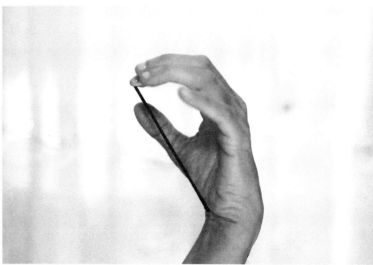

Figure 16.19 For a wrist vibrato, the fingertips aim in the direction of the wrist. *Photo credit to Eva Foxon Nicholas.*

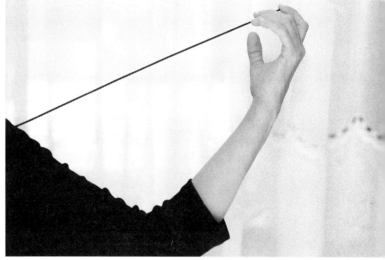

Left, **Figure 16.20** Aiming the fingertips toward the elbow. *Photo credit to Eva Foxon Nicholas.*

Above, **Figure 16.21** Aiming the fingertips toward the shoulder. *Photo credit to Eva Foxon Nicholas.*

Hand Vibrato

For hand vibrato, the fingertips are aimed in the direction of the palm. Envision the fan-shaped bones in the palm, the metacarpals. When firing the fingertips into the palm, avoid aiming at the firm barrier of bone. Instead, aim for the spaces between the bones to allow for more buoyancy in the vibrato. The finger extends energetically when pushing between the bones and, in so doing, accesses more range of motion than when bumping against the solid wall of the corresponding metacarpal.

Thinking of the fingers taken all together as orbiting the circumference of the thumb can improve vibrato. Poke your thumb through the hole in a metal washer, rest your fingertips against its perimeter and then vibrate each finger one at a time (refer to fig. 7.9). The first finger aims and vibrates to the left side of the thumb when vibrating, the second and third fingers aim more toward the center, and the fourth finger aims to the thumb's right side (on the arc). The fingers either engage with the palm during hand vibrato or the circumference of the thumb, depending on the rotational position of the hand.

Wrist Vibrato

For a supple wrist vibrato, the fingertips aim diagonally in the direction of the wrist (see fig. 16.22). The tip of the fourth finger aims at the part of the wrist underneath the base of the thumb, and the first finger aims at the wrist area underneath the fourth finger (lower outside corner).

Figure 16.22 The fingertips aim diagonally in the direction of the wrist. *Photo credit to Gail Taibbi.*

Bending the first- and fourth-finger large knuckles and lower corners of the hand inward toward each other secures the mold (ball shape) of the hand so that one motion does not compete with another. The vibrated fingers fire into the wrist (underneath the bottom of the hand) and then energetically wrap around the back of the hand as if securing a ball.

For a more rapid wrist vibrato, visualize a string affixed to each fingertip and running through each of four corresponding holes in the wrist just under the heel of the hand. For instance, when vibrating the first finger small knuckle, imagine drawing the fingertip, including the small, vibrated knuckle, down through the wrist opening underneath the first finger; when vibrating the middle-finger small knuckle, draw that joint into the hole beneath the second finger, and so on, each time creating a tight wrapping of the hand. Think of affixing a rubber band to the vibrated fingertip and the corresponding part of the wrist, drawing them toward each other. The elastic band reinforces wrist-to-fingertip balance and a wrist vibrato.

The Finger-to-Thumb Relationship to Gravity

It can be beneficial to think of each finger-to-thumb continuum as a boat; then balance the boat on an imaginary surface, depending on the hand's axis of rotation. The following are approximations that vary somewhat string to string. The idea is to notice the direction of your finger-to-thumb unit in relation to gravity and to experience its influence on the hand during various rotations. In lower positions, when the palm is facing up, the thumb and vibrating finger form the C shape of a boat on water. As you move up in position and balance your hand on the lower outside corner, picture the boat situated sideways on the wall, with the center of each of the boat's ribs pressing into the wall. In higher positions, the boat is capsized, suspended upside down, with the fingertip and thumb landing simultaneously against an imaginary platform. When you suspend the hand above the fingerboard, the thumb and finger balance equally on the same platform. Lift the center point between the tip of the thumb and fingertip, like holding a horseshoe, with the ends draping downward; then vibrate the finger-to-thumb band from that point of suspension. The higher the suspension, the deeper the application of weight in the fingers. This is because progressively more of the palm's weight is stacked on top of the relaxed fingertips. In lower positions, the C-shaped form of the thumb and vibrated finger also seeks its point of balance through a sense of its full weight, similar to the effect of a coaster (on snow) balancing and rebalancing on its changing landscape. The thumb is always the significant partner in that it deliberately counterbalances each vibrating finger.

Transitioning from Vibrato to Running Passages

Transitioning among slow and fast passages requires quick shifts in hand configurations. In fast passages, aim the fingers toward the center of the palm (or base of the thumb), whereas with slow, vibrated notes, aim the fingers at the wrist. When the fingers transition from a running passage into a vibrated note, sometimes there is a lack of carryover to the wrist (especially in the third and fourth fingers). In those cases, be sure to redirect the aim of the fingertips from the hand down to the wrist. For instance, on the sixteenth-note pickups at the solo entrance in the first movement of the Paganini Concerto No.1 (see ex. 16.3), aim the fingertips at the palm's center; then in the first full measure, they fire into the wrist to vibrate the half notes; then in beat two of the second full measure, the fingers redirect their aim back to the palm's center. Misdirecting the fingertips toward the wrist when articulating the six sixteenth notes distances the fingertips from the palm, potentially compromising speed. Conversely, vibrating while directing the fingertip toward the center of the palm can cause an excessively narrow vibrato and nasally tone. Vibrated fingers one and two are positioned to aim naturally in the direction of the wrist, but fingers three and four need to be consciously pointed at the wrist. What appears to be fourth-finger weakness can simply amount to not aiming the fingertip toward the wrist or the general area.

Example 16.3 From a transcription of the first movement of the Paganini concerto, the solo entrance.

Think of balancing the hand on top of either the radius or the ulna when vibrating, akin to centering a ball on a pole. For example, when vibrating fingers one or two, balance the bottom portion of the hand beneath either finger on top of the radius; when vibrating fingers three or four, tilt the hand sideways toward the bridge, balancing the bottom part of the hand beneath either of those fingers on top of the ulna. This lends stability to each vibrating finger, allowing the fourth finger to be as strong as the first. Mentally dropping weight inside the part of the base of the palm corresponding to the finger vibrated assists the bottom of the hand in tilting sideways from on top of the radius to on top of the ulna and back.

When rapid passage work follows a vibrated note, restore balance to the frame of the hand (thumb-to-fourth-finger curve). For example, if the last note you played was a vibrated third finger, the unadjusted hand remains balanced on the thumb-to-third-finger C shape (band). If you fail to reestablish balance to the full frame of the hand for a rapid passage, the fourth finger gets left out, creating uneven articulations in the passage. Anticipate transitions from vibrato to passage work so you can consciously leave behind the specific finger-to-thumb band for that last vibrated note, restoring balance to the frame of the hand to allow access to all four fingers; then run the passage. If, for another example, you form a thumb-to-first-finger band and then run a passage without establishing the frame of the hand (thumb and fourth finger), fingers two, three, and four are not housed in that frame. Or if you balance the thumb-to-second-finger band to support some expressive notes and then play a passage without transitioning, fingers three and four get excluded, and so on.

A good example of this transition exists in the first movement of the Mendelssohn concerto from the pickup into m.25 (see ex. 16.4). In the pickup, when you vibrate the second finger, the hand is balanced on a thumb-to-second-finger band. If you run the fingers on the triplet eighths following the half note with the hand still balanced on the thumb-to-second-finger band, the third finger is left outside the pack (as is the fourth, though there is not a fourth finger used in this passage). Before running the triplets, unless you affirm the frame of the hand when transitioning from vibrato to the fast passage, the division in the hand that balances and supports the vibrated finger upsets the hand's equilibrium for articulating the triplets. The frame of the hand unifies the four fingers, so if after a note is vibrated the hand does not reorganize to collect all the fingers for the triplets, the fingers outside the band will waver like unfastened cargo. The only time the transition from vibrato to running passages takes place without adjustment is when vibrating the fourth finger, by virtue of simultaneously accessing the thumb-to-fourth-finger band, the full frame of the hand.

Example 16.4 First movement of the Mendelssohn concerto, from the pickup into m.25.

Compressions That Enhance the Motion of Vibrato

Picture attaching a string to the lower outside corner of the hand. Pull the string to lift the lower outside corner up between the thumb and vibrating finger, suspending the hand. The upward compression of the lower outside corner against the downward pressure of the thumb and vibrating finger feeds the continuity of the vibrato. The finger vibrates more horizontally along the line of the string, so when you oscillate your vibrating finger toward the bridge, counter that oscillation with some pressure from your neck. The hand-to-neck compression also supports the instrument's suspension in a horizontal plane. Awareness of the counter pressures among the bow, the left thumb (somewhat vertical), and the vibrated finger and neck (more horizontal) supports the suspension of the violin—the receiver—from all directions, allowing it to float freely without domination from any one direction or influence.

When vibrating without a shoulder rest, especially in lower positions with the hand underneath the neck, if the hand assumes too much responsibility in supporting the instrument, the arm tends to become fatigued and lose altitude, sometimes even leaning against the torso in an effort to support the hand. Find an easy play back and forth between the thumb and chin that precludes clutching the violin and constricting the free flow (choking the life out) of your oscillating sound.

The understanding of the left arm is challenging, partly because the hand is on one kind of path in the first three positions and on another from fourth position, also because the circuitous path of support provides so many opportunities to acquire tension and lose facility. An awareness of the delicate interplays of balance benefits not just the complex synergies of vibrato and trills but virtually all the playing operations.

PART TWO

Right Arm

CHAPTER SEVENTEEN

Right Forearm

Part one of this book encompasses the development of form in the left arm and hand, mechanical (by observation) and kinesthetic (by direct experience) relationships that serve fine violin playing. Considering the many variables with the use of the right arm affecting the tonal outcome, part two focuses similar attention on bow arm formation, balances, and interactive relationships. Compartmentalizing balance issues and isolating them in the forearm or the hand or up in the shoulder enables you to quickly scan the various elements, find and adjust the imbalance, and then relax into the playing. The first step in this process is to properly balance the right forearm and then to get a feel for suspending it.

Forearm Balance

Inadequate awareness of how the forearm is best balanced frustrates the hand's efforts to negotiate the strings with the bow. Laying your bow arm on a flat surface and coordinating its physical components and multifaceted functions before floating it and setting it into motion generates a coherent form as well as a troubleshooting strategy for bow-arm obstacles.

First, it is helpful always to feel weight evenly distributed between the radius and ulna at the forearm's various points of rotation. Start to feel that balance by laying the forearm flat on a level platform with the hand pronated (palm down). Notice that the ends of the two bones of the forearm are level with each other on this flat surface. When crossing strings, imagine that platform now supporting the hand by tilting at an angle typical of the bow on each of the strings (see fig 17.1). Your forearm is at more of a right angle to the bow, but this image will remind you to keep a level wrist no matter the position of the bow. Maintaining an even distribution of weight across the forearm will set up the hand for effective bow control.

Figure 17.1 The tilted platform supports a continued even distribution of weight across the forearm. *Photo credit to Gail Taibbi.*

Locating the Balance Point

Once the forearm bones—radius and ulna—are integrated and continuous with the hand, lay the prone forearm on a fulcrum (try the back of a wooden chair) that divides it lengthwise such that the weight is evenly distributed between the bulk of the forearm and the wrist and hand (take the upper arm out of the equation to the best of your ability); you will know it is balanced when it easily rocks up and down with an even feel. We'll call this place of division inside the forearm the *balance point* (see fig. 17.2). Because the forearm is not evenly shaped and weighted, the balance point is about four inches beyond the elbow on an adult arm, not at the midpoint of the forearm's length.

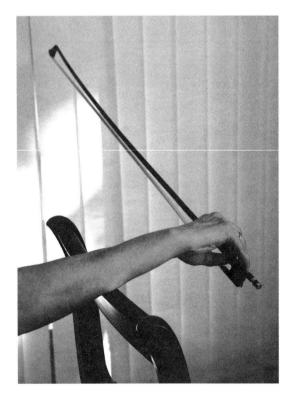

Figure 17.2 Balance the inner (anterior) aspect of the forearm on a fulcrum, such as the back of a chair. *Photo credit to Gail Taibbi.*

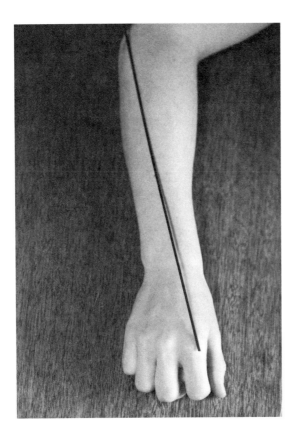

Figure 17.3 Picture a diagonal line from the lateral epicondyle of the elbow to the first-finger large knuckle. *Photo credit to Eva Foxon Nicholas.*

A good way to find that sense of balance is by identifying bony prominences that define the length of the forearm-to-hand continuum in playing position. Picture one end of a diagonal line connected at the elbow to the lateral epicondyle (bony protuberance) of the right humerus (upper arm bone), aka the outside bump of the elbow (though it is more on top in playing position) and the other end connected to the first-finger large knuckle (see fig. 17.3). Identifying these landmarks helps give a feel for the full extent of our excerpted mass (forearm and hand) as it rocks in and out on the hinge with the upper arm, up and down via abduction at the shoulder, or in some combination of the two, in all cases modified by accommodations in the wrist in service to the bow's contact with the string.

Unless the arm is properly balanced, the technical applications built on its functionality will be defective. If in your sensory experiment the weight is unevenly distributed across the fulcrum, the distribution of its motion will also be lopsided, and this choppy motion is disruptive to smooth bow changes while it causes sound volume inconsistency as well as tonal degradation and dissipation.

To get a feel for the more vertical component, the trickier dimension to conceive and incorporate, visualize that the forearm is a seesaw. If there is a heavy person on the elbow end and a light person on the hand end, the hand ascends without effort, but then much effort is required to lift the heavier elbow end. If the people reverse sides with the heavier person now on the hand side of the seesaw, this time the elbow end ascends with ease, but extra effort is required to lift the heavier hand. Similarly, when bowing a detaché, martelé, or spiccato stroke with the fulcrum placed too close to the hand, the upbow is relatively effortless, but the downbow requires undue force. And in reverse, when the fulcrum is placed too close to the elbow and the surplus weight is near the hand, the downbow is effortless, but the upbow is too much work.

Stand with your bow arm poised to play. To support the teetering motion of the forearm, bring to mind an image of someone standing to your right, palm up, extending two fingers from an otherwise closed hand—the index and middle. Rest the weight of your forearm at the balance point area in between those two fingers. Then imagine the person alternating effort from the fingers: lifting the first finger up while dropping the second one down, then lifting the second finger up while lowering the first finger. As the wrist drops, the elbow flaps upward like a wing, with all of its elevation and rotation coming from a passive shoulder. Or imagine that the edges of the forearm, at the balance point, are connected to a stationary stand that allows the outer ends (elbow point and hand) to move easily in countermotion (see fig. 17.4).

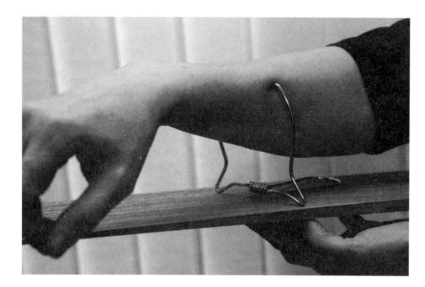

Figure 17.4 Connect the forearm to a stationary stand at the balance point. *Photo credit to Gail Taibbi.*

Balance Point Functionality

Having now gotten a general feel for the positioning and movement of the forearm via a sense of the balance point, its center of gravity, we can now explore the range of creative possibilities that gather in and emanate from the forearm's point of balance. Directives are more easily transferred to the bow hand with a growing awareness of the possibilities of this point of initiation and coordination, a feeling of a bending in all planes and directions (not just vertically), generating energetic expansions and contractions from this virtual joint area that, with complex string crossings and bow length fluctuations, constitute a perpetual dance of figure-eight variations. With this concept of fuller mobility of the forearm, normally considered relatively solid and inflexible, a new world of navigational opportunities opens up for the bow on the strings.

The following visual examples demonstrate its fundamentals. To create a fishtail motion of the hand for an effective horizontal bow stroke, trace the forearm on a piece of paper and cut it out. Then cut it in half widthwise (at the balance point area). Slightly overlap the paper—upper and lower forearm—and fasten the two halves together using a center metal ring. At Halloween, you may have noticed how a paper skeleton's limbs bend on a metal ring at each joint. If you then put your finger inside the metal ring and move it side to side, the paper forearm bends laterally from the midpoint. Similarly, when drawing a downbow, a new joint that energetically bends like the wrist can form momentarily at the balance point, with its sharpening angle point leading the forearm downbow before gradually opening back to a straight line. On the upbow, the apex of the new joint leads on the medial side, gradually increasing its angle to 180 degrees by the end of the stroke (see fig. 17.5).

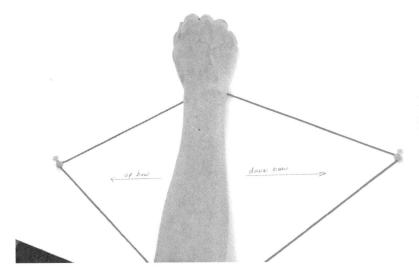

Figure 17.5 The forearm forms a new joint at the balance point that leads into the bow stroke. *Photo credit to Gail Taibbi.*

Place two sprockets side by side on a table, with the edges touching one another. Then transfer the two sprockets inside the forearm, intersecting at the balance point, with one closer to the wrist and influencing the hand while the other is closer to the elbow (see fig. 17.6). As the small sprocket turns clockwise, the other turns counterclockwise to support a simple downbow. This image temporarily ignores the restrictions of linear cables and the reality of bone, with the simultaneous movement of

Figure 17.6 Two sprockets inside the forearm oriented longitudinally, meeting at the balance point. *Photo credit to Eva Foxon Nicholas.*

both sprockets engaging the two halves of the forearm to allow for a more expansive lateral motion when drawing the bow. This time disengage the sprockets slightly and rotate the wrist sprocket both ways against a stationary elbow sprocket. Doing so prompts a fishtail motion in the wrist and hand.

Because a rigid forearm causes the bow to crush the string, encouraging the freedom and individuation of its many small muscles with this image is powerfully liberating for the bow arm. For quicker bow strokes, rest the right forearm flat on a table and then visualize a cross-section cut of the arm at the balance point, isolating the wrist half from the elbow half. Now place the delineated wrist portion of the forearm on the head of a vertical projection midway between the primary balance point area (where you made the cut) and the second set of knuckles to produce a new, secondary balance point (see fig. 17.7). The wrist portion of the forearm swivels on this new rotational point. Think of this portion of the forearm as functioning autonomously,

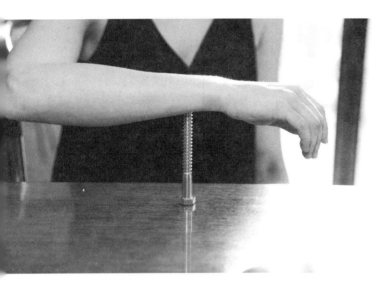

Figure 17.7 The bulk of the forearm and the hand move contrary to each other. *Photo credit to Eva Foxon Nicholas.*

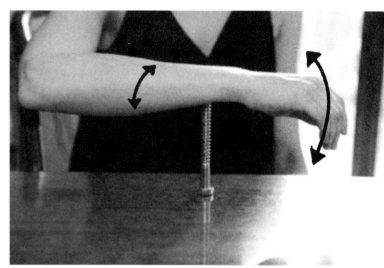

Figure 17.8 Imagine this shorter segment moving independently from the bulk near the elbow. *Photo credit to Eva Foxon Nicholas.*

with our newly excerpted element whirling like the ends of a propeller (see fig. 17.8). On the downbow (initiating motion from the area of the primary balance point), when you curve the hand away from the body, the wrist half of the forearm separates (energetically) from the more stationary elbow half, with the propeller rotating clockwise, looking down on it; on the upbow, with the propeller rotating counterclockwise, the hand moves toward the body, and our new mid-forearm end point rotates away. The possibilities of these smaller motions serve rapid, on-the-string passages.

Effective rotation at the primary balance point is crucial for simple string crossings, such as in the Bach Preludio, m.3 (see ex. 17.1). To facilitate smooth rotations, imagine that the forearm consists of two pipes, one inside the other (see fig. 17.9).

Rotating the pipes in contrary motion gives a feel for the counterrotations in the forearm that flip the hand one way and flap the wing of the elbow the other for nimble string crossings. The two ends alternate with a delicate interplay. Similarly, visualize someone taking two hands to the middle of your forearm, twisting opposite directions, one way and then the other (akin to wringing a towel), to approximate this subtle reciprocation.

Example 17.1 Bach's Partita No. 3 in E Major, Preludio, m.3.

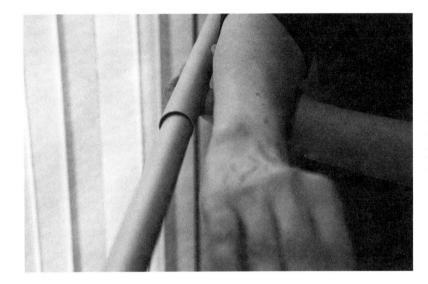

Figure 17.9 Imagine that the forearm consists of two pipes, one inside the other. *Photo credit to Gail Taibbi.*

Again, imagining that the forearm consists of two pipes, one inside the other, this time secure the elbow half and alternately rotate the other half. This application is effective in passages such as the slurred bariolage in the Bach Preludio at m.109 (see ex. 17.2).

For rapid string crossings, either rotate the arm/pipes at the secondary balance point or visualize the two pipes becoming narrower. Imagine each with a quarter-inch width. This narrower-pipes image facilitates a quicker rotation for maximizing speed, such as in the third measure of the Preludio (see ex. 17.1). To keep a passage crisp and clear, avoid losing your concentration and straying into larger rotations.

Example 17.2 Bach's Preludio, mm.109 into 110.

Picture that the forearm is hollow and separated into two parts at a crosscut at the balance point (similar to a pipe cut in half), but that strong elastic bands connect their cut edges and hold them together. Thanks to the elastic connection, the hand half stays close but separates from the elbow half easily enough to allow bending and rotating.

The possibilities with the balance point invite us to imagine a joint that is endowed with the same broad range of motion as the wrist. With these capabilities, in addition to moving the forearm in a fishtail motion horizontally and rotating at the cross section, we can imagine inducing a U shape and an upside-down U shape in the vertical plane. This image is useful in exploring the rebounding capacity of the bow. Allow the balance point area to sink downward on downbows, creating a bounced-upon trampoline U shape without lowering the elbow, and then allow a rebound back to a normal position or into an upward curve (upside-down U shape) on the upbow so the impetus of the single-motion downbow energizes both strokes: the downbow and the (rebounding) up. For example, in the first two notes of m.87 in the Preludio (see ex. 17.3), the downbow strokes the E-sharp, and the upbow rebound sounds the B-natural. Or you can imagine bouncing the balance point off the imaginary surface of a large ball for the upbow (B-natural). The upper arm muscles remain weighted and loose.

Example 17.3 Bach's Preludio, m.87.

Maintain an awareness of how the top, bottom, and edges of the right forearm in playing position correlate to the various aspects of the left arm. For example, depending on the musical application, simultaneously feel the anterior surfaces of each arm. Then experience each of the posterior surfaces (top of the right arm and the back of the left in playing position), or notice the thumb edge of one arm and the fourth-finger edge of the other, and so on.

Forearm Suspension

The height of the forearm relative to the string affects the bow's relationship to the string, including the gripped bow's ability to rebound. Just as the bridge supports the strings in the shape of an arc, imagine the balance point of the forearm resting on a curved support that is proportional to the arc of the bridge (see fig. 17.10). The arc-shaped support energetically fans the two bones in the forearm, generating a feeling of expansion and roundedness (akin to the expanded neck of a cobra). Always envision this support as higher than the bridge so the bow hand can lower itself from above, as opposed to the mechanics of starting with the bow on the string and then lifting off. The forearm must be elevated (energetically) to be able to drop and allow a rebound motion of the bow.

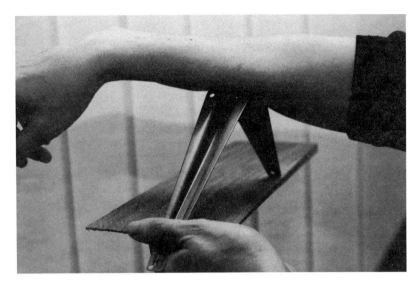

Figure 17.10 Fanning the two bones in the forearm. *Photo credit to Gail Taibbi.*

Imagine that the forearm is a long, flexible balance pole, the kind used by tightrope walkers; the center of the pole is at the forearm's balance point. Imagine using both hands to grip the pole in its center, first lifting it overhead and then pulling it back down (a military press). The ends of our flexible pole exhibit a certain natural response, illustrating as it bends the way energy flows toward the hand and elbow in a balanced forearm operating from its center, one alive with sensation, motion, vitality, and easy relaxation (see fig. 17.11), or draws energy back in as it curls up on the descent (see fig. 17.12). During extended use of detaché strokes, as required in the Bach Preludio, the bow arm tends to lock up. Using the pole image for the motion of lifting and lowering the forearm from the balance point area helps maintain

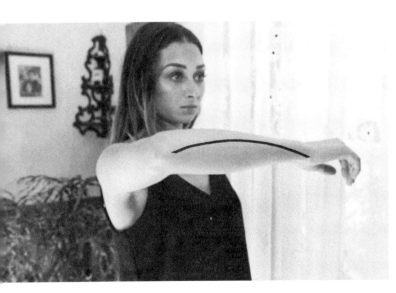

Figure 17.11 The ends of the forearm drape down on the pole's ascent. *Photo credit to Eva Foxon Nicholas.*

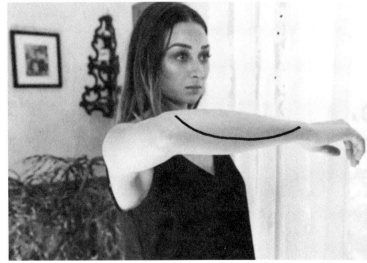

Figure 17.12 Feel the ends of the forearm curl back up on the pole's descent. *Photo credit to Eva Foxon Nicholas.*

flexibility, and from flexibility arises the opportunity for both a sense of freedom and its complementary flip side: control. Speaking of freedom, feel free at any time to transition (reset) your arm to adjust the position and feel of it, essentially by shaking it out around the balance point, working through from any uncomfortable holding posture to a place of balance and integration.

Forearm Application

Imagine that you make your bow changes entirely within the pause between the notes. Because of the challenges of quickly varying landscapes in rapid passages, it helps to find the shortest route (least motion) to get the bow from one string to the next without losing form. A way to approach this in your practice is this: play some notes and stop on the last note before the string change; then within an elongated pause, after having preconfigured the next move—including the optimal arm position, the proper angle of the bow, and the healthy placement of the hair on the next string—fire the bow to that next string in a singular motion back in tempo. The idea is to rely on your body's instincts to fulfill the criteria for the next position by forcing it to make snap decisions, therefore finding the most efficient route. With this exercise, you practice in the desired response so when it comes time to perform, the motion is reflexive (automatic and quick), and there is no need to pause. The efficient paths have been discovered and reinforced in the practice room, so the changeover feels natural.

For longer bow strokes, picture that the big end of the forearm, segmented at the balance point, has the indented shape of a nock, the bifurcated end of an arrow (see fig. 17.13). Hook your inner arrow onto the string and pull the string on the downbow the way an arrow would draw its bow string, and then let the restoring force of the string propel the upbow. Add to this natural momentum by firing the second set of knuckles on the upbow toward a spot underneath the violin (in the direction of the next string bowed); lead with the knuckles as if punching under the violin to the other side of the instrument (see fig. 17.14). On the completion of the upbow, adjust the bow arm to the proper string level (next string played), setting up for the next downbow. For instance, when you play an upbow on the A string followed by a downbow on the D, lead the upbow with the second set of knuckles, and then on the downbow, slightly rotate the arm clockwise and hook the inner arrow onto the D. On whole bows, begin drawing the bow from the elbow and then hook the arrow for the completion of the downbow. It also helps to imagine the right elbow hooking the left side of the strings and the left elbow hooking the right side of the same strings, and then pushing your elbows outward. Similarly, push your elbows out against two walls of resistance, in so doing squeezing out a core of sound. In general, the knuckles lead the way to the next string on the upbows; then the forearm reverses gears at the balance point and rotates, aiming for the next string played. For example, in the sixteenth-note pickups to m.1 (the solo entrance) in the Paganini concerto (see ex. 17.4), lead the upbow with the knuckles; then in the next measure (first full measure), hook the nock onto the E string and drag the E string (D-natural half note) while drawing the downbow; on completion, fire the knuckles into the A string (F-sharp) on the upbow. Then in the second full measure, hook the nock onto the E string and draw a downbow while articulating the dotted eighth and sixteenth notes (A to F-sharp). On the descending sixteenths (six to a beat), the knuckles fire into the E string on the D-natural (upbow) and the nock hooks onto the same string on the A; then the knuckles fire into the A string on the F-sharp and the nock hooks onto the A string on the D-natural; again, the knuckles fire into the open A string. The nock hooks onto the D string on the F-sharp (downbow), and the knuckles then fire into the open D string (quarter note); then the nock hooks onto the E string on the F-sharp (last note of the measure), and so on.

Figure 17.13 Picture that the end of the outer half of the forearm has the indented shape of a nock. *Photo credit to Gail Taibbi.*

Figure 17.14 Lead with the knuckles (second set) and scoop down underneath the violin on the upbow. *Photo credit to Gail Taibbi.*

Example 17.4 From a transcription of the first movement of the Paganini concerto, the solo entrance.

In the Fugue of the Bach Sonata No. 2, mm.18–20 (see ex. 17.5), the two eighth notes in beat two of each measure are upbow. Because the bow needs momentum to engage the one or two strings per stroke, dragging the string with the inner arrow (on the downbow) builds potential energy to add momentum to the upbow (see fig. 17.13). To rebound off the upbow instead of the down, picture the knuckles pushing against the string and the string's tension in response nudging the hand and wrist back down, propelling it back into the sleeve of the elbow half of the forearm.

Example 17.5 Bach's Sonata No. 2 Fugue in A minor, m.18 to the m.20 downbeat.

On the upbow, feel a developing resistance to the right hand, akin to sinking/driving your knuckles into softened clay. Drag a heavy, relaxed arm across the strings for the downbow. Avoid carrying weight from string to string—in other words, avoid holding up your arm with its own tension—it should be easily suspended from the torso and require very little work from itself. Feel that the arm musculature is 100 percent relaxed and ready for action. To experience that, draw the bow back and forth across all four strings without interruption as if the strings form one curved landscape you would find on the surface of a large ball.

Think of the hand as a facedown shovel and dig deeply, leading the upbow excavation with the second set of knuckles. Then on the downbow, pull the handle up, leveraging down the shovel face. The complete motion is one of digging with the knuckle end and dragging or pulling from the balance point (see fig. 17.15). For a heavier downbow, imagine that the neck of the shovel is caught on a root and that you have to drag the string with the arrow notch deeply and with great force. Even though it is tempting to pull from the wrist, drag the string with the balance point; otherwise, the arm goes out of alignment when drawing a whole downbow, and it runs out of range before completion of the stroke. To sustain a deep rich tone, as in the fourth movement of the Lalo *Symphonie Espagnole* at the pickup to nine measures after the solo entrance (see ex. 17.6), push against semisolid density of matter the consistency of clay with the knuckles while aiming them through and underneath the body of the violin. On the downbow (D-natural half note on the G string), stretch the G string with the inner arrow (see fig. 17.13). Because the D-natural quarter note takes up less time than the preceding half note, tighten the string's resistance on the downbow to allow the restoring force of the G string to propel the arm's inner arrow more quickly on the upbow.

Figure 17.15 On the downbow, pull the handle up. *Photo credit to Gail Taibbi.*

Example 17.6 Fourth movement of the Lalo *Symphonie Espagnole* in D minor, pickup to m.9 of the solo.

Hold the bow firmly with the fleshy parts of your fingers and zero in on the balance point area of your forearm. Because a spring expands and contracts but also easily bends and rotates, allowing a broad expansion of motion, imagine inserting a Slinky inside the balance point area (see fig. 17.16). During short, fast strokes, visualize that the coil at the balance-point area is high-gauge (thick and with little give), and that on longer strokes, the gauge is thinner and better able to expand. Fire the Slinky (from inside your balance point area) out toward the hand while securing the bow with your fingers; then snap it back into place, with the arm drawing into itself on the downbow. Expanding and contracting the forearm from the balance point area leaves the shape and tenacity of the fingers intact. After you project the Slinky forward, draw it back in before it completes its expansion to maintain momentum. On the upbow, throw the weight from the outer half of the forearm underneath the instrument in the direction of the bow; then at the moment of pause and maximum spring expansion, quickly set up the proper direction of the arm/balance point for the downbow stroke to be implemented, give a little tug, and let the accumulated

Figure 17.16 Inserting a Slinky inside the balance point area. *Photo credit to Gail Taibbi.*

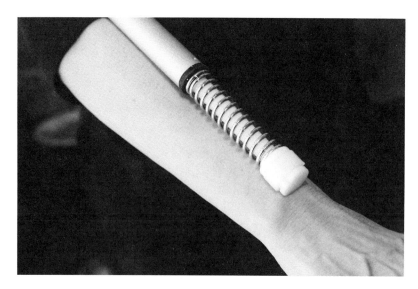

Figure 17.17 The pogo stick image is a representation of how energy builds and is released. *Photo credit to Gail Taibbi.*

potential energy do the work. The expansion and contraction dynamics of the Slinky are similar to those of hitting a paddle ball: you whack the ball (with a rubber band attached to the paddle); then you pull the paddle back, such that the loaded elastic returns the ball. Similarly, imagine propelling forward the outer half of the forearm on an elastic line; then let the stretched elastic snap the arm back into itself.

Think of the forearm as a pogo stick; then when drawing a downbow, energetically compress the outer half of the forearm / pogo stick into the inner half, building potential energy; on the upbow, release the compression. This twofold action supports the building and releasing of energy inside the forearm (see fig. 17.17). Motion is active from the balance point to the hand and passive toward the elbow. Initiate motion from the balance point and then always experience the complementary motion of the hand.

CHAPTER EIGHTEEN

Right Hand

The fundamental transaction of an effective bow arm is a relaxed transfer of weight down the arm to the hand, so we shift attention from the right arm balance point to the pertinent territory of transfer for that weight: the wrist. The wrist acts as a bridge or suspension system between the forearm and the hand, securing itself and staying level such that weight crosses over easily and without collapse.

Stabilization of the Wrist

The position of the hand on the wrist affects the stabilization of the whole limb as well as the power and control of the bow stroke. As a palm-up hand rotates into a palm-down position, this pronation is a flopping of the forearm's radius bone on the thumb side over a stationary ulna bone on the pinkie side. As it turns down, the palm should also be slightly abducted, that is, shifted a small amount toward the thumb. When the hand leads the forearm in this complex rotation into pronation, it counters the tendency of a lazy arm to unconsciously laterally rotate. That energized intention ultimately sets up the default hand position establishing flat hair on the string and maximum influence for sound production.

To get a feel for the configuration of the hand slightly abducted, set your forearm and hand palm down on a table. Then place the edge of a small dish against the curve of the wrist into the base of the thumb. The circumference of the plate supports a good curvature of this edge of the wrist, and the outer edge forms more of a straight line, together delineating a hand that is properly pronated on the wrist (see fig. 18.1).

The longitudinal slope of the forearm is significant in that, properly considered, it provides weight with a clear direction and pathway to travel. Rest your arm on a board tilted such that the hand is lower than the elbow. The two bones of the forearm are level (at their cross section), and the forearm is in the same plane as the hand and wrist. The board stabilizes the forearm from the balance point to the knuckles. If the wrist collapses, overextending, the bow disengages and becomes floppy. Maintain a level wrist connection that is strong but flexible, one that allows weight to shift down the arm to the fingertips without the unnecessary exertion (contraction) of other muscles. When playing on the G string, such as in m.79 of the Bach Preludio (see

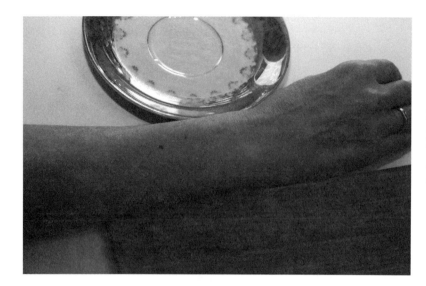

Figure 18.1 The curve of a plate supports curvature of the wrist; the lateral edge is more of a straight line. *Photo credit to Gail Taibbi.*

ex. 18.1), more energy is generated and more weight is transferred than for similar bow strokes on the D, A, or E string. Keep wrist suspension firm enough to support weight traveling to the bow, but not locked. When transitioning from mm.28 into 29 (see ex. 18.2), it helps to restore the forearm's balance before bowing the downbeat of m.29 (and in other strategic places) to avoid having to muscle your way through to the end.

Example 18.1 Bach's Preludio, m.79.

Example 18.2 Bach's Preludio, mm.28 to 29.

Playing a work such as the Bach Preludio from beginning to end requires a good right arm suspension system, including mobile joints that transfer weight and energy but also act as shock absorbers, proper alignment of the arm through the wrist, and a feeling of weight pooling in the fingers. If you place a weighted box on our tilted board, gravity will cause the box to slide to the ground. If you then crack the board so it is no longer straight, the package will get trapped in the crook of the board and fail to reach the ground. Bending the wrist—either the arch of overflexion or the cave of overextension—similarly creates an impediment to the smooth flow of weight traveling to the fingers.

If you tilt the board sideways, rotating it one way or the other on its long axis, the package will fall off to the side before reaching its destination. Similarly, without a level forearm (cross-sectionally), expect the relaxed weight of the arm to slide sideways before it reaches the fingertips.

Bow Hand

The right hand is responsible for receiving and transporting the arm's weight to the bow. For this reason, the right hand needs to be strong and balanced enough to disallow the tendency for weight to roll off one side or the other or otherwise dissipate on the way to the frog.

Balancing the Hand

Once the wrist is secured and the forearm stabilized, we move on to balance the right hand. Position your hand on a small, round, rubber tube (an inner tube) the size of the palm's circumference. Imagine sinking the tube into a body of water by pressing on the back of the hand at the midpoint. Notice the resilience around the frame of the hand and the yielding countermotion at the palm's center. The palm-sized tube isolates the palm's buoyant response in a balanced format while dispelling knuckle tension and generally freeing the hand from the negative consequences of clutching the bow. Focus your awareness on the follow-through response of the liberated fingers and thumb.

Now, insert a vertical, semicircle-shaped wire in the center opening of the tube. The top of the curve aligns with and supports the large knuckles while the tube facilitates a perfect distribution of elements around the circumference of the hand, including balancing the fingers with the heel of the hand as well as the fourth finger with the opposing thumb (see fig. 18.2 and fig. 18.3). The wire promotes mobility in

Figure 18.2 A small, inflated tube. *Photo credit to Gail Taibbi.*

Figure 18.3 The top of the curve supports the large knuckles while the tube distributes the peripheral hand. *Photo credit to Gail Taibbi.*

the large knuckles without the disruption of form that might otherwise accompany that freedom. During on-the-string bowings, as in m.7 of the Bach Preludio (see ex. 18.3), set the right hand on top of the tube and then drag the tube with the frame of the hand through water to the left and then to the right—upbow, and then down. The first- or fourth-finger large knuckle leads the other large knuckles, which in turn drag the fingers, together trailing like the wake of a boat. When a stiff hand disallows this natural knuckle response, the bow changes become points of interruption in the sound. To achieve deeper dimension of tone, visualize that the tube is submerged in water and partially filled with sand. When you want lighter, quicker notes, imagine that there is no sand inside the tube so that it floats higher on the water's surface. Or visualize moving the tube back and forth on the surface of ice. With less resistance, you can access speed.

Example 18.3 Bach's Preludio, m.7.

To balance the right hand, superimpose the base of the thumb by moving it slightly to the center of the base of the palm; then touch the tip of the thumb in its new position to the tip of the middle finger, forming a circle. Imagine bisecting both the thumb and middle finger vertically with half of the thumb and half of the middle finger to the right side of the frog and the other half of the thumb and middle finger to the left. Then balance the hand around the stick, countering the fingers with the thumb in a four-way divide. Like a roof, the palm is now balanced on the digital structure underneath.

Now, think of the right hand in playing position as a globe, and then distribute weight evenly with the suspended center of the palm as the north pole and the south pole where the middle finger and thumb contact the bow. Then draw the bow into the center of the planet/palm. If you then tighten the coil of the hand by pointing the thumb toward the radial (left) side of the middle finger's small knuckle, it will quicken all sorts of responses.

If you overrotate your bow hand one way or the other on the long axis of the bow, or if you use the fingers without counterbalancing them with the heel of the hand, the sound loses quality and volume. Passages such as the chord progression 43 measures after the solo entrance in the Paganini concerto (see ex. 18.4) demonstrate it well. When the bow strikes a chord, the sound quality is compromised if it is backed up with only part of the hand.

Example 18.4 The chord progression 43 measures after the solo entrance of Paganini's concerto.

While performing, the feeling of weight can dissipate from your hand and shift up into your wrist or elbow, or get hung up in the muscles of the arm (especially during pieces that require extended bowing, as in the Bach Preludio). When this happens, imagine that your right arm, hand, and fingers are hollow; then picture pouring sand through the funnel of your arm and filling the silos of the fingers, adding weight all the way to the fingertips.

In skeet shooting, there is a device called a trap that hurls clay disks into the air. Akin to the trap, the right arm can shoot the disclike palm out from the balance point, spinning it one way on the upbow and the other on the downbow. Snap the palm/disc quicky to fire the motion into the fingers and to avoid distorting the bow stroke with a lasting rotation of the palm. The motion suggested by the disk image requires—and generates—movements and flexibility involving all the joints of the hand and all but guarantees an effective transfer of weight and momentum to the bow.

The Right-Hand Spine

There are symmetrical comparisons between the left and right violin-playing hands. In the same way as described for the left hand, the right hand can be centered around the hand's spine (the kitty-corner hand division), with the lower outside corner (its origin) energetically resting on top of the bow. From the lower outside corner, the spine extends to the first-finger second knuckle (see fig. 18.4).

Projecting the spine to a position directly on top of the frog provides a backbone that lends strength to the hand and an ability and readiness to dive deeply into the string with the bow. In the first movement of the Mozart concerto, on the transition from beat 1 to beat 2 at 20 measures after the second solo entrance (see ex. 18.5), the spine dives from the A string to the left of the G on the upbow, at which point the forearm at the balance point engages the G string and reverses the hand for the downbow; in the succeeding measure, the spine dives from the E string to the left of the G on beats one and two. Like the backbone of a bird, when the hand ascends with the bow, feel the hand's spine rising and falling in response to natural fluctuations.

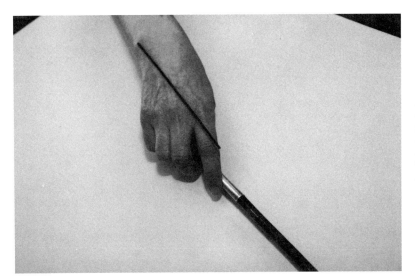

Figure 18.4 Feel a correspondence between the hand's spine and the longitudinal line of the bow. *Photo credit to Gail Taibbi.*

Example 18.5 First movement of the Mozart Concerto No. 4, 20 measures after the second solo entrance.

Hand-to-Thumb Rotation

Tuning into the rotational relationship between the thumb and the rest of the hand expands the range of motion. As we did with the left hand, picture a solid, round cookie cutter, and imagine punching out a circular hole in the middle that allows the insertion of the thumb; experience the rest of the hand rotating around the perimeter of the cookie cutter. The thumb rotates with the hand, but not in a one-to-one correspondence; the palm moves semi-independently, conforming to the musical task while continuing to harmonize with the adapting thumb. During multiple string crossings, as in the bariolage in m.76 of the Bach Preludio (see ex. 18.6), allow the palm to rotate on the curved thumb, effecting a seesawing motion of the bow.

Example 18.6 Bach's Preludio, m.76.

Explore a secondary balance where you imagine centering the fingers on top of the upright thumb tip. This creates a strong vertical relationship that supports an effective seesawing motion at the frog. Because we want the fingers farther apart when playing legato and closer together when playing spiccato or a fast detaché, visualize expanding and contracting the size of the thumb tip to accommodate the spread of the fingers.

Bow Fingers

The Bow Hold

Just as the correct balancing of the forearm enables the hand, the apt positioning of the fingers supports the stabilization of the bow. Hold the bow with the last set of joints in fingers one, two, and three, and then place the fourth finger on the near incline of the hexagon, not directly on top. Direct the tip of the thumb toward the small joint of the second finger (see fig. 18.5). Energetically draw the thumb and fingertips into the palm's center, bringing the bow with them. When the hand is in a natural position with the fingers angled in and well distributed relative to the thumb,

Figure 18.5 Right hand position. *Photo credit to Gail Taibbi.*

Figure 18.6 The second and third fingertips on one side of the platform and the thumb on the other. *Photo credit to Eva Foxon Nicholas.*

bow response is quicker. To heighten awareness of that, press your thumb and fingers against the bow and feel the thumb pressure counterbalancing the finger pressure.

The horizontal equipoise of the bow is lost with the thumb's tendency to push the tip away while the fingers can drag the frog inward, together resulting in an involuntary angling of the bow. To reinforce a better counterbalance, think of a horizontal platform that extends out beyond the base of the frog, like a lip on each side (or modified stirrups); balance the second and third fingertips on one side of the platform and the thumb on the other (see fig. 18.6).

The fingers can support a buoyant response by adding a vertical sense of balancing the bow underneath the palm. To take that a step further and feel secure without holding on tightly, imagine poking the fingertips and thumb through a flat piece of balloon material; then place the bow inside between the small knuckles of the fingers and the thumb. The bow bounces inside the opening between the fingers and the membrane, confining motion to the fingertips and guaranteeing a relaxed, light touch (see fig. 18.7).

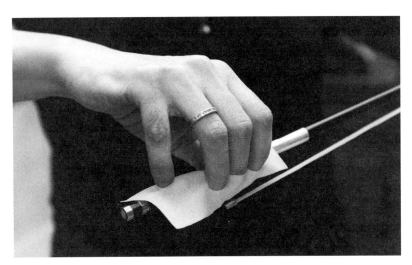

Figure 18.7 Poke the fingers through a flat piece of balloon material and hold the bow with the small knuckles. *Photo credit to Gail Taibbi.*

Example 18.7 Fourth movement of Beethoven's Symphony No. 9, from m.543.

In the off-the-string triplet passage beginning at m.543 in the fourth movement of the Beethoven Symphony No. 9, Op. 125 (see ex. 18.7), balance the first and fourth fingers with the thumb centered between; the rubber barrier image enables you to maximally let go of tension throughout the hand without losing your grip of the bow. If you lose the sensation of elasticity in the palm, the fingers lack a rebound response and the bow clunks down onto the string.

Although the physical principles are different, the bow hand has a challenge similar to a jockey's need for aerodynamic efficiency: if the head lifts or the foot sticks out, flow is impeded, with the resistance to the flailing mass affecting performance. Like the jockey, our skillful fingers huddle into the bow as the hand draws them into the palm, as a result avoiding the extraneous influences of straying digits.

It is common to let go of the bow at the end of a downbow, releasing the fingers in the shape of a bird's beak (see fig. 18.8). Straightening the fingers during bow changes means having to backtrack to retrieve them (and the bow), and as a result you lose time and risk adding unwanted vectors to the bow stroke. Keep the fingers flexed and the wrist slightly abducted. Let the flexibility occur in your joints and in the way that the bow moves back and forth against and with the flesh of your fingers. Otherwise, the bow hold becomes unstable, and you end up with a distorted grip, such as the bird's beak, or with an inadvertent rocking on the longitudinal axis with each change of stroke.

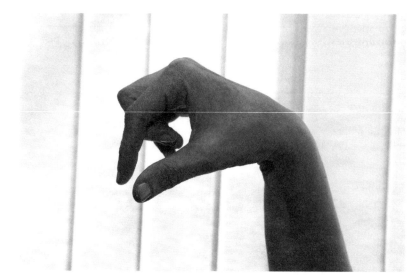

Figure 18.8 It is common to let go of the bow, releasing the fingers in the shape of a bird's beak. *Photo credit to Gail Taibbi.*

Finger Action

When playing slower passages, the shape of the phrase can benefit from extra emphasis on certain notes. To deepen the contact or even pulsate notes within a slow bow stroke, imagine a small wheel parallel to the frog that rotates but with some resistance. The curved shape of each fingertip takes a turn inside the bottom of the wheel. On the downbow of the solo entrance in the Bruch (see ex. 18.8), lead with the fourth finger, gradually urging the wheel counterclockwise on the longer note. On the upbow, lead with the first finger, rotating the wheel (fingers one, two, three, and four) clockwise, as in the triplet pickups to m.3. Ease into the rotation for each note, spin the wheel more quickly in the middle of the note, and then ease back out.

Example 18.8 Bruch's Scottish Fantasy in E-flat Major, Op.46, the solo entrance

Projecting the Sense of Touch

What is the most efficient way to transfer the fingers' directives to the bow's point of contact with the string? In experiments at Harvard, Hungarian biophysicist György Békésy placed a vibrator on each arm of experimental subjects. Whenever the vibrators moved at different speeds or with different strengths, the subjects recognized the presence of two vibrators. When moving at the same speed and with the same strength, the vibrators produced a surprisingly different experience. Subjects reported perceiving the vibration in a single location in between the two arms but beyond the skin. A similar experiment on each knee produced the same result.

When we write with a pen or pencil, we routinely perceive the contact of pencil point to paper and not skin to pencil. If we become overly concerned with the pressure or placement of our fingers holding the pencil, however, we lose the feeling and control of the pencil's contact point. Békésy's concept applies here, arguing for a secure and relaxed bow hold that we can ignore as our attention stays at the singular point of articulation. Once efficiently set up, think only of the left-hand fingers and the contact point of the bow to the string.

CHAPTER NINETEEN

Total Right Arm

Right Arm Presentation and Directing Points

To fully enable the operations of the balance point, the wrist, the hand, and the fingers that are now established, our attention turns to suspending the right arm. Initiate the lift from a presentation point a few inches below your shoulder blade (refer to fig. 2.3) and then extend it forward from a directing point behind the upper arm (refer to fig. 2.4). Direct your arm around toward the front of your body as if to rest the energized forearm on a chest-high shelf out in front. To get a feel for a fully relaxed arm floating and alert for an impulse, you can also imagine the arm as a wing drifting on a current of wind that gracefully lifts and lowers it from underneath. As with the left arm, the more efficiently and consciously the trunk muscles are used to initiate and support arm movement, the more relaxed the arm can be, especially the more peripheral muscles, which are designed for fine motor control.

Insert an imaginary hinge into the back of the upper arm, several inches above the elbow (see fig. 19.1); the hinge creates the feeling of a crook or second elbow to assist the arm in positioning itself out in front of the body, carrying the dead weight of the relaxed muscles in the upper arm farther away from the body. Then place a

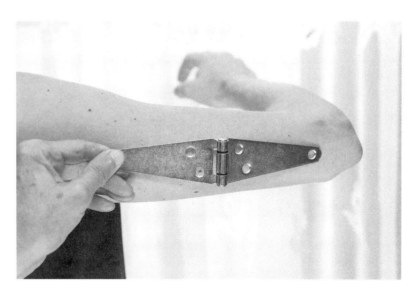

Figure 19.1 Insert an imaginary hinge into the back of the upper arm, several inches above the elbow. *Photo credit to Eva Foxon Nicholas.*

large exercise ball under your upper arm; the large ball supports a relaxed shoulder and maintains the position of the upper arm.

Right Elbow

The elbow leads the way from one string to the next. It secures the location around which the rest of the arm assembles.

Taking the Lead

Anticipate string changes by adjusting the height and the angle of the plane of the arm ahead of the bow's change of string. The full arm rotates in anticipation of string changes and without the elbow ever sinking below the hand. If the elbow is operating lower with the hand or wrist leading, because weight does not fall uphill, the transference of weight gets caught in the crook of the elbow. When that happens, only weight from the wrist to the fingertips reliably transfers down to the bow.

To systematically build the right arm formation, begin by placing the bow on the string; then line up the forearm parallel to the violin. Lift the arm just behind the elbow when you begin to draw a downbow; the deltoids in the upper arm and the forearm muscles, running toward the wrist, pulsate in synchronicity, all without an appreciable lifting of the shoulder. The elevating arm draws up the hand and shoulder the way the feet of a bird are suddenly swept up on an ascending flight. Dropping the elbow below the level of the bow causes weight to migrate only to the frog instead of a healthy transfer of weight all the way to the bow's contact point on the string, as a result causing the bow stroke to chop. Once a minimum altitude and angle for the bow arm is established, the full arm engages with the same degree of gyroscopic independence as the hand on the wrist. The collaborative positioning of the level wrist and the arm's wingspread spawn the blend of freedom and mechanical advantage necessary for effective bowing. The angle of the arm is especially critical with complex string crossings, in the bariolage at m.17 in the Bach Preludio, for instance (see ex. 19.1). Elevate the elbow above the lowest pitched string—the D in this case. To achieve a feeling of rebound that supports evenness and speed, keep the arm poised to play on the D string while an impetus of motion coming from the balance point area thrusts the bow hand to the E string, with the uncompromising angle of the arm inviting its return. During multiple string crossings, don't undercut the effectiveness of the arm's position by adjusting it to each string played because the balance point will lose its orientation to the elbow and therefore its ability to rebound without retracing its steps and wasting time in the process.

Example 19.1 The bariolage in the Bach, m.17, beginning in fifth position.

Figure 19.2 Loop a rubber band around the bow and the lowest-pitched string to encourage its return. *Photo credit to Gail Taibbi.*

Visualize that the contact point of the bow is attached to the string with a rubber band; loop the rubber band around the bow and the lowest-pitched string to encourage its return (see fig. 19.2). This image is especially helpful with multiple string crossings.

Right Shoulder

The right shoulder is passive in its response to right arm motion. It participates, but think of it more as an afterthought.

Multiplicities of Suspension

When presenting the left and right arms, there is a tendency to raise either one or both shoulders. Imagine suspending the shoulders via the trapezius muscles on either side of your neck, letting them widen as they drop to counteract any tendency to habitually lift them up and in or to push forward or pull back. Do not lift or hold the arms with the shoulders but rather from the trunk. Feel the initiation of the lift of each arm from its presentation point (several inches below the shoulder blades), including a widening of the shoulders in the motion. Establish the torso as the foundation for the head (structural) and the arms as fueled by your body's natural inspiration: a deep breath (functional).

Comprehensive Right Arm

The right arm is a vessel through which weight migrates. As the receiver, the bow converts substance into beauty of sound.

An Overview

With an alert awareness in your arm, coordinate the following structures: the shoulder (disengage), the arm (suspend), the balance point (motion dominant toward the hand), the wrist (level), the hand (in balance), the knuckles (large knuckles firm, middle knuckles diving under the instrument), and the fingers (silos filled with sand).

Right Arm Suspension

Experience a good bow arm placement above the string by wrapping your arm around the branch of a tree or a horizontal pole (see fig. 19.3). The pole supports your arm just beyond the elbow, leaving the forearm relaxed and buoyant. Now poise the arm and hand as if ready to reach for a thrown baseball. Reaching for and drawing a ball into your palm calls for the muscle patterns necessary to draw in the bow. When you reach down from above to engage the strings with the bow, the pole prevents the elbow from dropping down with the full weight of the arm. Maintaining support midarm allows for a rebound motion of the hand to the forearm. Having home (where you return) located off the string not only liberates motion and ultimately sound but also frees the mind and body more generally, whereas when the bow arm's resting point is on the string, the sound's projection possibilities are constricted.

Figure 19.3 A pole to your right supports the crook of your arm. *Photo credit to Gail Taibbi.*

Experiencing weight rolling down the slope of the bow arm is a way to feed momentum to the bow strokes. To create this invigorating flow, the elbow needs to be energetically (experienced and operating as-if) positioned higher than the wrist and hand. To maintain aliveness and balance in the arm (with your bow on or off the string), picture two springs sitting vertically on a board: one taller, thicker, and with far less give, and one shorter and more flexible (see fig. 19.4).

Figure 19.4 Two springs with very different characteristics supporting the arm. *Photo credit to Gail Taibbi.*

Place your elbow on the taller spring and your palm on the shorter spring (see fig. 19.5). While the elbow stays relatively stable or situated (moves less) in comparison to the hand, the spring underneath the hand easily rises up and down, sways side to side, and rotates, with these motions individually and in combination lending buoyancy and flexibility to your bow arm in a controlled format.

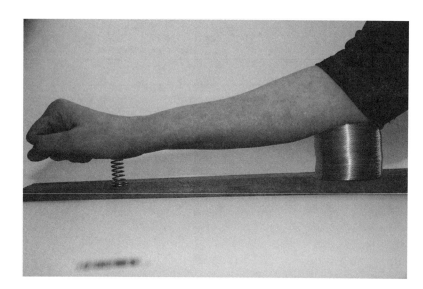

Figure 19.5 Place your elbow on the taller spring and your palm on the shorter spring. *Photo credit to Gail Taibbi.*

Moving weight to the fingers is crucial, but be sure to keep them animated with good arm suspension; burdening the hand with dead weight chokes out the sound. As it would have been easier for Michelangelo to paint *The Creation* on the walls of the Sistine Chapel instead of the ceiling, so it is easier to control relaxed weight as it touches down from suspension.

Know Thyself—The Bow Arm

It is critical to right-arm coordination for the bow arm to stay contained. As with the left arm, experience the right arm playing into itself, with a feeling of the hand teaming up with the underside of the arm. The contained integrity of the arm is lost when, for instance, you carelessly cross sides with one arm straying out and playing to the opposite side of the body, such as bowing to the left shoulder with the right hand or directing your left hand toward your right shoulder. Visualize an elastic string: if you affix one end to the palm's center and the other end snugly to the elbow, this reinforces the arm's firm but flexible connection to itself (see fig. 19.6).

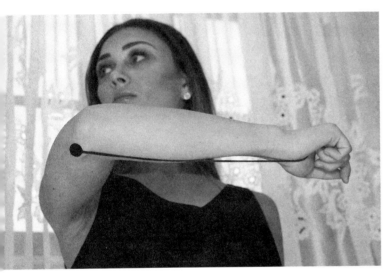

Figure 19.6 Affix an elastic string from the palm to the elbow to keep the arm contained. *Photo credit to Eva Foxon Nicholas.*

Figure 19.7 The suspended elbow forms the highest peak, and the balance point creates a secondary peak. *Photo credit to Eva Foxon Nicholas.*

As with the left arm, form an alliance of the forearm with the upper arm by conceiving of two bones in the upper arm to match the skeletal anatomy of the lower arm. Align the two forearm bones with the two imaginary bones in the upper arm. If you think of the arm as a suspension bridge, the elbow forms the highest peak, and the balance point creates a secondary peak; each point of suspension integrates with the other, reinforcing the hand playing into itself (see fig. 19.7).

Poise your bow arm as if to play. Place your left thumb underneath the fuller part of the forearm and push upward; then with your left-hand fingers on top and further toward the hand, pull out toward the hand (mostly) and down (slightly), in that way attempting to bend the forearm (see fig. 19.8). This is the implied direction of the lower half of the forearm in relation to the upper half.

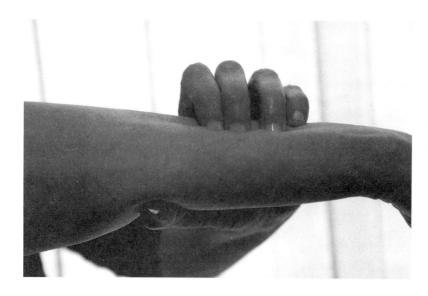

Figure 19.8 Push up with your thumb and pull the fingers out and down. *Photo credit to Eva Foxon Nicholas.*

Envision holding a beach ball under your right arm. Now imagine the volume of the ball expanding while you draw the bow. Press the ball into the body to counter the ball's expansion. This image supports a healthy bow arm formation, reinforcing the arm's dynamic relationship both to itself and to its foundation in the torso while protecting the elbow from lateral flexing (improper sideways deviation).

Arm Shape and a Coaster Full of Weight

Again building a suspension bridge using your right arm, consider the elbow as the pinnacle from which the shoulder and hand suspend. The area from the balance point to the knuckles then becomes a slide through which gravity draws weight to the fingertips (see fig. 19.9). It is not that the elbow is always literally the highest point, but experiencing it as the point from which all else is suspended creates a

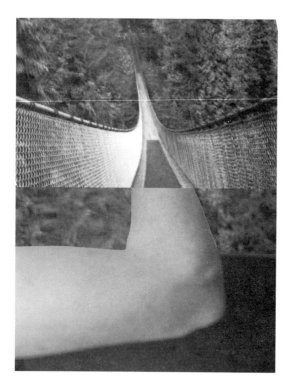

Figure 19.9 The area from the balance point to the knuckles becomes a slide. *Photo credit to Eva Foxon Nicholas.*

Figure 19.10 Form a bow arm structure that allows downhill migration of weight to the bow's point of contact. *Photo credit to Eva Foxon Nicholas.*

sensation of being functionally higher, allowing weight to travel easily into a relaxed hand to give it the most potential energy for momentum and control.

Energetically speaking, the arm has to be higher (operate from a feeling of being higher) than the frog, and the frog has to be higher than the contact point so weight can continue to travel downward with gravity. If the bow arm drops too low, it becomes difficult to get the bow off the string or to bow evenly when implementing on-the-string strokes. Experiencing the effective downhill migration of an imaginary ball conveys a sense of the energy and weight moving progressively down the arm to and through the fingers enroute to the bow's point of contact with the string (see fig. 19.10). Consider that your whole body supports the positioning of the bow. As an alternative, imagine connecting a string to the elbow—the lateral epicondyle (bony protuberance) of the right humerus (upper arm bone)—and then lift and suspend the right arm from that point.

Weight Transference

In the same way weight travels from the arm to the frog, a sense of unimpeded weight must transfer from the frog to the bow's point of contact with the string. To maximize the transfer of weight from the hand to the contact point of the bow with the string, imagine turning a bicycle upside down on an incline, with the back wheel positioned higher than the front. Place the bow on top of the wheels (see fig. 19.11). The higher back wheel supports the frog, and the lower front wheel receives

Figure 19.11 Imagine your bow on top of two bicycle wheels, one higher than the other. *Photo credit to Gail Taibbi.*

the bow at its moment of music making. The tilted wheels slant the bow so weight can migrate from the frog downhill to the bow's contact point at the lower wheel. The frog spins one wheel (the higher), and the hair spins the other wheel (the lower). When you spin the two wheels with a single bow stroke, the connections of the hand to the bow and the bow to the string deepen. Instead of the bow moving the bicycle wheels, try the reverse, with the spinning wheels propelling the bow up and down. If the frog's position becomes subordinate to the contact point, the bow's home gets relocated from a point above the string to a point on the string, and the lowered arm loses the control it has when reaching down from above. With this disrupted suspension, each upbow motion feels like pushing a rock uphill.

Hand and Arm Placement Relevant to the Violin

Taken together, the positioning of the right arm and shoulder in conjunction with the bow and violin outlines the shape of a square. The line from the bow's midpoint contact with the string to the bow hand forms one side of a square, the forearm forms a second side, the upper arm and shoulder is the third, and the violin constitutes the fourth side. As a way to monitor the square shape, pay particular attention to the forearm's alignment, keeping it parallel to the violin when averaging out its motions. Otherwise, the square-shaped relationship of the bow and arm to the violin is easily lost, especially the stability from the default right-angle position of the right elbow. This interdependent support system is gained or lost together, the way the integrity of a door frame either succeeds or fails all around.

Bowing to the left of each string (see fig. 19.12 and fig. 19.13) is a good way to generate sonorous tone. One advantage is that it effects a steeper arm slope, and that maximizes the arm's potential to transfer weight. If you think of weight as a ball with potential energy, the steeper the slope, the more potential to transfer and use that

Figure 19.12 Bow to the left of the string for reliable resonance. *Photo credit to Gail Taibbi.*

Figure 19.13 Bowing to the left of the E string. *Photo credit to Gail Taibbi.*

weight to increase the vibrating string's amplitude. And the steeper angle requires a robust arm suspension, encouraging more of a pulling of the string as well as the use of speed instead of relying on dead weight as is so easy when playing on top of the string. Always be sure to draw out the sound, however; the more weight, the easier it is to crush the sound, even when bowing on the side of the string.

Even though tone quality can benefit from bowing to the left of each string, often there isn't time to do that in rapid passages, where instead it can be beneficial to imagine playing within the inner walls of two strings. For example, in the next to last measure of No. 16 in the Violin II part of the Handel *Messiah* (see ex. 19.2), the A-natural downbow is bowed to the left of the E string with the C-sharp upbow bowed to the right of the A string; then on beat 3, the F-sharp downbow is to the left of the E string and the D-natural upbow again to the right of the A. Thinking of the strings as walls and then navigating within these walls shrinks the motion, in that way increasing the speed of the bow.

Example 19.2 Handel's *Messiah*, Violin 2, No. 16, next to the last measure.

Imagining the violin level with the ground, place a wooden platform on top of it and then rest the right forearm and hand on the platform. Tip both the violin and platform (bow arm) at an angle, rotating clockwise (see fig. 19.14). The angled instrument is the new ground zero for the bow arm. Always keep the elbow above the bow in this new orientation, with the weight rolling down into the hand with respect to its new floor in the quadrant of this tilted microcosm. Adding pressure, sometimes by torquing the bow in a vertical plane, is another way to keep the frog subservient to the elbow.

Figure 19.14 The right elbow appears lower than the strings but is not lower relative to its new ground-zero. *Photo credit to Gail Taibbi.*

Bow-Arm Rotation

Awareness of fundamental rotations in the bow arm allows the forearm to operate either more horizontally or more vertically in a semi-orbit. Without well-grounded points of rotation in the forearm, the fingers become distorted in compensation.

Right Forearm

It is easy to keep your right arm relaxed and balanced while playing in the middle of the bow. The challenge is to adjust the arm to create the same quality of engagement at the tip of the bow as in the middle. When drawing a whole bow, picture a vertical axis projecting up from a table. Place the center opening of a bicycle wheel on the vertical axle; then place your bent arm across the wheel while locating the rotational point of the axle underneath the arm at the elbow. When you rotate the wheel one way and then the other, the bow hand moves contrary to the shoulder, an effective contrast for a horizontal bow stroke (see fig. 19.15, fig. 19.16, and fig. 19.17). Because the ball of the shoulder isn't perfectly spherical and the remaining joints have individual intricacies, and because the motions of the body are neither perfectly round nor linear as a result, hand and arm movements do not fit in a single anatomical plane but rather in a more complex, real-world combination in three dimensions. That said, one plane sometimes defines the movement well enough. As such, the mentioned images approximate the motion of the bow arm in a somewhat horizontal plane.

Figure 19.15 Picture your bent arm across the wheel, with the rotational point underneath the elbow. *Photo credit to Gail Taibbi.*

Figure 19.16 The bow hand moves contrary to the shoulder, supporting an effective horizontal bow stroke. *Photo credit to Gail Taibbi.*

Total Right Arm

Figure 19.17 The bow hand moving contrary to the shoulder supports effective movement for an upbow. *Photo credit to Gail Taibbi.*

Three Points of Rotation for the Bow Arm

To maintain efficient and effective bow work regardless of the musical landscape, it is useful to imagine three functional bow-arm lengths, each anchored on the axle of a wheel. The size of the wheel depends on how much arm, relative to bowing length, you wish to use (a shorter arm length rotates more quickly than a longer one). The first and longest length is shoulder to knuckles with the axle placed underneath the elbow (see fig. 19.18); the second longest is elbow to knuckles with the axle situated at the primary balance point (see fig. 19.19); and the third, the shortest, is balance point to knuckles with an axle centered underneath the secondary balance point (see fig.

Figure 19.18 Shoulder to knuckles with the axle placed underneath the elbow. *Photo credit to Eva Foxon Nicholas.*

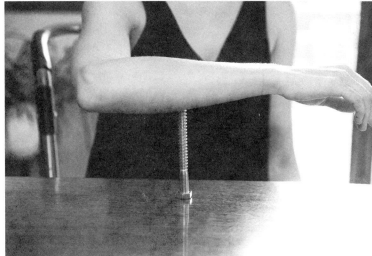

Figure 19.19 Elbow to knuckles with the axle situated underneath the primary balance point. *Photo credit to Eva Foxon Nicholas.*

19.20). Each wheel is sized to correspond to each arm length. For the largest circles with lengthy bow strokes, use a rotational point at the elbow delineating the curved path for the hand and shoulder (see fig. 19.21). A good application is in the first movement of the Brahms concerto, 47 measures after the solo entrance (see ex. 19.3).

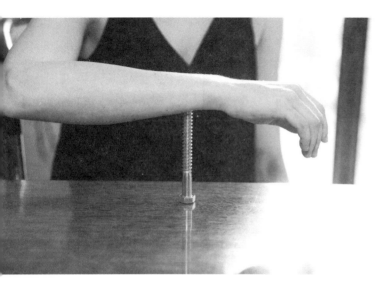 

Figure 19.20 Balance point to knuckles with an axle centered in between at the secondary balance point. *Photo credit to Eva Foxon Nicholas.*

Figure 19.21 Using a rotational point at the elbow delineating the curved path for the hand and shoulder. *Photo credit to Eva Foxon Nicholas.*

Example 19.3 First movement of the Brahms, 47 measures after the solo entrance.

Next, you have the primary balance point that centers the hand to elbow (see fig. 19.22). That rotation creates moderate-sized circles, which is appropriate in the Fuga of the Bach Sonata No. 2, from the first measure to the downbeat of m.3 (see ex. 19.4). And finally, you have what was described in part one as the secondary balance point that splits the line from the knuckles to the primary balance point (see fig. 19.23) imposing the smallest circle.

Example 19.4 Bach's Sonata No. 2 in A minor, Fuga, from m.1.

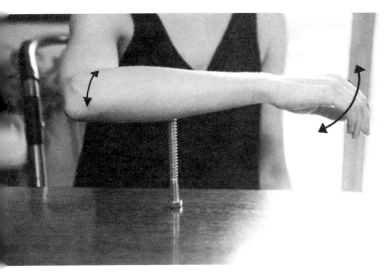 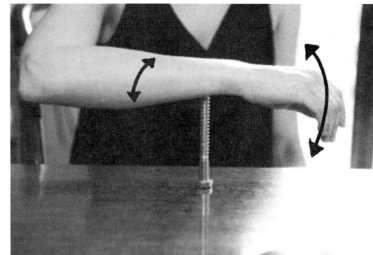

Figure 19.22 The primary balance point centers moderate-sized circles of the hand and elbow. *Photo credit to Eva Foxon Nicholas.*

Figure 19.23 The secondary balance point imposes the smallest circle. *Photo credit to Eva Foxon Nicholas.*

During fast passages, such as beat 2 in the first measure of the second movement of Schumann's Symphony No. 2 in C Major (see ex. 19.5), it is advantageous to limit the range of arm motion by imposing the rotation onto the smallest bicycle wheel. Organizing around the secondary balance point effects the small-scale rotation to facilitate the speed necessary for this passage.

Example 19.5 First two measures of the second movement of the Schumann Symphony No. 2 in C Major.

Side Arm Rotation

To effectively rotate the right arm in more of a vertical plane, supporting a more vertical seesawing motion during string crossings, think of a rubber screw jutting out from the wall approximately chest high. At the point on the lateral edge of the arm closest to the balance point, press the right arm against the screw (see fig. 19.24) and then rotate the arm on that screw. The functional forearm of knuckles to elbow seesaws up and down. Then, drawing a transverse line that bisects the forearm at the secondary balance point, between the knuckles and the primary balance point, press

Figure 19.24 Press the right arm against the screw lateral from the balance point. *Photo credit to Gail Taibbi.*

the right side of the forearm (at the end of that line) against the screw and seesaw from that point. The ends of each shorter arm length touch down more quickly than the rotations of the longer arm lengths from knuckles to elbow to access greater bow speed. This rotational point assists the bow arm for multiple string crossings, as in the bariolage in m.17 of the Bach Partita No. 3, Preludio (see ex. 19.1). The knuckles and balance point teeter, like the ends of a seesaw, and the elbow, despite being required to negotiate some rotation in the upper arm to support this motion, nevertheless remains poised above the D string. For multiple string crossings, place the rotation point at a level such that the elbow is positioned above the base of the three strings.

The Bow

Rotations

If you spin the propeller of a plane that is not well secured to a center-pin, its revolutions spin out of control as it loses its center. Imposing the restraint of a rotational point at the middle of the bow allows the bow to seesaw without flying out of its semi-orbit. Conceive of a hole in the stick of the bow at its point of balance (see fig. 19.25). Then rotate the bow from that point. Always be aware of the balance point of the bow, especially when rotating from another point where it becomes necessary to negotiate an uneven weight ratio.

Figure 19.25 Conceive of a hole in the stick of the bow at the balance point. *Photo credit to Gail Taibbi.*

To keep the hand relatively stationary while the bow rotates, drill a phantom hole through the side of the frog and insert an axle. The thumb holds one end of the axle, and the middle finger's point of contact with the bow holds the other. In beats 2 and 3 at m.29 of the Bach Preludio (see ex. 19.6), when crossing back and forth between the D and A strings, the axle image suggests bow rotation that doesn't disrupt the balance or shape of the hand. If you then attach two silver-dollar-size wheels, one to each side of the frog, the larger surface engages fingers two and three in a way that enables a more muscular motion and tone.

Example 19.6 Bach's Preludio in E Major, m.29.

To better balance the bow from the frog end, form a picture of an actual bow and an imaginary bow to the right but in the opposite direction of the actual bow, with only their frogs overlapping. Drill a hole through both frogs and insert an axle. When you hold the ends of the axle between the middle finger and thumb, there is now a single axis of rotation. Once more, attach two wheels (see fig. 19.26). Now contemplate in the imagination that the axle (running through both frogs) is the body of a bird and that the two bows—one actual and one imaginary—are wings. When you lift the axle (bird's body) up, the tip of both the actual bow and its mirror image drops down equally, like the downward flap of wings (see fig. 19.27). And when the axle/bird's body descends, the tips of both the actual and phantom bow ascend like (V-shaped) wings in perfect balance and weight (see fig. 19.28). Raise and lower the axle when playing the Bach Preludio at m.3 (see ex. 19.7) so the actual bow

Figure 19.26 Insert an axle; then attach two wheels, one to each side of the frogs. *Photo credit to Gail Taibbi.*

Figure 19.27 When you lift the axle (bird's body), both tips drop equally, like the downward flap of wings. *Photo credit to Gail Taibbi.*

Right Arm

traverses the D and A strings. Exaggerate the lifting and sinking motion of the frog/axle even more when playing m.67 (see ex. 19.8) so the bow navigates the arc of the three strings—the G, D, and A.

Figure 19.28 As the axle/bird's body drops, the sticks/wings ascend in perfect balance and weight. *Photo credit to Gail Taibbi.*

Example 19.7 Bach's Preludio, m.3.

Example 19.8 Bach's Preludio, m.67.

Integrating the Arms through Visualization

To integrate the motion of the hands and arms in relation to the neck, imagine that the combination of your arms, the bow, and the neck outline the shape of a butterfly. Draw a line connecting the left-hand fingers to your left shoulder to outline one triangle-shaped wing; the right arm, including the stick, outlines the other. The point where the bow touches the fingerboard from the right wing and the left-hand fingers from the left side is where the wings connect to the body of the butterfly/violin. The arms are the wings, and the neck is the body of the butterfly (see fig. 19.29 and fig. 19.30).

At times, a butterfly suspends motion in one wing—the left arm—as in the Preludio, m.76 (see ex. 19.9) and moves the other, or the reverse, as in the first movement of the Brahms, pickup to 16 measures after the solo entrance (see ex. 19.10), where the right wing/arm is essentially passive and activity takes place primarily in

Total Right Arm

Figure 19.29 The arms are the wings, and the neck is the body of the butterfly. *Photo credit to Gail Taibbi.*

Figure 19.30 The wings are the arms, and the body of the butterfly is the neck. *Photo credit to Gail Taibbi.*

the left arm wing/fingers. At other times, the wings move in parallel to the left, such as when playing same-position slurred passages downbow going from the G to the E string, or to the right when staying in position to move from the E to the G with slurred upbows.

Example 19.9 Bach's Preludio, m.76.

Example 19.10 First movement of the Brahms concerto, pickup to 16 measures after the solo entrance.

To reinforce the synchronicity of elbow movement, imagine affixing one end of a string to the inside of the left elbow and then attaching that same string to the right elbow before extending the string further. Then imagine someone off to the right pulling and releasing the end of the string, rocking the two arms in parallel (see fig. 19.31). Notice the synchronicity of movement of the two elbow points during practice and performance.

Figure 19.31 Attach a string to both elbows and imagine someone off to the right pulling and releasing the string. *Photo credit to Eva Foxon Nicholas.*

Figure 19.32 Imagine attaching one end of an elastic string to each elbow point. *Photo credit to Eva Foxon Nicholas.*

To intensify the movement relationship of one elbow point to the other, imagine attaching one end of an elastic string to each elbow point (see fig. 19.32). Observe the tension and release of each elbow, one to the other. Or imagine the elbow wings flapping and displacing a semisolid density of matter surrounding the arms.

Musical compositions consist of smaller phrases within an outer, larger form—in my mind, flesh to bones—with unique shapes resulting. Through a dexterous and expressive usage of the left-hand fingers and the bow (with backup support from the entire body), a master player can do justice to the composition by staying true to the broader lines and textures while lovingly sculpting the musical shapes within them. And even though at first glance, the fingers seem to relate to the bow and strings merely with straightforward, material contact, the sensitive anterior of the body—of the hands, the arms, or even the torso—is simultaneously in continuous pursuit of ecstasy by manipulating various densities of matter to invoke the spirits of sound.

CHAPTER TWENTY

Bow Form and Application

Bow: the lifespan of sound.
—Maureen Taranto-Pyatt

Autonomy of the Bow Hand

Once the bow's relationship to the string is understood, it is important to back up a bit to more finely attune the fingers to the bow's response. Call to mind an image of throwing a stick in the air and imagine that an owl swoops down, opens its claws, grasps and retracts it, and then ascends. The motion of the owl securing the stick in its claws is analogous to drawing the bow into the palm as part of the normal course of adjustments in bowing. If the owl accidentally releases the stick and catches it again midair, for a moment the stick bottoms out inside the talons (fingertips) as it is caught, and when ascending the owl once more retracts the stick, this time more deeply in its clutches. Now, imagine releasing your grip on the bow. If in that moment you ignore the hand and connect primarily to the falling and ascending motion of the bow with less focus on habitual strategies for the hand, you can enjoy more of an instinctive interaction with the stick, tossing it up, following it where it is going, then descending with it and gravity before snapping it up, with the arm and hand anticipating the bow's every move.

Connecting to the minimally controlled ascent and descent of the bow creates a tremendous feeling of freedom in the bow arm, especially when crossing from one string to another with the bow skirting over the strings in between, as when playing an upbow on the E string followed by a downbow on the G. With a similar configuration in the Bach Preludio, mm.119–120 (see ex. 20.1), as you play the last note of

Example 20.1 Bach's Preludio, mm.119–120.

m.119, let the bow continue to ascend, support it just enough to feel its weight, and then guide its rotation into the downbow contact on the G, like the touchdown of an airplane. This application is also useful for the transition to the chord on beat 3 of m.3 in the Bach Violin Sonata No. 2, Grave (see ex. 20.2).

Example 20.2 Bach's Sonata No. 2 in A minor, Grave, m.3.

Martelé

Form and Application

Developing a solid martelé stroke is essential because its straight-line orientation establishes the fundamentals for the other, more multidimensional bow strokes. The mechanism operates as follows: on the downbow, hook the inner arrow at the balance point onto the string to give a clear bite at the onset; then drag from that point to be in the string for good resonance. The balance point's inner arrow feels perpendicular to the string as if poised to be fired from the string (refer to fig. 17.13). The stroke is a fast-slow motion. The full forces of the arm and upper body support this engagement. At the end of the stroke, the hand leads the upbow with the second set of knuckles, firing into the underside of the violin. If you throw a punch leading with the knuckles, the knuckles lead the compressed forearm as it expands forward from the balance point area. So it is when implementing an upbow: the knuckles lead the punch, and then you want to allow the extension. On release, the forearm snaps back into itself in a rebound motion that initiates the drawing of a downbow. The downbow then finishes with a release to the upbow.

Kreutzer's Caprice No. 7 (see ex. 20.3) is a good practice tool to develop the martelé bow stroke. In m.1 the upbow fires into the higher strings, A and E (lead with the knuckles), and on the downbow, the balance point (inner arrow) drags the lower strings, D and A. To expand the core of each articulation, imagine on the downbows dragging the lower strings to the right of the higher ones. In m.3 (see ex. 20.4), envision the balance point dragging the G and D strings to the right of the A and E. M.23 (see ex. 20.5) from beat 2 onward is particularly challenging with the consistent engagement of the outermost strings. In m.27 (see ex. 20.6), begin the A-natural upbow (G string) and its octave A (on the D string) downbow, bowing backward to the end. Doing so requires the negotiation of extreme and severely contrasting forearm angles, in this way stretching the martelé technique to its limit. This is particularly evident seven measures before the end (see ex. 20.7) where you drive the upbow into the G string and hook the downbow onto the E. After practicing the Kreutzer No. 7 with this reverse bowing, when you implement the recommended down-up orientation, the martelé stroke is much more efficient and less arduous.

Bow Form and Application

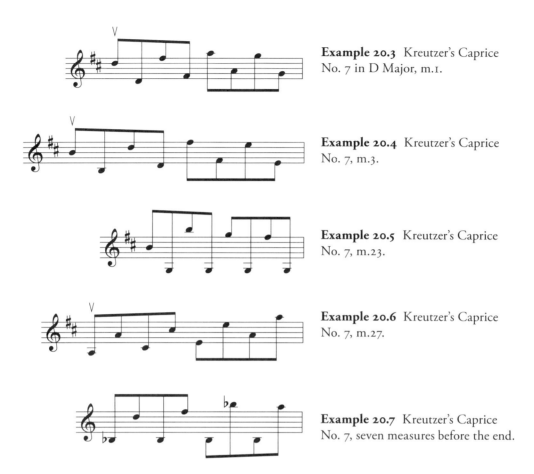

Example 20.3 Kreutzer's Caprice No. 7 in D Major, m.1.

Example 20.4 Kreutzer's Caprice No. 7, m.3.

Example 20.5 Kreutzer's Caprice No. 7, m.23.

Example 20.6 Kreutzer's Caprice No. 7, m.27.

Example 20.7 Kreutzer's Caprice No. 7, seven measures before the end.

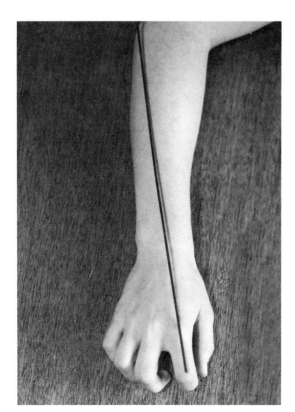

Consider firing the second set of knuckles underneath the instrument on the upbow, with the large knuckles remaining somewhat flattened to lend strength to the bow hand. To secure the strength and balance of the hand and arm, envision a thin rod running diagonally from the outside bump of the elbow (though it is more on top in playing position) to the first-finger second knuckle (see fig. 20.1).

Figure 20.1 Support martelé strokes with a rod running from the outside elbow to the first-finger second knuckle. *Photo credit to Eva Foxon Nicholas.*

Spiccato

Fundamentals

Spiccato is a bouncing stroke, unlike on-the-string strokes with supple but minimal vertical motion. As a result, spiccato requires a more involved and refined vertical process with the fingers suspending the bow, extending it down and retracting it up into the palm.

To set up the arm for an effective spiccato stroke, again imagine wrapping your right arm around the branch of a tree (horizontal pole). The pole supports your arm just beyond the elbow, leaving the forearm poised to drop and rebound off the string for the perfect spiccato. When you reach down from above to engage the strings with the bow, the pole stops the arm from crashing down with full weight but allows a buoyant freedom of motion. Operating from the primary balance point area with the full weight of the forearm supports more moderate tempo passages that are usually expressed anywhere from the frog to the middle of the bow. When playing at the frog, tilt the bow to play more on the side of the hair. For a more rapid spiccato, center the action farther out toward the secondary balance point and bow somewhere from the middle to the upper half, using flatter hair.

To get a feel for the vertical motion, think of the bow as a yo-yo on a short string that unwinds and then snaps back into the palm. Or curve your hand around a ball that is smaller than your rounded hand. If the palm bounces against the ball, the ball rebounds off the floor formed by the fingertips (see fig. 20.2 and fig. 20.3). Similarly, find a perfect balance between freedom and restriction with the bow so that the spiccato stroke is allowed to dance but not out of control. As the bow dances on the string for the spiccato, it doesn't have the same linear intensity and hammered onset as the martelé stroke; rather, the quality of motion is more pliant and bouncier, and the onset can vary from sharp to soft. From 23 measures after the solo entrance in the

Figure 20.2 The palm bounces against the ball. *Photo credit to Eva Foxon Nicholas.*

Figure 20.3 The ball rebounds off the floor of the fingers and back into the palm. *Photo credit to Eva Foxon Nicholas.*

first movement of the Brahms (see ex. 20.8), the ball rebounds off the secured fingertips and back into the center of the palm for the downbow and upbow rebounds, ensuring substantial depth in sound.

Example 20.8 First movement of the Brahms Violin Concerto in D, 23 measures after the solo entrance.

For endurance in extended spiccato passages, visualize that the right hand is a ball suspended on a rotisserie and that the spit running through the center of the tunnel formed by the flexed fingers and opposing thumb is the bow. Chuck the bow through the tunnel, one way and the other, propelling the full mass of the bow in a balanced format. Then imagine a rubber barrier at the thumb and fourth finger end of the tunnel that can catch and rebound the bow, the effect of which is to reduce the effort in long passages (see fig. 20.4 and fig. 20.5). This image is especially useful with smaller, more rapid strokes coming from the secondary point of balance that have more of a linear orientation.

Figure 20.4 Chuck the bow through the hand's tunnel, imagining a rubber barrier at the end of the tunnel. *Photo credit to Eva Foxon Nicholas.*

Figure 20.5 A rubber barrier at the thumb and fourth finger end of the tunnel. *Photo credit to Eva Foxon Nicholas.*

To support a bouncy, U-shaped spiccato, as in the fourth movement of Beethoven's Symphony No. 9 (see ex. 20.9), the off-the-string bowing is assisted by experiencing the full, relaxed weight of the forearm while maintaining a healthy suspension of the elbow. Bowing closer to the frog generates the desired fortissimo.

Example 20.9 Fourth movement of the Beethoven Symphony No. 9, m.543.

For a slower, more rounded off-the-string stroke, it helps to feel the impetus of motion coming from the forearm's point of balance. For example, in the *poco piu lento* chord passage in the first movement of Tchaikovsky's violin concerto, again at the frog but this time either with the bow hair flattened or to the side (see ex. 20.10), first balance the fingers on one side and then counter that weight carefully with the thumb. Now, lift the bow without using the second and third fingers while balancing the hand's four corners. Using fingers one and four to pick up the bow, rather than fingers two and three, gives a broader and more stable hold. A hold that overemphasizes fingers two and three is less stable and is likely to lead to the end of the bow tipping onto the string. Practice the bow stroke on open strings, balancing the hand and focusing on motion coming from the forearm's point of balance. Then follow that by applying the left-hand articulations.

Example 20.10 Opening measure of the chord passage in the Poco piu lento of Tchaikovsky's violin concerto.

Often there is a tendency to move the bow more quickly than the fingers, especially in rapid, off-the-string passages. Make sure each articulating finger is cleanly on the fingerboard before bowing the note. Regardless of the bow stroke, a note can't speak well unless the fingers are firmly in place. It is helpful to think of the fingers galloping slightly ahead of the bow to establish a rhythmic pace.

In slower strokes, as with the off-the-string triplet passage at m.543 in the fourth movement of Beethoven's Symphony No. 9 (see ex. 20.9), visualize a ball held in your hand and a larger ball secured to a spot underneath your forearm's balance point to shift weight toward the fingertips (see fig. 20.6). Simultaneously drop the hand and balance point area together onto a board and lift them together, all the while maintaining a feeling of suspension of the elbow. When the bow lifts off the string, the hand and balance point area stay in the same plane; otherwise, if the wrist is too high or low, interference with the transference of weight down the arm to the hand results.

As in the left hand, bending the first- and fourth-finger large knuckles and lower corners inward secures the rounded mold of the hand. Because a sturdy palm provides a foundation for a freer spiccato, connect one end of a wire to the large knuckle of the first finger (palm side) and the other end to the lower outside corner; then affix

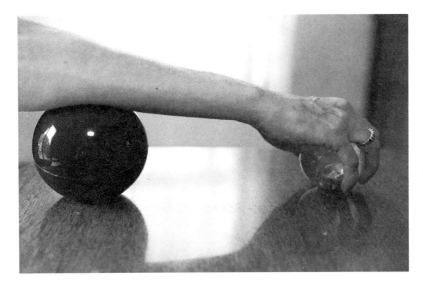

Figure 20.6 Visualize a ball held in your hand and a larger ball underneath your forearm's balance point. *Photo credit to Eva Foxon Nicholas.*

a second wire, one end to the fourth-finger large knuckle and the other end to the lower inside corner (refer to fig. 5.3). Pulling the corners closer together to tighten them molds the hand while it isolates and liberates the fingers from the palm.

Legato

The physics of the legato bow stroke is similar to the martelé stroke in that both use the balance point and middle knuckles. With legato, however, the initial bite is missing, and the bow is in continuous motion at a steady pace. Drop the relaxed hand, and brush the nails of the thumb and fingers back and forth on a flat surface to feel a firm and flowing connection.

Awareness of the string's resistance and amplitude of vibration dramatically affects the quality of the tone. Exerting too much or too little pressure with the bow (or the left-hand fingers) impedes the string's vibration. It is easy to articulate notes on the E string, but because of the width of the G string, a choppy sound occurs if the initial attack is not lengthened; the G string needs more time to sound because of its thickness. You want to add slightly more pressure, but gradually. If the bow gets bogged down with overemphasis, the intonation suffers. The E string is thinner, and the angle of the attack can be greater, whereas on the lower strings, you exert more effort with a smaller angle, pulling or pushing the string with more weight. Awareness of the varying string thicknesses informs the choice of bow pressure and speed, with adjustments made note to note (string to string). Imagine that each string is a rolling pin varying in thickness relative to the actual strings, with the E string being the thinnest and the G string the thickest. Being larger and having the ability to rotate, the cylindrical rolling pin thwarts the tendency to crush the string. Now imagine that the bow hair is a strip of rubber. When you draw the bow across the rubber string, rubber against rubber creates a smooth, connective contact throughout each stroke. To assist tone production, concentrate on the bow's period of contact, not on the spaces in between. Picturing the rotation of various sized rolling pins while drawing the rubber bow across the strings illuminates the nuanced bow weight and speed application relative to each string.

To deepen the bow's contact with the string, imagine that the neck is an axis around which a medium-sized rubber ball rotates. Picture that the body of the violin is nonexistent, and all that is left is the axis that runs through the middle of a rotating ball. Draw a legato bow stroke, rotating the ball one way and then seamlessly into the other with consecutive strokes. To increase the production of tone, imagine that the ball is slightly deflated. This allows the bow to sink more deeply into the string. Slowing the stroke can improve the contact with the string and increase its resonance. When playing faster, deliberately nudge or slightly bounce the bow against the arc of a fully inflated ball, redirecting its spin for each change of bow. Adding velocity to each bow stroke often produces a better sound, especially to counteract any momentary reluctance or lack of confidence. Using the ball image is valuable because it propagates a more nuanced approach to encountering the string with the hair.

The following visualization ascribes an independent physical existence to each note to elucidate the influence of bow speed and weight on each note. Imagine that the notes in a piece of music are rubber balls, the size of each ball determined by the note's length and its significance within the structure of a phrase or passage. Each ball has the capacity to rotate on the string in the area between the fingerboard and the bridge (see fig. 20.7). Because a smaller ball spins more quickly than a larger one, envision the rubber-haired bow spinning smaller-sized balls that are quicker notes and rotating larger-sized balls that are longer notes. When implementing a whole-bow crescendo, picture a small ball that expands as you draw the bow. On a whole-bow fortissimo, the ball is beach ball sized or larger. For slurred notes, spin a sequence of various-sized balls, each in ratio to the note value and significance.

When executing on-the-string strokes, the fingers can carve out notes the way a sculptor's tool shapes clay. To develop greater dimensions of tone, sculpt curves with the bow on the inside of an imaginary sphere, with the frog curving away from your body on the downbow, as with the tied half and dotted half at the solo entrance in

Figure 20.7 Each note is represented by a rotating ball, its size a function of its duration and significance. *Photo credit to Eva Foxon Nicholas.*

Example 20.11 Opening measures of the solo entrance of the Bruch *Scottish Fantasy*.

the Bruch (see ex. 20.11), and then toward the body on the upbow, as in the triplet in beat 4. Scooping out the inner curve of a ball on the downbow by leading with the fourth finger supports good form with the hand's downbow adjustments. Create micro (convex) curves by pulsating the bow on the outside of a smaller ball for each triplet note, in this way emphasizing their dimension. Or imagine that the violin is situated on top of a giant ball filled with helium. Now picture the ball elevating, with the giant ball lifting the violin. Drawing the bow across the strings while consciously sustaining resistance against the ascending force lends a throbbing quality to the tone.

Envision holding a beach ball under your right arm. Now feel the volume of the ball expanding while you draw the bow. Use the arm to counter the ball's expansion by pressing it into your body. This image supports a healthy bow-arm structure while reinforcing the arm's relationship with itself.

To maximize bow-arm weight, form, and application when drawing a whole bow, imagine enclosing the violin inside a horizontal cylinder; then picture a medium-sized ball to its right. Flop the bow arm over the ball and roll the ball against the cylinder's surface in both up- and downbow directions, with both the ball and arm orbiting the violin/cylinder. (Imagining that the underside of the arm is sticky lends traction to the arm's rotation of the ball.) At each point, the ball supports a good curvature of the right arm and the cylinder creates resistance, allowing the right arm to relax sideways (against the ball), thus deepening the tone.

Detaché

Detaché refers to separate strokes that are even and smooth, often in the upper half of the bow. Speeding up or slowing down the bow during detaché strokes affects the integrity of sound, such as when speeding up creates unwanted accents, or when the tendency to add weight in slowing down crushes the string. When you want to access speed during detaché (on-the-string) strokes, align the spine with the bow to lend additional backbone to the rigors of small, fast bow strokes in works such as the Bach Preludio. Visualize that the right-hand spine is a kitty-corner log that extends out farther, from the lower outside corner all the way to the first-finger middle knuckle (refer to fig. 18.4), and that when you tap the end of the lower outside corner of the hand (one end of the log), the other end (first-finger middle knuckle) is propelled forward. The hand then rebounds back to its natural state, all together creating a back-and-forth, straight-line route of detaché, the log in the hand acting as a (horizontal) pile driver. During prolonged periods of detaché, sustain the extended spine to maintain the more linear orientation and avoid lapsing into a rounder configuration.

Points of Rotation in the Hand

To increase bow speed for a variety of strokes, imagine a circular indentation into the center base of the right hand. Slide this opening (palm down) onto a vertical pole projecting up from a platform and then fishtail the knuckles side to side (see fig. 20.8). The first-finger large knuckle pushes the fourth-finger large knuckle via the knuckles in between, and the same in reverse. This time, picture a similar indentation in the middle of the palm, or farther out into the large or middle knuckle of the middle finger. Again, slide the facedown hand onto the vertical pole (see fig. 20.9). Moving the point of rotation farther out on the arm incrementally isolates the motion of the fingers, in turn inducing progressively greater bow velocity. Even though holding this image while playing tends to sacrifice tone because the hand motion is more horizontal (moving in the flat plane instead of scooping into the string), it is worth the cost. Placing the palm or large or middle knuckle on a vertical pole or rotational point to access greater velocity (due to the economy of motion) is useful in works such as in the opening two measures of the Presto in the Sinding Suite in A minor, Op 10 (see ex. 20.12), where tempo takes precedence over tonal depth and volume. It is also effective in generating quick bursts of bow energy, as in the third movement of the Grieg Concerto for Piano and Orchestra at m.38 (see ex. 20.13). When you whip the hand (on a rotational point) for the first note in a downbow direction, you can get a double rebound—upbow and downbow—for the next two notes, with the single gesture encapsulating the triplets. The forearm then snaps the hand upbow on the eighth note that follows the triplets, reestablishing the position of the hand to articulate the next set of triplets. Drawing shorter bow lengths supports bow speed because less distance traveled allows for a quicker turnaround, so try bending the thumb's small knuckle and placing the tip of the thumb against the

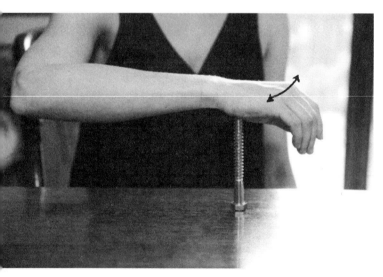

Figure 20.8 Place the heel of the hand on a vertical rotational point to access greater velocity. *Photo credit to Gail Taibbi.*

Figure 20.9 Slide the opening of the hand onto a vertical pole projecting up from a platform.

nose of the frog (see fig. 20.10). The thumb tip creates a wall of resistance to restrict the upbow rebound.

Example 20.12 Sinding's Suite in A minor, Op 10, Presto, mm.1–2.

 **Example 20.13** Grieg's Concerto for Piano and Orchestra in A minor, Movement 3, m.38.

Figure 20.10 Bending the thumb's small knuckle and placing the tip of the thumb against the nose of the frog. *Photo credit to Eva Foxon Nicholas.*

To elicit a larger follow-through response of the bow, as with passages on one string, impose a vertical pole into the forearm balance-point area (refer to fig. 19.22); then fishtail the hand from that point. The forearm swings side to side in a horizontal plane with the feel of a pendulum. For an even wider hand swing, insert the pole just below the elbow (refer to fig. 19.21). To lend buoyancy to the bow stroke when swinging the forearm side to side, imagine holding a rubber ball in the palm of your hand.

Imagery with the Bow as a Conduit

Always look for ways to sculpt the flat surface of sound into a multidimensional landscape, a deadpan tone into expression. To enhance the depth of sound during rapid, off-the-string strokes with minimal loss of speed, form a picture of a ball the size

Figure 20.11 Spin a tiny ball affixed around a vertical axis using the bow. *Photo credit to Eva Foxon Nicholas.*

of a grain of sand and affixed around a vertical axis that can travel along the string (see fig. 20.11); its placement moves along the string length between fingerboard and bridge in accordance with the change in sounding point. Spin the tiny ball with each stroke of the bow. On slower passages, the size of the ball expands. Just as the size of the ball changes, imagine the length of the arm and bow extending and contracting relative to the length of the bow stroke.

String Crossings

Circles and Figure Eights

For simple string crossings, as in m.42 of the Bach Preludio (see ex. 20.14), avoid rotating your arm for each change of string. Float the arm/wing into position to play the lowest-pitched string level and maintain it to force a rebound back to that position after playing on higher strings. Draw ample bow on the first note of the sequence to avoid constriction. If you give an initial push, the rest of the motion, whether it is a circle or figure eight, will take care of itself. The initial push of the bow is similar to the initiation of swinging a jump rope or pushing a swing. Once you establish a stroke for simple or multiple string crossings as in mm.17–28 of the Preludio (see ex. 20.15), back off on the length and volume of the stroke to maintain endurance. Motion stays consistent like a car set on cruise control. Do not stop the bow; if you stop pushing, the bow stops on its own. It is like releasing a gas pedal as opposed to putting on the brakes, or like a rallentando versus a ritardando. When the bow stops, make sure it is straight and on the same track for the change of direction.

Example 20.14 Bach's Preludio in E Major, m.42.

Example 20.15 Bach's Preludio, mm.17–28.

The control of motion in the right hand is put into play in the beginning and end of notes; the hand eases in and out like a plane landing and taking off. The bow maintains solid connection to the string during the middle of the stroke as does an airplane moving down the runway. (Maintain pressure between strokes by calling to mind an image of someone's hand and forearm resting on top of yours, disbursing weight evenly from your elbow to your fingertips.)

When crossing strings and picking up the tempo, as in the clockwise rotation in m.42 and counterclockwise in m.43 of the Bach Preludio (see ex. 20.16), there is a tendency to shrink the bow's circular path, constricting and choking off the sound. In mm.17–28 (see ex. 20.15), leave the arm suspended in the same place. Make sure that the stroke is not too fast for your bow and that your arm is not moving too fast. When the bow arm is used properly, each bow change creates a clear articulation, thanks to the string's restoring force, its natural proclivity to return to its original state between strokes. When things become difficult, avoid tucking in your arm, a move that degrades the bow's contact with the string.

Example 20.16 Bach's Preludio, mm.42–43.

CHAPTER TWENTY-ONE

The Bow Stroke—Speed, Balance, and Mental Projection

The structural underpinnings for the comfortable suspension of a readied bow arm are now established and the fundamental bowing styles have been explored. A closer look at factors that affect the bow's relationship to the string is in order.

Bow Speed

With a stabilized elbow, you can access greater bow speed by using smaller strokes and keeping steady pressure (similar to a tremolo) without pressing. In conjunction with proper balance and suspension and an even downward pressure, besides adjusting the actual lengths of the bow strokes, experiment with varying the lengths of the arm and bow in your imagination to increase your speed range on both the high and the low ends. As with all things related to violin playing, effective employment of the right arm requires a complex balancing of mind and body—yoga postures for the bow.

Bow Imagery

With creative visualizations, you can negotiate the bow's natural weight with the transfer of that weight in support of greater traction on the string. There is a unique abstraction that creates effective resistance and supports balance. Picture two bows playing from opposite sides of the violin on the same string, making an X shape, with the violin in the center. The imaginary bow is coming from the left side (see fig. 21.1).

As you engage the left side of the string with your actual bow and attempt to drag it to the right, envision someone else to your left engaging the right side of that same string, drawing the imaginary bow to your left, which counteracts the direction of the string with equal application. On the downbow, you are essentially creating a controlled feeling of a tug-of-war between you and your imaginary partner, whereas on the upbow, the two of you are pushing against each other. Absorbing this image creates a sensitivity to resistance while reinforcing even weight distribution throughout the stroke, all together allowing you to exert maximum pressure while stabilizing the bow's relationship with the string. In passages where the bow stroke is counter to

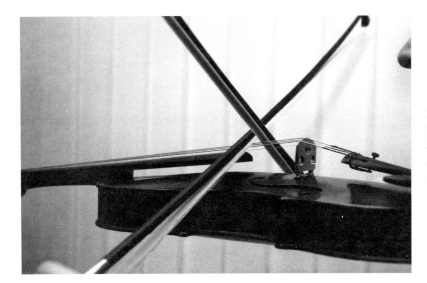

Figure 21.1 Imagine two bows playing from opposite sides of the violin on the same string. *Photo credit to Gail Taibbi.*

what feels natural, as in mm.98–99 of the Bach Preludio (see ex. 21.1), the countermotion of the two bows grounds and balances the stroke. This image also creates stability drawing slow, whole bows, especially when shifting or changing strings, as in the opening four bars of the solo in the second movement of the Brahms concerto (see ex. 21.2).

Example 21.1 Bach's Preludio in E Major, mm.98–99.

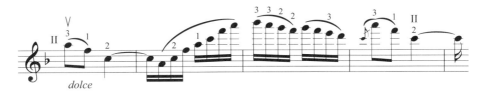

Example 21.2 The opening four bars of the second movement solo in the Brahms concerto.

When you place the tip of the bow on the string, there is often a struggle among holding the bow, controlling it, and relaxing the arm. Imagine doubling the length of the bow by extending it to the left of the actual bow. This creates a feeling of more weight at the tip, relieving the arm of the burden of having to add weight by way of a muscular rotation of the hand. Another application of this image is in multiple string crossings. The lowest-pitched string tends to get slighted, so lengthening the bow to the left strengthens the connection to that string. When you want to favor weight at the frog, visualize the bow length extended to the right. It is more difficult to be at one end of something and navigating its balance than from an imaginary midpoint, so when you double the length of the bow to the right, your hand energetically navigates to a comfortable position in the middle of a five-foot bow instead of struggling at one end of the bow of normal length. Without a sense of counterbalance, the burden of holding and directing the bow can eventually overwhelm the fingers.

Now imagine shrinking the bow to a five-inch length, and picture the thumb as a fulcrum underneath the short bow. From on top, the fingers seesaw the ends of the bow in various combinations: the tip of the thumb acts as a fulcrum to fingers one and two, one and three, or one and four, as well as all four fingers together. This image supports the rotation of the bow and fingers relative to the thumb in off-the-string passages. Imagine lengthening or shortening one end of the bow or the other to create a sensation of better balance when the bow's contact point is off-center.

Gravity's Influence on the Bow

Using an awareness of gravity offers respite to the playing. Ideally, motion is not an unceasing continuation of muscular effort but rather an alternation of exertion and release, including relaxation to allow weight and momentum to do some of the work. With a downbow on the two higher strings, the A and E, the angle gives you the greatest benefit of gravity (gravitational potential energy); then on the upbow on the A and E, you can draw on some momentum from the movement of the mass of the bow to help counteract gravity. With a downbow on the lower strings, the D and G, again you counteract gravity, mostly with your own effort (pulling is easier than pushing), and on the upbow you benefit one more time from gravity. The bow that is pushed or pulled against gravity is the motion that requires most effort, an awareness that heightens your sensitivity to its weight, just as the relaxed feeling of its weight conversely clues us in to the efficiency of our efforts. The knuckles lead the upbow against gravity on the A and E strings, and the forearm (from the balance point) leads the downbow against gravity on the G and D strings.

Tracking the Bow

In traditional training, the student is taught to practice drawing a straight bow in front of a mirror and then to transfer that feeling to other playing situations. There are arm mechanics that can be learned that make it possible to draw a straight bow without using the mirror, however. During a relaxed detaché bowing, hook the forearm onto the string at the balance point and then feel the arm shortening as it contracts into itself on the downbow; release the compression and then lead with the knuckles for a straight upbow. Picture everything consolidating into itself as needed: the arm, the wood of the bow moving into itself like one pole telescoping into another, and the bow hair moving into itself like a mat on a treadmill, all combining into a more compact bow.

When drawing lengthy bow strokes, keep the long line of the bow perpendicular to the string at the start and end of a stroke to avoid losing solid contact with the string and to minimize the sound of bow changes (there is a healthy amount of latitude in the middle). Do not release the fingers from the bow. Maintain pressure and stay in the string, with the bow playing to a point centered between the feet of the bridge. Imagine that in playing position your right biceps muscle is a heavy ball, and a miniature bowling ball is glued to your right hand; combined, this weight draws the bow into the string while stabilizing the bow arm's balance.

Think of the frog propelling the point, just as rear-wheel drive propels a car. While steering the bow from the frog, push it upbow while pushing a mirrored counterpart underneath the instrument so the actual and imaginary bows travel above and beneath the center bout in parallel. Use the bridge and the big end of the fingerboard as guiding walls. This image helps solidify tone in long, drawn-out passages.

Experiencing the bow hand carving out curves transmutes into the effective shaping of musical landscapes. Imagine standing inside a large, hollow ball, the curved surfaces of which come in as close as you need them. To achieve deeper dimension of tone when drawing a downbow, scrape the fourth-finger edge of your hand along the curved surface in front of you; leading with the tip on the upbow, the thumb's metacarpal cuts a path that corresponds to the rounded surface behind you. Prepare each impulse while on the previous note, but initiate the new motion inside the pause between notes. As the downbow progresses, slightly flatten the bow hair while lifting the frog, in that way adding both weight and surface area for more traction at the lighter end of the bow. The om of violin playing.

The Sounding Point

Consider that the fingerboard measures approximately ten and a half inches in length and that the area between the end of the fingerboard and the bridge where the bow is drawn is approximately two and a quarter inches. Now think of playing a scale from an open string to the top of that same string (see fig. 21.2). A microcosm of that scale exists for the bow on the line between the fingerboard and the bridge, fully

Figure 21.2 D major scale beginning with the open D string to the top of that same string. *Photo credit to Eva Foxon Nicholas.*

Figure 21.3 The D-major scale exists for the bow in microcosm between the fingerboard and the bridge. *Photo credit to Eva Foxon Nicholas.*

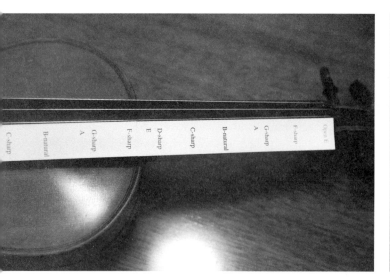
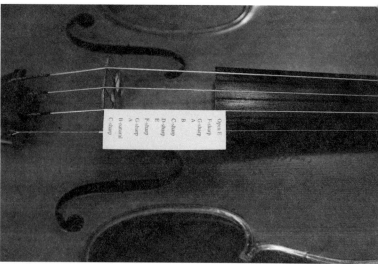

Figure 21.4 Thirteen-note scale on the E string. *Photo credit to Eva Foxon Nicholas.*

Figure 21.5 Thirteen-note microcosm of scale between the fingerboard and bridge on the E string. *Photo credit to Eva Foxon Nicholas.*

represented, but in smaller proportion (see fig. 21.3). Whether it is a short phrase or a full two-octave scale on the same string, reflection of those intervals exists in miniature proportion in that space (see fig. 21.4 and fig. 21.5).

When the position of each bow articulation between the fingerboard and bridge properly corresponds (in reduced scale) to the relative position of the fingers on the fingerboard, then each sound pops out with greater clarity. That ideal longitudinal location is the sounding point. How it works is this: as the articulating finger moves higher, closer to the end of the fingerboard, the bow correspondingly moves higher, closer to the bridge. As the articulating finger moves lower toward the scroll, the contact point of the bow moves lower toward the fingerboard.

When you play open-string D, the bow is close to the fingerboard; for the first finger E, the bow moves closer to the bridge. The bow moves still closer for F-sharp, the bow is closer yet for the third finger G, and it is closest for the fourth finger A. Then when you articulate B-natural with the first finger on the A string, the bow drops back farther away from the bridge and closer to the fingerboard, and it repeats its proportional placements on the next string, collaborating again with the ascending left-hand fingers. Do not create extreme angles by leaping between a low contact for an open string and a much higher one for an articulated finger, as in beat 3 of m.17 to beat 1 of m.18 in the Preludio (see ex. 21.3).

Example 21.3 Bach's Preludio, m.17 into m.18.

Again, on string crossings that incorporate the use of open strings, as in m.76 of the Bach Preludio (see ex. 21.4), it is not necessary to move the bow away (backtrack) from the bridge on the open strings because they speak well without adjusting. Keep the bow straight on the sounding point of the moving notes (or with a stationary finger on one string and moving fingers on another), as in m.3 of the Preludio (see ex. 21.5). To optimize a smooth bow transition, it helps to envision traveling on arcs that connect one note to the next and allow for that fluctuation. The bow remains mostly parallel to the bridge while it navigates the moving notes, as in m.55 of the Preludio (see ex. 21.6).

Example 21.4 Bach's Preludio, m.76.

Example 21.5 Bach's Preludio, m.3.

Example 21.6 Bach's Preludio, m.55.

The exact location of the sounding point is affected by pressure, speed, the length and angle of bow stroke used, and the string played, so it is important to keep a conscious, coherent bow grip. Use the contrary motion of the third and fourth fingers on the bow to change from one sounding point to another, rather than disrupting the full right hand. When the bow is improperly positioned relative to the location of the fingers on the fingerboard, the string rejects the bow, causing the sound to be fuzzy. To adjust or soften volume, it's OK to place the bow away from the sounding point for that section, closer to the fingerboard; sound quality is affected but is less crucial and less evident in a whispering passage. Just as the shifting left-hand fingers ascend and descend on arcing paths above the fingerboard, the bow concomitantly travels over smaller arcs, adjusting its location relative to the left hand.

Right- and Left-Hand Synthesis

The following image helps to synthesize left- and right-hand movements. Place the bow across the strings in first position where the left-hand fingers articulate with the string. Using a ball to represent the left hand, imagine positioning the ball on top of the bow where the bow meets the string. As the bow changes strings, it stays in contact with the string, with each string serving as a fulcrum to the bow (see fig.

21.6). When the left hand and bow travel from the G string to the E, the bow acts as a movable rail on which the left hand slides down (with gravity) to the vertically lower E string. When you raise the frog, the bow lifts the left hand slightly and slides it toward a vertically higher (but lower pitched) string destination. When you lower the frog, the bottom of the hand slides back toward the frog and across the width of the fingerboard toward the E.

Figure 21.6 Imagine the bow providing a rail for the hand to slide to the next position. *Photo credit to Gail Taibbi.*

***Left,* Figure 21.7** On a scale ascent, imagine placing the bow behind the left hand at the wrist. *Photo credit to Eva Foxon Nicholas.*

***Above,* Figure 21.8** On the scale descent, project the bow either against the front of the wrist or the fourth-finger corner. *Photo credit to Eva Foxon Nicholas.*

Now imagine placing the bow behind the upright left hand at the wrist in the area underneath the thumb and first finger (see fig. 21.7). Then coax the wrist with the bow to transport the hand toward the bridge. On a scale ascent, use the bow to drag the hand bridge direction, and on the scale descent, project the bow underneath the fourth finger at the wrist, carrying the hand via the wrist toward the scroll (see fig. 21.8). These exercises help relate the placement of the bow (with its changing sounding points) and the position of the left hand (with its shifts) along the line of the strings, synthesizing the bow and hand motions.

Right-Hand Chords

The top of the bridge is curved, so the curved line of the bow stroke by contrast is its mirror image. A feel for that scooping motion of the bow is crucial for playing chords. With two-note chords, the bow arm scoops a small arc; with a three-note chord, a bigger one; and with a four-note chord, the biggest curve.

When practicing four-note chords, as in the downbeat chord of the Fuga of Bach's Sonata in A minor at m.13 (see ex. 21.7), lean on (bias) the G string and play the D string, pause; then lean on (bias) the A string and play the E. Then practice eliminating the pause time between the two. Angle the bow on the sounding points relative to the fingers articulated. Pull the bow with the second and third fingers and the palm while vibrating the left-hand fingers. Weigh down the center of each hand to reinforce center balance and strength. The weighted right hand follows through the duration of the chord. The arm also stays heavy (weighted). When you pick up the bow to play a four-note chord, do not reduce weight in the arm, only in the hand. Throw your body weight from the right side of the torso into the stroke.

Example 21.7 Bach's A minor Fuga, m.13.

On an upbow, as in the pickup to beat 2 of m.154 in the Fuga (see ex. 21.8), fire the balance point out through the hand, leading with the second set of knuckles; as the arm retracts back on the downbow into beat 2, drag the balance point (indented end of arrow) across two, three, or (in this case) four strings of the chord. Practice four-note chords as if they are three-note chords, and then play the fourth note as an afterthought, starting with a slow bow and then moving fast as if in a throw-away motion. Increase the speed of the bow if you wish to crescendo as the bow follows through (G, D, A, E). During chords that turn around, for instance in m.40 (see ex. 21.9), bow speed is the same on the turnaround as in the beginning of the stroke. To approximate the motions of a bow negotiating a four-note chord, imagine inserting a skewer across the fingerboard into both the lowest and highest pitched strings (see fig. 21.9).

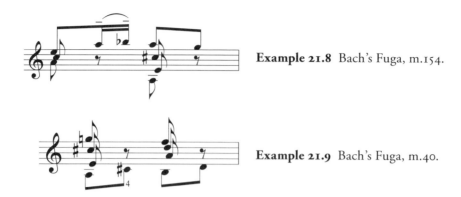

Example 21.8 Bach's Fuga, m.154.

Example 21.9 Bach's Fuga, m.40.

The middle string or strings that are raised above the skewer are accommodated in the process. In beat 2 of m.154 of the Fuga (see ex. 21.8), the skewer impales the G and E string, leaving the D and A strings above the line of the skewer. If the chord consists of three strings, as in beats 1 and 2 of m.70 (see ex. 21.10), the skewer would intercept the G and A string, leaving the D string above the line. Do not roll the bow with the curve of the bridge; instead, impale the bottom string and the top string of the chord with the bow. Or visualize that akin to a needle, the string has an eye, and then thread the eyes with the bow.

Figure 21.9 Insert a skewer across the fingerboard into both the lowest and highest pitched strings. *Photo credit to Eva Foxon Nicholas.*

Example 21.10 Bach's Fuga, m.70.

Two Hands Ascend

Before releasing the hands to play, hold them up with palms facing you. Draw a line from the large knuckle underneath the first finger to the lower outside corner of each hand (the spine). The spine divides the hands in half, kitty-corner. Now imagine that the two hands are two birds and that the spine of each hand is the backbone of a bird. The thumb is one wing and the fingers the other. The wings are balanced. In the right hand, the thumb and fingertips (wing tips) balance on an imaginary lip placed on each side of the bow. In the left hand, the thumb leans against an imaginary string while the fingertips articulate with an actual string.

The left hand works the perimeter of the neck like a woodpecker on the bole of a tree. Either wing, thumb or fingers, can flap their way out of awkward positions, with the spine flexing and extending in response. Or sometimes the spine leads the effort. The bird is in a continuous state of flux, inhaling, exhaling.

In both hands, the spine drops and lifts, engaging the wings. The bow hand soars while the left hand glides and rolls, together floating sound on a whisper of wind.

PART THREE

Integration

CHAPTER TWENTY-TWO

Full Body Balance

Counterbalance can be found on all levels of our musculoskeletal anatomy in action. On a smaller scale, the fingers counterbalance the thumb, and in a larger context, the torso and hands are in continual collaboration while the feet or sitting bones are relentlessly informing the shoulders.

Arm-to-Body Expansion and Contraction

There is a reciprocal interplay between arm weight and a relaxed and grounded spine that supports playing facility, achieved through a healthy distribution of weight. Experience it by extending your arms in front of you and joining your right and left fingertips, forming a horizontal circle at heart level (see fig. 22.1), as if hugging air out in front. Notice that the heavier the hand and arm weight out in front, the more the corresponding part of the spine can relax back and down to create a relatively tension-free counterbalance of support for the arms. When playing in first position, the left hand is farther away from the body, requiring a larger circular expansion to balance.

Because there is a tendency to overwork the muscles in the back by using tension instead of weight distribution to counterbalance the extension of the arms, always

Figure 22.1 Form a horizontal circle at heart level with your extended arms. *Photo credit to Eva Foxon Nicholas.*

consider the circular formation of the torso and arms to create a more harmonious configuration of support. Shifting back while extending the arm engages the muscles of the torso. Then allow the weight in your low back to drop down through your legs and feet and into the earth for a feeling of support and an overall sense of connectedness. Extending the arm (say, shifting down to first position) from a vertically rigid position isolates the hand and places too much responsibility onto the smaller muscles of the arm while it strains the shoulders and back. As a counterintuitive exercise, lean back slightly and take the instrument with you during shifts into first position. By extending your torso away from your arm instead of the other way around, the fine motor movements keep a connection with their fundamental impulses in the torso. When the back remains unyielding in its upright posture, the natural flow of support is stymied by superficial tension. When playing in higher positions with the hands closer to the body, the back is naturally more vertical—the circle smaller (see fig. 22.2).

Figure 22.2 The circle is smaller with the hands closer to the body and the back more vertical. *Photo credit to Eva Foxon Nicholas.*

All that said, some fine players do lean forward on a descending shift, allowing the arm to dangle, despite the risk of dragging down the scroll. Although there is a freedom and a maneuverability of the arm and hand in this position, unless this move is part of a graceful choreography that integrates it with counterbalancing moves, accommodating this setup is eventually stressful for the back and shoulders.

Full Body Balance

Feel the body circle expanding as a sequence descends the line of the string, and then feel it contracting again with a migration back up the fingerboard. In first position, imagine hugging a large ball. In higher positions visualize squeezing a smaller ball, or use a ball that expands and contracts, automatically accommodating the changing relationship of your arms to your torso.

When standing to play the violin, the feet are the foundational support. When sitting, the sitting bones are usually the primary foundation of support with the feet secondary. Whether standing or sitting, locate the body's operating center of gravity as a function of its primary foundation. When the body is both grounded and center balanced or in neutral, you have laid the groundwork for a psychophysical state that allows for the most possibilities of both movement and awareness, in the process inviting an opening of the emotional and musical channels.

Balancing the Body and Violin

Envision yourself *suspended* on a horizontal axis, the spindle passing through the front of the body and intercepting your body's center of gravity just under the navel (see fig. 22.3), allowing rotation in the frontal plane (akin to a pinwheel). When a different horizontal axis penetrates the center of gravity through the side of the body, the rotation is in the plane of a head nod or formal, full-body bow (see fig. 22.4). When a vertical line this time spears the body through the top of the head, the body

Below, **Figure 22.3** Imagine the horizontal axis passing through the front and intercepting your center of gravity. *Photo credit to Eva Foxon Nicholas.*

Right, **Figure 22.4** A different horizontal axis penetrates the center of gravity through the side of the body. *Photo credit to Eva Foxon Nicholas.*

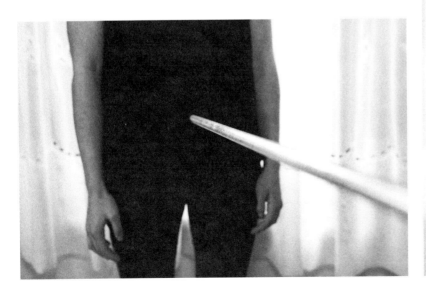

Figure 22.5 Even the vertical axis intercepts the center of gravity. *Photo credit to Eva Foxon Nicholas.*

spins around it clockwise or counterclockwise (looking from above) in a horizontal plane (see fig. 22.5). To optimize the ability to perform from any point of balance, consider all the possible angles among these three fundamental axes, imagining all possible playing positions.

Next, think of the instrument as part of your anatomy while standing and playing. Combine the mass of the violin and bow with the mass of you; then find the center of gravity of that totality. When holding the instrument while sitting, that is yet another composite totality with a new center of gravity due to the functionally new center for the sitting body. Again, the violin and bow become part of the new anatomical outline. Find the center point of this fuller content of mass and play from that point of balance.

When imagining that the violin is part of the anatomy, the balance point is slightly in front of the body's center of gravity, not as deep inside the body's core. There is much more mass back in the body, however, and that keeps the center of total mass much closer to the body's center than the violin's. If you then hold the instrument while sitting, there is yet another overall configuration with a new center of gravity. Most of the mass is in the torso because the legs are less engaged and the instrument and arms are relatively light, but the force of the instrument in motion is a function of its distance from the center of the body, so keep that in mind.

There is a sense of stability in playing posture and motion that is somewhere between being too contained and too splayed out. Stand in a performance position and imagine a vertical axis running down through your center of gravity. With any luck, your body is organized pretty well around it. This is your place of return—your core line. Now imagine encasing yourself in a vertical rubber cylinder with a perimeter large enough to allow a circular motion of the torso, a gentle leaning at a slight angle in any direction or a bouncing off (the arms are able to move through the constraints of the cylinder). The vertical axis provides a center line while the cylinder sets limits, a healthy perimeter containing a good range of movement of the torso.

If, after you stand and lean forward, assimilating a feel of reaching and supporting something heavy that is held away from your torso, you then stand upright at less of an angle and hold that same object close to your torso, you will find that it is easier to support that object. Likewise, if you absentmindedly let your weight drift forward when performing, placing undue stress on the body, you can reduce that stress by shifting your weight back over your feet. It is fine to move your upper body toward the violin, but not so far that you lose the backup support of your pelvis. Losing that support disrupts delicate playing balances.

Imagine two large, heavy bowling balls inside the rib cage, each of them attached to the shoulder. Divide the torso down the spine and sternum and think of each side of the torso as the base of one arm. The massive weight of each ball allows an arm to extend without losing touch with its firm foundation. To effectively transfer weight to the hand and not lose your balance, imagine holding a small bowling ball in the hand while the larger, heavier bowling ball continues to secure the arm's base of support (see fig. 22.6). The small ball lends weight to the hand, but because it is lighter than the larger-sized ball grounding the torso area, the hand still floats and easily finds its destination. Learn to transfer weight to the hands without compromising the body's balance. Feel like an elephant that easily extends its trunk and lifts a log with no sense of tipping over.

Figure 22.6 Imagine holding a small bowling ball while the larger, heavier ball continues to secure the arm's base. *Photo credit to Eva Foxon Nicholas.*

Application

Still feeling a separation of the right and left sides of the torso, imagine them as two root systems that are primarily independent but somewhat interrelated. Focus your attention on the full volume of the right side of the torso. As you present your right arm, extending it out and around (see fig. 22.7), initiate the movement from deep in the right side of the torso, feeling the momentum accumulating in the rib cage and traveling into the shoulder, out through the arm and into the bow. Like the root ball of a tree, the torso's influence travels into the branch/arm (because of its many connections), contributing to the arm's weight and supporting its intensions. For a heavier bow stroke, consider accessing back-up support across the body from the outer left side of the torso (see fig. 22.8), the left arm perhaps taking this opportunity to get backup support from the outer right side. For a lighter left-hand touch, initiate from the left side of the torso (see fig. 22.9).

Figure 22.7 Access the right side of the torso. *Photo credit to Eva Foxon Nicholas.*

Figure 22.8 Accessing backup support across the body from the outer left side of the torso. *Photo credit to Eva Foxon Nicholas.*

Figure 22.9 For moderate left-hand movements, initiate from the left side of the torso. *Photo credit to Eva Foxon Nicholas.*

In the solo entrance of the Brahms concerto (see ex. 22.1), initiate the left-hand movements from the right side of the torso (see fig. 22.10), with the demands of the passage necessitating even greater involvement from the biggest muscles of the torso. The solo entrance begins with a powerful two-note unison (on the lower strings); the next measure transitions dramatically from ascending motion into descending octaves, followed by a heavy martelé stroke, with the bow in each instance calling on substantial strength and weight to back up the strokes. For maximal support to the bow arm, picture the roots of the root ball wrapping around the left rib cage. And for giving utmost support to the left arm and hand, as is appropriate in the opening of the passage (see ex. 22.1), picture the roots wrapping around the outer right side of the torso (see fig. 22.11).

Example 22.1 Opening solo of the Brahms Violin Concerto in D.

Figure 22.10 Initiate the more vigorous left-hand movements from the right side of the torso. *Photo credit to Eva Foxon Nicholas.*

Figure 22.11 For maximum right- and left-hand strength, access both opposite sides of the torso. *Photo credit to Eva Foxon Nicholas.*

Creative Division of the Body

A good way to integrate the violin into the body is by exploring some body balances *without* the instrument in hand. Imagine dividing each finger in half lengthwise, extending into the palm. Similarly, longitudinally divide the wrists, the forearms (the radius from the ulna), and the upper arms (see fig. 22.12). The division travels into the shoulders, splitting the collarbones from the shoulder blades, before moving down the spine through the sacrum and cutting diagonally into each leg. The division continues through the weight-bearing bones of the legs, the femur of the thigh and the tibia of the shin (slicing front to back, lengthwise), into the ankle, and out the feet (each foot separated from the heel to the web space between the second and third toes). This sagittal division also travels up the neck and into the head, equally dividing the head into two halves (including left and right brain). This three-dimensional, full-body experience of lengthwise separation creates a broader awareness of total body balance, breaking through and deepening the superficial perception of the body as a patchwork of surfaces. On a smaller scale, each finger plants itself on the fingerboard (or on the bow) as if with the balance of two feet, each microcosm of bipedal balance supporting and reflecting the macrocosmic bilaterality of the whole body.

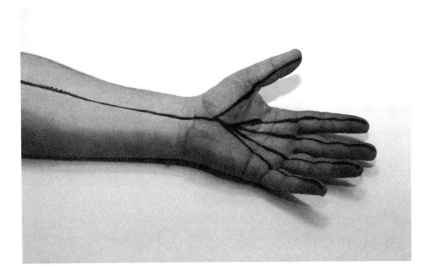

Figure 22.12 Longitudinally divide the fingers, the wrists, the forearms, and the upper arms. *Photo credit to Gail Taibbi.*

Conjure up an image of a breeze swirling around each half of the body's now-divided segments, starting with the fingertips; minifunnels swirl around each half of the fingers, arms, and legs. Then picture two larger funnels moving inside the body and surrounding each half, the left funnel swirling clockwise and the right counterclockwise. To further heighten a sense of the body's expansion, picture a breeze flowing through each of the joints, giving all the bony connection areas a sense of expansion—a larger space for the bones to relate, especially for the vertebrae of the upper torso and neck, considering the tendency to compress the head, neck, and shoulder areas while securing the violin.

Again, divide the torso in half along the sternum, leaving the two sides connected by their relationship to the spine, neck, and head. Imagine that each half is a vertical cylinder with space in between. Insert two vertical poles, one centered inside each cylinder. To effectively facilitate either bow-arm or left-arm motion, allow each cylinder to spin clockwise or counterclockwise on its respective pole. When drawing a downbow, imagine the clockwise (looking down from above) rotation of the cylinder lending backup support to the bow arm's direction of motion. The cylinder continues to rotate after the completion of each bow stroke, displaying the fullness of the gesture with attunement to the degree of effort needed to affect the cylinder's (bow's) complete turnaround. Let the left cylinder spin slowly counterclockwise as the left hand descends a three-octave scale, gradually extending out and around the fingerboard.

Synchronized Compressions

A helpful way to appreciate and explore the proprioceptive affiliations within ourselves and between player and instrument is through the concept of oppositional compressions. Attuning to the rhythm of compression and release, the concentration and subsequent liberation of energy, is the invitation into a space of full artistic connection. Compressions are coordinated exertions from the periphery, collectively pushing inward toward energies emanating organically from the center.

Compressions constitute healthy tension; their natural exertions bear the outbreath of playing and, when released, invite the inbreath. Building and releasing energy, somewhat a function of the diminution and expansion of physical movements, feeds continuity to the playing. Employing compressions is especially significant when used to enliven the fingers, hands, arms, and sometimes the entire body, whereas the lack of compression—the dearth of either natural or deliberate concentrations—is experienced as a sensation of atrophy in the fingers, limbs, and trunk.

Elbow to Palm: Two-Way Compression

With palms facing each other, place your hands on the outer ends of a Bullworker and push inward; the pole compresses. Imagine that the Bullworker is small enough to fit inside your right forearm and that one end is the elbow and that the other end projects an inch beyond the center of the palm. While bowing, feel an external exertion of pressures from the ends of the Bullworker, with the hand and elbow compressing inward with the counter pressures meeting in the center, the balance point area. Experience the balance points in both arms receiving vectors of longitudinal compression. The quality of sound can be adjusted by manipulating pressures. A flaccid arm creates a loose sound. When that is experienced, adjust the pressure to get a robust arm creating a firmer sound.

Forearm to Hand: Four-Way compression

Visualize a T-bar about a foot long that is made from springs. Wrap the large knuckles of your right thumb and fourth finger around the ends of the horizontal part of the T and place the vertical part (as in the Bullworker image) inside your arm (see fig. 22.13). The thumb and fourth-finger knuckles compress the cross piece toward the center line while the elbow and center of palm compress longitudinally, inward toward the balance point, all together creating four-way compression. These compressions solidify the bow arm structure, providing a buoyant backup to the bow handling.

Employing a four-way cross-compression of thumb to fourth finger in conjunction with elbow to palm can also unify the left hand and arm, reinforcing awareness of the important elbow-palm axis and the hand's frame of support. The opposite is an unfocused hand with the renegade fingers getting jammed up manipulating the neck. Maintaining patterns of pressure throughout the completion of a scale or arpeggio enhances continuity in running passages. The constant state of readiness paired with thoughtful compression patterns enlivens both arms and hands, feeding them energy.

Restoring Force

When a rubber band is stretched, it returns to its unexpanded state on release, thanks to its restoring force. If it is stretched to the left, and that left side is then fixed, the restoring force pulls anything attached to the right end back toward the left until

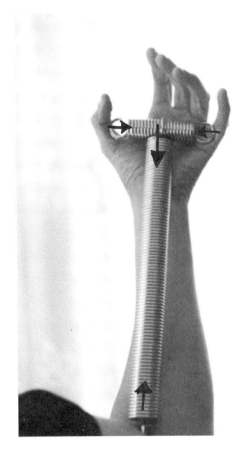

Figure 22.13 Compressing a T-bar that is made from springs. *Photo credit to Eva Foxon Nicholas.*

the band has returned to its original, contracted position. Create an elastic feeling of controlled expansion and contraction to explore the interaction of the two violin-playing arms, first visualizing an elastic string connected to two balls. Run the string through the pulley, forming an L-shape with the pulley in the middle and each ball on the string jutting out at right angles to each other (see fig. 22.14). Hold one ball in your left hand and the other in your right. When the left hand descends

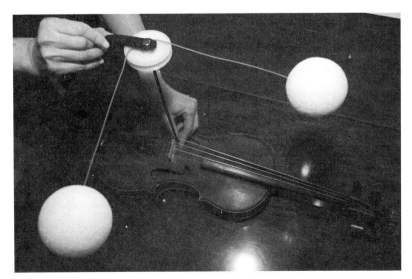

Figure 22.14 A vertical pole is attached to the bridge, with a (horizontal) pulley on top. *Photo credit to Gail Taibbi.*

Integration

a scale and the right hand draws a downbow, the two hands stretch the elastic; as the left hand ascends the scale and the right hand pushes the upbow, the elastic retracts, the two hands acquiescing together. Often, a scale passage ascends on a downbow and descends on an upbow, in which case one hand can drag the other. Imagining that the heart is a pulley is a way to deeply connect your emotions to the notes.

Envisage an eye screw affixed to the center of each palm; then connect the ends of an elastic string to each eye screw. Again, feel the relationship between the left and right hands and, this time, the subtle response of the concave and convex motions of each palm's center as they alternately pull and release each other.

Try envisioning a pogo stick of eye-level height when playing a passage. Grip the handles with the left hand facing toward you and the bow hand facing away. Now imagine pulling down on the handlebars while drawing the bow and articulating the left-hand fingers. As the hands descend, the rib cage expands despite the shoulders, which separate in accommodation, with this shift of weight and position drawing the full weight of the body into the playing.

By raising the lower ribs and pulling down on the head of the humerus, a strong contraction of the latissimus dorsi muscles forces a lateral expansion of the rib cage that both benefits breathing and disallows a chronic hunching of the shoulders. Add in their primary function (which involves the extension and rotation of the arms) and their large mass, and there is no doubt that they should be deliberately recruited to assist with the coordination of motion and breathing in violin playing. Integrating the sublime sensation of expansion via the increasing volume of the rib cage and horizontal widening of the shoulders with well-considered contraction along the muscular core line from the shoulders to the hips helps to ready the body for performance.

Coordinating the Periphery

On a macro scale, the peripheral body is a rich source and mediator of energy. With their complex architecture and dense innervation, the hands and feet are especially full of creative possibilities. On the downbows in the Brahms, 47 measures after the solo entrance (see ex. 22.2), when you exert bow pressure to the left of the string, let the right foot absorb the impact, and on upbows in the next bar, let the left foot absorb the impact. That said, you can interact primarily with either foot on the down or the upbow, so long as the foot countering the exertion of bow pressure acts as its foundation.

Draw a diagonal line from the bow's contact point on the left of the G or D string to the right foot. Now imagine that the diagonal line is a pogo stick. With one end stabilized at the foot, the pogo stick invites a compression from the other end

Example 22.2 First movement of the Brahms violin concerto, 47 measures after the solo entrance.

that connects the contact point of the bow to the right foot. On slurred, downbow, G-to-E-string ascents, the bow compresses into the right foot, and on slurred, upbow, E-to-G-string descents, the bow compresses into the left foot.

Your feet respond to many influences, including the subtle side-to-side rocking motion of the bridge's feet in response to the bow. To magnify the balancing and rebalancing of the feet, picture yourself standing on a shoulder-width seesaw that is a couple of inches off the floor. Then while playing, notice the side-to-side shifting of body weight and the resultant compressions. The bow jockeys weight back and forth between your feet, creating either same-side or crossing compressions between the contact point of the bow and your feet.

The head can move in counterbalance to the direction of the bow, especially in response to elongated bowing. It may tilt to the left, away from the downbow stroke, to create a long line of full extension through the neck and shoulder; then the weight of the head would relax back toward the upbow stroke, at times more deliberately to support a vigorous upbow, and at other times simply to return to a neutral position for the next downbow.

To experience a great feeling of fluidity, start by standing on your right foot, feeling your full body weight against the floor. Contemplate in the imagination that your legs are the bole of a weeping willow and that your body drapes sideways and backward, like a branch/sprig hanging down (see fig. 22.15). Do not fall back onto

Figure 22.15 Your legs are the bole of a tree, and your body drapes back. *Photo credit to Eva Foxon Nicholas.*

your heels; push off one or both balls of your feet to maintain the extension all the way from your toes to your nose. When you lean back and to the left side, the table of the violin becomes level. At times, the right foot anchors the body. At other times, the left foot is out in front, acting as the support, and the right leg is at ease. When sitting, a way to experience a sense of expansion is to ease the weight of your upper body into the spine, with the heart tilting slightly toward the heavens.

Supporting the Violin with Compression

The violin is effectively suspended through the surrounding body's coordinated use of compressions. The body adjusts and readjusts to balance and support our involvement with the instrument—the musical requirements being the ultimate determinant of the precise choreography.

Just as we can use compressions to increase the energy to a functional area, such as the hand, we can add energy more directly to the violin. When ascending a scale, visualize that the ends of the violin on the longitudinal axis—scroll and button—compress inward like bellows, with both the left hand and chin/neck assisting. Or similarly, imagine the violin as a horizontal spring that you can compress when ascending the scale; then intentionally release compression. During scale descents, as the distance between your neck and your hand expands, generate a feeling of extending the length of the violin.

Creative Use of the Bow

Another component of support/suspension is a counterintuitive lifting motion of the bow to counter the weight of the instrument (see fig. 22.16). When drawing the bow across the strings, imagine urging the bow hair underneath the feet of the bridge and lifting against the gravitational pull on the instrument: the violin becomes stabilized,

Figure 22.16
When bowing, imagine tucking the bow hair underneath the feet of the bridge. *Photo credit to Gail Taibbi.*

the left hand is liberated, and tone production is maximized. Doing so transfers the sense of support from taking place primarily at either end to the middle, thwarting the tendency of the left thumb to excessively squeeze the neck or the chin to clench the chin rest. This projection of the hair under the bridge feet also deepens the relationship of the bow to the violin, enabling the more penetrating bow strokes to carve out a more profound depth of tone. Assume for this exercise that the longitudinal balance point is close to the bridge.

To add more dimension of sound, picture carving out a generous scoop with the bow hand, uprooting an area of imaginary matter either underneath the bridge or between the bridge and fingerboard. As another variation, imagine that the bow hair has miniscule barbs that have the capability to grab onto the string (there is no evidence that this is the case, popular myths notwithstanding). Keeping this in mind, draw a downbow from its left side that lifts the string; the lifting helps suspend the violin and deepen tone production.

This time, as an exercise, actually slide your bow underneath the strings between the bridge and fingerboard area and then suspend the violin by holding the ends of the bow, tip and frog. When the bow is near the end of the fingerboard, the instrument balances longitudinally (see fig. 22.17). Back in the imagination, zero in on the specific point of balance for the instrument, considering length and width, and then place it on a pinnacle. The violin teeters back and forth, allowing a more comfortable exchange of weight between the hand and the chin.

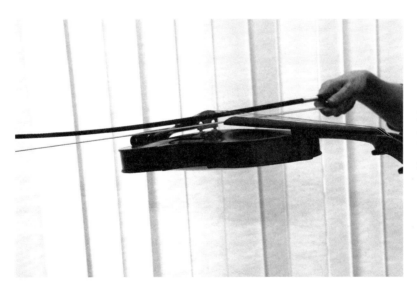

Figure 22.17 Suspending the violin with the bow between the bridge and fingerboard. *Photo credit to Gail Taibbi.*

Imagine placing the violin against the sternum (breastbone) and then inflating the upper body, expanding the head, neck, shoulders, and arms upward and over the top of the violin. When drawing a downbow, generate a sensation of using the pressure of the bow against the strings to further elevate the upper body. Transferring upper-body weight and influence to a position above the violin lends backup support to both the left-hand fingers and the bow hand. Likewise, visualize a giant ball encasing the suspended instrument; then imagine draping your body around and over the top of the ball. The big ball image supports the transference of upper-body weight to a position above the violin and allows both hands to reach down from above. The spherical barrier prevents the arms and hands from collapsing in and around the instrument.

Using the Restoring Force of a Ball

Imagine that the violin rests on top of a giant ball that is floor-to-violin height. When the bow bounces on the strings, it sandwiches the ball between the floor and the instrument. The ball's compression response contributes to the rebound from the violin to the bow. When bowing, you can also visualize bypassing the violin and bouncing the bow off the ball.

This time imagine that there are four balls filled with helium; the left hand rests on one (on top of the fingerboard), two larger ones are wedged in each underarm, and once more the violin is situated on top of a giant one. Now picture the four balls elevating: the ball beneath the left hand elevates the hand, the balls in the underarms maintain a good position of the upper arms relative to the torso, and the giant ball lifts the violin. Raising the hand and arms (a pair of wings) along with the violin itself supports a sense of physical freedom.

There is a dull quality of pressing down on something inanimate that contrasts with a more vital feeling of pressure on something lively that responds. The first tends to create unwanted tension; the latter is likely to solicit the integrated use of the muscles. Draw the bow across the strings while consciously sustaining resistance against the animated energy of the still-elevating violin. The pull of the bow and the left hand restraining the ascending ball and violin support the potent production of tone.

Consider pulling energy directly from the ground to vitalize your playing. When sitting, stack the vertebrae one upon another, beginning with the tailbone and ending with your head balanced on top. When sitting in playing position, the sitting bones serve and respond to the balanced upper body the way the feet react when standing. In thinking of the sitting bones as feet, consider the related muscles lifting, lowering, shifting weight side-to-side, adjusting on the floor of the chair in counterbalance to the upper body's fluidlike motions. For more intense playing, imagine that your chair is the back of a horse: bend your knees while straddling the outer sides of the seat and call on the inner thigh muscles (the adductors) to raise you up as if posting (English-style riding) to the musical pace. That motion supports the lifting of the spine out of the pelvis, even a sense of it lifting out of the body, in that way generating a feeling of being in flight.

Performance Energy

What we learn from Békésy's demonstration of the projection of touch, in combination with an awareness of the body's energy field and its ability to expand, reminds us that our sensory experience often breaks the confinement of our own perceived periphery. Examples include the sensation of pain in acupuncture that can radiate beyond the physical perimeters of the actual body and the phantom limb experience with an amputation.

During a particularly intense period of my life, I intuited a body of flames projecting outward around a dark silhouette larger than my actual body within. Using this expanded experience of my body, I experimented with following a motion into and through this outer body, like a flamethrower, and as a result I was more fully projecting my actual physical motions. Brought to violin playing, consider that an upbow is not just an upbow but a core experience of energized material in motion, mobilized substance led by the projectile of the outer-flamed knuckles.

Anatomical position shows the body in standing position with arms at the side and palms facing forward. Everything that faces forward in this position is called anterior or ventral, and it tends to be the feeling side of the body. The ventral side of the body can express tender feelings through an embrace, with the dorsal side or the back of the body responding more in a supportive and often protective manner—for example, holding the back of the forearms up with fists clenched as a way of blocking assault to the front, protecting the vulnerable person who dares to love.

Because of the careful wrapping of the instrument for technical efficiency, the most fundamental playing position is also the one that best supports an embracing of the instrument that brings warmth of expression to the playing. Each finger is structured like a violin scroll or a fiddlehead fern, spiraling into itself as part of a larger spiraling of the hand into the arm and the arm into the body, with the circular overlapping continually reinforcing its connection to itself in a way that builds both great strength and sensitivity.

The images in Progressive Form are designed to assist in overcoming the challenge of balancing the inner, embracing-of-the-instrument vulnerability with good structural support to reliably attain abundant sensitivity and expression in the playing. Try visualizing a galaxy of varying sized balls that are strategically placed in the flexed finger, in the palm, in the bent arm, and under the upper arm (refer to fig. 16.6); the balls lend structure and add buoyancy and responsiveness to the entire arm and hand. If you then drape your body on top of and around a large ball as if in a hug, that ball supports the overall weight and roundedness of good form while enhancing and protecting the natural vulnerability of that position. Think of this largest ball as taking the playing into the most personal and profound realm of the torso, expanding and contracting with the breath, pumping life into the playing, with your heart at the core of the system.

The ventral side of the body surrounds or embraces itself and the violin, manifesting the delicate transmission of emotions from the heart through the instrument with a responsive sound feeding back to the body, completing the circle of this intimate continuum. From that perspective, we can play the instrument, embrace a lover, cradle a newborn, or grasp at souls of loved ones slipping away—blessed water spilling through our open fingers (see appendix I).

Integration

Energy and Balance

Implied Spiral Motion of the Head and Torso

From embryological stages to maturity, the body develops in spirals. Many of the visualizations in Progressive Form are circular because those circular suggestions help liberate the spiral rotations of both the static body and the body in motion. Visualize that your head and torso is hollowed. Roll a metal ball around inside your head in a Hula-Hoop fashion; the direction of the ball assists the shift of weight of the head on the neck and transfers that feeling of motion and freedom down into the body.

Motion and Energy Pathways

Buddhist and Hindu traditions use a psychophysical system of energetic vortexes known as chakras, which line up along the vertical axis of the body, with their swirling currents feeding energy to their physical counterparts (see fig. 22.18).

With the chakras in mind, visualize two energetic spheres heart level. Each sphere is a mass or energy field that radiates in all directions, including sending energy down the arms to the fingertips and to the bow's contact points with the string. Supported by the spheres, the hands navigate the instrument.

Figure 22.18 Chakra System.
Photo credit to Eva Foxon Nicholas.

Now visualize that the left and right arms individually encircle their suspended spheres and that each arm movement influences the rotation of that ball of energy. This grounds and synchronizes both arms, and it fuels the playing. When performing, gently coaxing energy in a circular motion toward the body's energy centers, especially the heart, can heighten emotional and spiritual states.

We humanize the instrument through a symbiotic exchange of energy that pulsates the strings, giving the notes a voice. I've written a poem that expresses this sentiment.

> Sinking into awareness of the fingerboard, feeling the tingle, my spine at its base, I ponder my familial roots, all four fingers and the four strings. I juggle the polarity of love and hate and the in-between of second position. From third, I leap on top of the instrument and feel the thunderous pulse between the heavens and earth. In fifth, we communicate. Venturing into vagueness—impressionism—nonmatter, alone, eventually through letting go, I find seventh . . . Coils of energy fuse like tentacles to the spines, the violin's—and mine.

Forces of Nature in Motion

The larger forces of nature are powerful and commonly understood, so they make inspiring images. Inject the exuberant feeling of natural forces to enhance particular aspects of movement. For instance, picture miniature tornadoes bumping against the edges of the hand, moving the hand up and down the fingerboard (at the desired wind velocity) during ascending and descending shifts. Or feel the wind lift the hand off the wrist and spin it as the fingers articulate same-position passages descending from E to G string.

The following maps out the pathway of a funnel that supports motion of the left hand during a three-octave E major scale ascent (see ex. 22.3). Beginning in first position, contemplate in the imagination a funnel spinning counterclockwise, bumping against the back of the left-hand third and fourth fingers of the left hand (the large knuckles). The funnel rotates the hand clockwise, propelling it up the tiers supporting the finger-pattern of the scale—one-two-three, shift, and then one-two, shift—with the bottom of the hand returning to first-finger position between each tier, once more to be bumped forward.

Example 22.3 Three-octave E major scale.

When the hand reaches the top of the scale, the funnel reverses the direction of its spin (to clockwise) and rotates the hand counterclockwise, supporting repeated articulation of fingers—three-two-one, shift—on each descending tier. When the hand reaches first position, aim the wrist toward the D string (in this instance) or G string (depending on the final destination). Each time, the funnel lifts the hand up and off the wrist foundation, spinning it counterclockwise and supporting the four, three, two, one, finger rotation of the hand on each descending string (the hand restores balance to a point underneath the fourth finger between string changes), carrying the bottom of the hand to the left of its destination of the lowest string.

Let the funnels brush against your right hand or arm (or the middle of the bow) to access speed. The idea is to interact with larger energies, whether turbulent or gentle, affecting the degree and quality of movement.

Once you get a feel for conjuring up natural forces, be creative with it in small and big ways. On a particular day, like a bird with an immense wing spread, ride massive currents of air, sumptuously transcending earthbound limitations.

CHAPTER TWENTY-THREE

An Expanded Approach to Scales and Arpeggios

Elaborating the E Major Scale

Rather than presenting a teaching lesson on how to practice, this is a guide to incorporating the techniques developed in Progressive Form into your practice. Through the repetition of a three-octave scale, a concept of overall motion evolves, so it becomes a useful template to demonstrate Progressive Form's imagery in the context of disciplined practice. Playing a scale requires a plethora of tools to successfully establish left- and right-hand balance throughout our migrations around the instrument (see ex. 23.1). This exercise will involve adding a feature each time you play a scale until the hands and arms are optimally balanced.

Example 23.1 Three-octave E major scale.

Each of the seventy-five scale presentations here demonstrates a combination of thought processes using imagery from Progressive Form. Our set-up steps will serve as examples. First, place the violin against your neck while imagining that the neck portion of your spine is a vertical pole about three inches in diameter. Then visualize that the soft tissue of your neck is ghostlike and that the tailpiece end of the violin can slide between your head and shoulders and lean directly against the spine/pole. Refer to chapter 3, "Positioning the Violin."

Align the fingers with the string via a well-distributed rotation of the arm. Refer to chapter 2, "Forearm Rotation—The Radius and the Ulna."

Present your left arm by initiating the lift from the presentation point, an area several inches below the left shoulder blade (refer to fig. 2.3). Then continue the lift from a *directing point* behind the upper arm, several inches below the shoulder socket

Integration

(refer to fig. 2.4), poising the hand in first position. Refer to chapter 2, "Presentation and Directing Points."

While presenting the hand, focus on its height and rotation, in that way placing the neck deeply enough in the hand so that the fingers can flex into a relaxed square shape. To keep the fingers efficient, bend (flex) them at the middle and small knuckles so the inside forms a square room (refer to chapter 6, "Structure and Weight"). It is helpful if all the joints are relaxed, especially in the fourth finger and thumb, two digits that tend to hold tension.

Then to monitor the balance of the left hand on the wrist, imagine shifting the base of the thumb into the base of the palm across from the second and third fingers. Balance all three around the extension of a line that splits the two forearm bones, the radius and ulna. The thumb's weight and strength counterbalance the fingers on top of the properly positioned forearm. Refer to chapter 7, "The Hand's Stabilization of the Fingers."

Imagine placing the back of the hand against the left side of the neck of the violin and, by so doing, relaxing the whole hand (refer to fig. 15.1). Feel the fingers dropping into the palm as they then move up and down with ease. Refer to chapter 15, "Hand Position." When the hand falls forward in the higher positions (fourth), feel the weight of each finger moving longitudinally toward the tip's articulation with the string, with each segment leaning into the next one.

1. On the first time playing the scale, adjust the lateral angle of the violin to support a continuous relationship of the hand with the thinnest aspect of the neck. Refer to chapter 8, "Poised Fingers."

2. Sense the subtle sideways rotation of the violin as it responds to the left hand's ascent and descent of the scale. Think of your spine as a vertical pole, secure the button end to it, and picture the scroll swinging right to left in a slow, pendulumlike motion when the hand ascends a scale—and then continue left to right during the hand's descent. Refer to chapter 3, "Positioning the Violin."

3. Now experience your upper body and left hand moving toward each other when ascending the scale (refer to fig. 22.2), and then experience their expansion when descending to first position (refer to fig. 22.1). You can envision hugging a ball that expands and contracts to accommodate this dynamic relationship of the arms and hand to the torso. Refer to chapter 22, "Arm-to-Body Expansion and Contraction." While bowing the sounding points, coax the violin toward your neck, even when the left hand and bow are moving away from the bridge in the descending shifts. Refer to chapter 22, "Creative Use of the Bow."

4. This time, shift your attention to finer subdivisions of the anatomy, starting by gazing at the palm of your vertical hand and imagining that the bottom of the hand is the bottom of a rocking chair that rocks lengthwise on top of the fingerboard (refer to fig. 4.2). When the fingers are firing away, notice the side-to-side rocking motion of the hand via the wrist and how it lends snap

and speed to the drop and release of the fingers. To intensify the motion, ponder turning the rocker blade upside down, this time rocking the bottom of the hand along the now-convex arc. Refer to chapter 4, "Wrist Motion in Position."

5. Picture the thumb encompassing not only its meaty first segment but also the base of the palm. Refer to chapter 8, "Imagery That Supports Finger Rebound." Superimpose the thumb onto the center of the base of the palm; then visualize a solid, round cookie cutter, and imagine punching out a circle that allows the insertion of the thumb; the peripheral hand rotates around the perimeter of the cookie cutter. As it moves, the hand balances and rebalances itself around the circular cutout for the thumb, continually shifting weight underneath any finger eager to act. Refer to chapter 10, "Thumb-to-Finger and Thumb-to-Palm Rotational Relationships." Avoid rocking the hand too far one way or the other when firing the fingers. Refer to chapter 2, "Forearm Rotation—The Radius and the Ulna."

6. If the left arm is lackadaisical and your fingers aren't above the string well enough, think first of the rotation as evenly distributed between the hand and the whole arm and combined into one flowing gesture of presentation. Refer to chapter 11, "The Home Position." Then, as the left hand rotates clockwise (from an aerial view) approaching the violin, picture a line segment from the large knuckle of the middle finger to the hand's lower outside corner becoming more vertical until it is aligned with the pinky side of the forearm, the ulna. Now the hand is in position to play (refer to fig. 11.2).

7. To feed more energy to the hand or to lend additional weight to the fingers, experiment with steering the elbow along its circular path, adding energy, support, a slight shift of direction, whatever improves the hand's positioning (refer to fig. 1.3).

8. If your fingers aren't connecting well to the string, try conjuring up the image of a clasp attached to each fingertip that is fastened around the string (refer to fig. 7.11), which helps maintain a consistent proximity of the fingertips to the string. Then articulate the fingers with the string using this guiding restriction. Refer to chapter 7, "Finger Placement."

9. If your fingers are connecting but feel sluggish, envision four rubber bands, one end of each attached to a fingertip and then running along the back of the hand and down to a corresponding part of the wrist (refer to fig. 8.7). After the finger articulates with the string, the stretched rubber band lifts the finger to support its rebound. Refer to chapter 8, "Imagery That Supports Finger Rebound." When lifting and dropping each finger, maintain weight on the fourth-finger portion of the hand to anchor its balance.

10. Imagine that the neck of the instrument is a cylindrically shaped water balloon. Then rest the four fingers on the balloon as you would on the string. As each finger drops, it displaces enough fluid to slightly elevate the remaining fingers: the articulating fingers are discharging the others from the string. Refer to chapter 8, "Imagery That Supports Finger Rebound."

11. Imagining an open space between the forearm and hand, insert a platform underneath the bottom of the hand, and then let it elevate. You may find that pulling the hand upward to the neck, rather than drawing the neck down into the hand, intensifies compression between the bottom of the hand and the collective fingers without bogging down the fingers, as a result fueling the acceleration of the freely flexing fingers. The finger rebounds the moment note contact is made due to the slight release of that compression. Refer to chapter 8, "Imagery That Supports Finger Rebound."

12. Likening the palm to the body of a bird in flight, observe it orbiting the neck without landing prematurely on top of the fingers. Refer to chapter 5, "Migration of the Hand."

13. Picking a set of knuckles (the same one from each finger), imagine that the fingers are powered by them. Now picture that the rest of the finger extending beyond the knuckle used is nonexistent, leaving the full knuckle as the end of the finger. Use the nicely rounded and weighted knuckle that is now at the end of the finger to easily articulate notes by hammering the string. This has the added benefit of positioning the neck more deeply in the hand, reinforcing a proper relationship of the hand to the neck. Refer to chapter 8, "Support for Finger Action."

14. To further secure the hand's proximity to the violin, imagine that the hand can play an imaginary violin to the left of the actual one (refer to fig. 12.5), securing the hand's position in relation to the actual instrument. Then articulate the fingers with the string from this position of greater potential.

15. To access more of the thumb side of the hand, and in so doing to achieve the strength and facility that good balance promotes, bend the thumb with a curve similar to the fingers and draw in the base knuckles of the thumb and fingers to provide equal back-up to both. Refer to chapter 9, "Balance of the Hand and Thumb."

    When playing the scale, confirm that your thumb is functionally centered between fingers one and four. Direct the fingers through the string at angles determined by the articulation while pushing the thumb upward against the side of the neck so that neither aims at each other (refer to fig. 9.1).

16. Imagine balancing a vertical pole with a ball on top on the open palm of your left hand. Now capture that feeling in your arm in playing position, beginning with simple support through your elbow that allows the hand to float freely on top of your forearm (refer to fig. 1.9). Elbow position determines the height and location of the forearm, with the hand's position and distribution of weight counterbalancing the angle of the forearm. Refer to chapter 1, "Facilitation of the Hand in Passage Work."

17. Similarly, think of the hand as a ball nestled in the wrist. To stabilize the upright position of the hand during a continuum of passage work, visualize pulling a string that is attached to the center bottom of the hand through the center of the wrist and down the hollow of the forearm, securing it to the elbow (refer to fig. 7.5 and fig. 7.6).

When descending the scale, thrust the ball-shaped hand to its calculated destination while attempting to retrieve it and retract it back into the wrist's pocket. Eliminating extraneous motion with this image allows you to connect primarily to the descending and ascending motion of the hand on the fingerboard. The responsive arm anticipates the hand's every move.

18. When ascending from first to fourth position, travel an imaginary line extending from the scroll to the outer shoulder of the violin (refer to fig. 11.5). There is a tendency for the left hand to track the line of the neck rather than a better, diagonal line extending from the scroll to the shoulder.

19. This time you may want to picture the metal rim of a bicycle wheel positioned horizontally (floating like a halo), and then insert the violin inside the rim, securing the scroll and button to the wheel's inner surface (refer to fig. 11.6). Acting as an invisible guide, the rim redirects the hand, preventing a collision with the shoulder.

20. During the third-to-fourth-position transition of the scale, as the hand ascends above the violin, exert equal pressure from the thumb and fourth fingertips on the same platform, like a person starting to do a split. Refer to chapter 14, "Combining Imagery for Left-Hand Support."

21. Think of the elbow, the thumb, and the fourth finger forming a V (refer to fig. 14.1); then push the elbow in the direction of the thumb and fourth finger. This creates an overall feeling of cohesion, with the elbow assisting in the expansion of the hand.

22. At the top of the scale, if you want a wider expansion of your fingers and thumb, first shift the base of the thumb into the center of the base of the palm. Then to maximize your reach, expand the space between the centered thumb and middle finger large knuckles like a person doing a split.

23. To create a sense of balance and stability, imagine suspending the back of your hand above the fingerboard from its midpoint. Then counter the weight and balance of the fingers by feeling the thumb as dead weight. The fingers and thumb teeter over the fingerboard like a five-footed person, with the feet symmetrically balanced around the palm, dangling, and touching down from above. From this suspended position, articulate the notes at the top of the scale.

24. On the scale descent to first position, maintain as much of an upright forearm position as possible. If you tilt the forearm too much to play in first position, the hand has to overflex to find its verticality and bring the fingers in closer to the fingerboard. Refer to chapter 2, "Balance of the Forearm." To offset this, you can visualize that you are suspended from the top of your shoulders as if hanging midair from a parachute (refer to fig. 2.6), and now you can easily direct your elbow away from your torso in support of the more vertical forearm position.

25. Your neck and shoulders may be free, but now you may find yourself clutching the neck with your hand. If so, this time picture being submerged

in water up to your chin, and visualize that the violin is floating like a raft on its surface just underneath your chin. Weight is distributed roughly evenly throughout the instrument, side to side and scroll to button, so the instrument floats quite horizontally. The purpose of this visualization is to generate support for the violin without soliciting help from either the hand or the shoulder. Refer to chapter 3, "Setting Up without Tension."

26. To create a sense of suspension, visualize four suction cups, one attached to each fingertip; then use them to lift the light end of the violin. As you articulate notes, pass the fingerboard from one suction-cupped fingertip to the next. This secures each finger's tonal connection to the fingerboard while supporting the neck. Refer to chapter 7, "Finger Placement."

27. If your forearm and upper arm lack a feeling of cohesion during transit, you may regain a solid feeling of balance by calling to mind an image of holding a ball in your left palm (face up) while imagining that the left biceps muscle of your upper arm is also a ball (refer to fig. 2.5). Sense a direct correlation of balance between the biceps ball and the hand ball while negotiating ascending and descending passages. Refer to chapter 2, "Upper-Arm-to-Hand Balance."

28. If there is division in the hand such that your thumb gets left behind in the third-to-fourth-position changeover, you have to compensate by extending your fingers to reach the notes, disturbing the proper formation of your left hand. To remedy this, again imagine balancing both the biceps/ball and the ball in your hand, and then, while transitioning from third position to fourth, imagine a force field emanating from within the hand that preserves its organization, preventing any collapse or lean or distortion during transit. Refer to chapter 2, "Upper-Arm-to-Hand Balance."

29. In your imagination, flex the forearm toward the upper arm until the violin is pressed in between. During ascending and descending passages, this feeling of the arm's unity creates a stable platform for the hand while better supporting the instrument, as a result averting the danger of the hand getting involved with holding onto the neck. Refer to chapter 3, "Forearm and Upper Arm Mutuality."

30. Then visualize enclosing the violin inside a ball and navigating by way of its surface. The spherical barrier prevents the arm from collapsing in and around the instrument. The surface of the ball also helps you to bypass the crook of the neck, a place where the hand often gets trapped when ascending a three-octave scale. Refer to chapter 3, "Setting Up without Tension."

31. If your hand lacks stability, imagine resting the center of your palm on a post projecting up from the fingerboard (refer to fig. 5.7).

32. If you are beginning to loosen up and want to express more buoyancy of motion, try projecting your elbow to a spot underneath the scroll and imagine placing it on top of a pogo stick. Ease the elbow downward on the pogo stick; then on the pogo stick's rebound, quickly ascend the scale. This effectively

An Expanded Approach to Scales and Arpeggios

reduces left-arm tension while feeding continuity to the passage. Refer to chapter 1, "Reducing Hand and Shoulder Tension."

33. The hand's progression starts in its fundamental home position, a place of maximum range of motion but minimal reach—some lateral rotation of the arm and hand plus a bit of clockwise rotation with the palm. If your finger-to-thumb relationship is not tight enough to secure running fingers, add a small amount of rotation at a time in all three planes until the hand is sitting on its lower outside corner, with the spine continuous with the line of the ulna, a position of less freedom at the wrist but maximal reach, especially for the fourth finger. Balancing on the lower outside corner is a way of miniaturizing the healthy motions of the hand for the efficacy of the fingers as they travel further from home. Refer to chapter 12, "Hand Balance."

34. This time, connect one end of a wire to the large knuckle of the first finger (palm side) and the other end to the lower outside corner; then cross that with a second wire, one end to the fourth-finger large knuckle and the other end to the lower inside corner. Pulling the corners closer together molds a coherent configuration (refer to fig. 5.3) while it differentiates the fingers as it liberates them from the palm.

35. If, while focusing on a renewed feeling of muscularity in the fingers, you lose your sense of direction when transitioning from third to fourth position, concentrate on catapulting the hand from its bottom center. Refer to chapter 14, "Catapulting the Hand from the Bottom Center."

36. During the hand's third-to-fourth-position changeover, exert downward pressure on the tip of the thumb to rotate the hand counterclockwise, lifting the fingers against both gravity and the hand's natural resistance to this motion. On the descent, feel the thumb's release and the hand settling back under the neck. Refer to chapter 9, "Thumb-to-Fingertip Rotation."

37. Imagine four strings (which we'll call G^1, D^1, A^1, and E^1) underneath the neck, spaced farther apart than the actual strings (refer to fig. 9.10). Then lean the tip of the thumb on the imaginary string that is diagonally underneath the string being played. Refer to chapter 9, "Invisible Props for Thumb Support."

38. If your hand is unified, but the transition from third to fourth position and back is not as rapid as you would like, imagine that the hand is a ball suspended on a rotisserie and that the spit runs through the center of the tunnel formed by the fingers and opposing thumb (refer to fig. 11.13); then affix a string to the bottom center of the hand (refer to fig. 11.14). When transitioning from third position to fourth, pull the string (out the back of the hand) toward the ceiling, with the hand flipping around the rotisserie/axis to a position above the instrument and the fingers dangling down. Then when you pull the string toward the floor, the hand flips back underneath, the fingers now upright. Refer to chapter 11, "The Sphere of the Left Hand and Its Axes of Rotation."

Integration

39. Modifying a previous image, imagine poking your thumb through the hole in a metal washer and resting your fingertips along its circumference (refer to fig. 7.9). Playing on the washer's edge supports an expansion of the fingers that is maximized at the second set of knuckles. Play the scale focusing only on the fingertips to the string, benefiting from that resultant expansion of the second set of knuckles. Articulating the fingers on the washer's edge also keeps the hand well centered while retaining a sensation of the outer corners balancing equally on the wrist.

    Now envision the washer with an edge that is grooved, like the wheel on a train. Imagine that the washer moves along the line of the string, supporting the position and suspension of the thumb (inside the washer) and the fingers (on top). Refer to chapter 7, "Direction of the Fingers."

40. It is likely that muscle memory is beginning to take over with these new patterns. Now, to access more of the left hand's potential energy, visualize a T-bar about a foot long that is made from springs (refer to fig. 22.13). The thumb- and fourth-finger knuckles compress the cross piece toward the center line while the elbow and center of palm compress longitudinally, inward toward the balance point, altogether creating four-way compression. These compressions unify the arm and feed energy to the fingers. Refer to chapter 22, "Forearm to Hand: Four-Way Compression."

41. Envision pressing a ball in your hand against the fingerboard; then imagine bending the forearm at its longitudinal midpoint, akin to a backhoe's arm (refer to fig. 3.6), and pushing the ball through the center of the palm toward the hollow of the forearm. The resistance from the ball dissipates tension in the fingers but leaves the hand with a feeling of great strength. Refer to chapter 3, "Strength versus Tension."

42. Because of how far the hand extends and rotates away from the torso as it crosses or ascends the fingerboard, it may help to envision the elbow navigating the inside of a sphere (refer to fig. 1.5), actively carving a path that at first scoops slightly lower and away but then quickly higher up the sphere's inner wall as the hand ascends the scale. Refer to chapter 1, "Transporting the Hand."

43. During the final descent from first position E to the D string, imagine the fourth-finger edge of the upright hand pushing through clay to create a feeling of resistance during the hand's rotation from one string to the next. Refer to chapter 11, "The Home Position."

44. Now to fine-tune the micromotions within the hand, again using the first position E-to-D-string descent, first conjure up an image of a ball inside a hooded caster turned upside down. Visualize placing the hood part of a caster against the thumb and the large knuckles on top of the ball—which is cradled in the hood (see fig. 10.2). While staying in the same position on the same string, rotate the ball with the palm to transfer weight from one large knuckle to the next, in that way lending backup support around the thumb

to the articulation of each finger. Refer to chapter 10, "Thumb-to-Finger and Thumb-to-Palm Rotational Relationships."

45. If you notice that your fingers need more snap, visualize four strings running up along the back of the hand, one affixed to each of the four large knuckles, and four strings attached to the top of the second set of knuckles. To assist finger action, with your hand in playing position, envision someone simultaneously pulling a string attached to one of the large knuckles downward and one attached to the related second knuckle upward, and then releasing (see fig. 8.3). Alternating the pulling of the strings with the influence of gravity on the release allows the first segment to flex and extend more vigorously, in that way sending more power and precision to the point of articulation.

46. When lifting each finger, be careful to keep the fingers parallel with each other and the tips of the fingers in a nice alignment with the string. Then strike the string with the middle of the fingertip in such a way that the padding is equally apportioned on both sides of the string. Refer to chapter 8, "Finger Position."

47. Again, modifying a previous image, balance the finger laterally by imagining feet on either side of a bisecting line that splits the nail face in half. The feet (extending from each side of the fingertip) bolster a balanced connection of the fingertip to the string (see fig. 16.3). Refer to chapter 16, "Balancing the Hand."

48. When playing the scale, if the last or third segment of your finger is flapping, imagine leaning your fingernails against the constraint of the inner wall of a cylinder surrounding the string and move them up and down by guiding the small segment on the same trajectory each time. Refer to chapter 8, "Finger Position."

49. To further secure the strength of the finger and revitalize its buoyancy at the point of articulation, imagine flexing the finger into a square shape around an imaginary miniature ball (refer to fig. 16.4) before articulating the finger with the string.

50. You may find that you can provide backup support for the fingers by drawing strength from the large knuckles. When playing the scale, think of each large knuckle as a ball; then imagine bouncing that knuckle/ball off the string, in that way articulating each finger. The limited motion from the joints at the large knuckles in a flexed hand provides for a fast knuckle bounce, which translates into rapid articulations. Refer to chapter 6, "Knuckle Support for the Articulating Finger."

51. To effectively present each finger, envision the top of the wrist as a pedal similar to the one on a trash can. When you press down the pedal, the bottom of the hand rotates down and the metacarpal leaps forward, almost as if out of the palm, helping extend the finger before the now-cocked finger

can snap down onto the fingerboard from its heightened position. Refer to chapter 4, "Wrist and Finger Collaboration."

52. More elaborately, instead of thinking of each finger individually, roll your foot back and forth on the four imaginary pedals, tipping over and releasing the fingers with counterpressures from the wrist. Refer to chapter 4, "Wrist and Finger Collaboration."

53. To implement a plucking articulation, which requires a strengthening of the relationship of the finger to itself, visualize a miniature C-bar made from springlike material. Insert it inside the square of your flexed finger and then compress it; the C-bar's wanting to return to its original state supports the pluck and the fingers' return to a more relaxed, extended position. Refer to chapter 13, "Guiding Imagery Using the Violin String."

54. Now imagine wrapping a bungee cord around your wrist and lifting your hand from the loop (refer to fig. 11.18). Then experiment with touching down and running your fingers. The suspended hand tips weight toward the fingertips, providing greater facility. Use the up motion of the finger push-off to guide the hand's weight toward the next finger articulated. During rapid articulation, the motion is not preconceived; the fingers simply run. Refer to chapter 11, "Left-Hand Suspension."

55. To effectively distribute weight to the fingertips, imagine that the hand in playing position is hollow; then envision four metal balls, one inside each fingertip. As you glide your fingertips along the string, experience the smooth connection. Refer to chapter 7, "The Hand's Stabilization of the Fingers."

56. With your hand in an upright position, this time form a picture of a circular wire running inside the flexed hand, just above the large knuckles (an equator for the rounded hand). Wrap your upright thumb and the crease formed above the large knuckles of the fingers around the circular wire, and then lasso a string around the hand and underneath the large knuckles before tightening it (refer to fig. 8.6). The wire holds the round form inside the hand, and the lasso creates an environment where the natural state of the fingers is off the string. Refer to chapter 8, "Imagery That Supports Finger Rebound."

57. Imagine the fingertips pushing down on an actual string while the thumb (tip or small knuckle) pushes upward against an imaginary string that is parallel and to its left (refer to fig. 10.12). This image reinforces the compression between the thumb and fingertips and strengthens the fingers' ability to rebound while maintaining their respective independence.

58. To deepen the contact of your fingers with the string, aim your fingers for both the string played and the inner edge of the thumb (refer to fig. 10.5). Refer to chapter 10, "The Left-Hand Bow Hold." If the fingers lose their connection to the thumb or if the thumb disengages from the rest of the hand with a sensation of isolation below the fingerboard, the fingers can sink into the fingerboard and get bogged down. To avoid that, project your hand, thumb included, above the string played to support a more liberated and

coherent articulation. Also, imagine that the neck of the violin is round and sculpted with indentations, pathways for the fingers to travel. Refer to chapter 8, "A Dream."

This time, with your fingers flexed, imagine that the thumb is wider than in actuality, with this area now providing the fingers with a stable platform on which to balance during their articulation. Refer to chapter 7, "The Conjoining of the Fingers and Palm."

Whether your fingers aim for both the string played and the inner edge of the thumb or the string played and the widened platform of the thumb, each image provides a healthy sense of balance in the hand. Try them both and see if one works better than the other for you.

59. During the scale descent from fourth position to first, imagine someone using their fingers to lift the area between the elbow point and the triceps on the back of the arm upward and out (refer to fig. 1.7), causing the hand to catapult scroll direction. Because lifting the shoulder interrupts a healthy transfer of weight to the fingers, focus on relaxing your left shoulder.

    Next, think of the strings as guiding rails with which the thumb aligns and travels. On the repeat of the scale, notice how the thumb's rotational position reflects the position of the fingers on the string, with some adjustments providing support and others minimizing string access.

60. To more effectively ascend and descend the scale, explore the mechanics of the ever-changing configuration of the hand. Imagine that the left hand in home position is rolled up like a shade around the vertical thumb. As the hand ascends the scale, it begins to open, with the shade unrolling and stretching out until it is fully expanded; then it slowly retracts to its home position, with the thumb once more wrapped in the palm. Refer to chapter 14, "Combining Imagery for Left-Hand Support."

    When shifting, imagine a sensation of the back of your thumb leaning against and pivoting off the right side of the neck to support a healthy connection to the thumb's actual point of contact, the left or underside of the neck. Doing so allows the thumb to relax without falling away from the neck, and it thwarts the tendency to lean the finger side of the hand against the neck. Refer to chapter 10, "The Thumb's Suspension of the Fingers."

61. Now, imagine that the fingers and thumb of the cone-shaped hand form a coil (refer to fig. 11.19). When ascending the fingerboard, push the smaller first-finger end through the larger end. When descending the scale, reverse the direction of the cone with the smaller end at the fourth finger pushing through the now larger first-finger end to transport the hand down the fingerboard. Whether ascending or descending a scale, pushing the narrow end of the coil/fingers through its wider end propels the fingers to their new location without disrupting the shape of the hand.

    Similarly, form a tunnel in your left hand by flexing the fingers and opposing thumb. Then imagine a rubber barrier at the thumb and fourth finger end of the tunnel (refer to fig. 20.5) and envision slipping the rubber barrier around the scroll and neck. As the hand ascends the scale, the rubber barrier stretches, in that way creating a healthy resistance inside the hand. Then it retracts on the scale descent.

62. This time, approach the scale with three basic strategies. First, focus on the scale segments where the hand moves back and forth, first between the D and E string in first position. The hand can flex forward (toward the left side of the fingerboard), causing the fingers to expand accordingly, supporting D-string finger access, or fall back, with the fingers dropping naturally into the palm, positioning the fingers above the E string. Refer to chapter 4, "Optimum Wrist Placement." After descending the E string in the context of the full scale, relocate the hand across the fingerboard without disrupting the shape of the hand and fingers by catapulting from its bottom center to the D string. Refer to chapter 14, "Catapulting the Hand from the Bottom Center." Also refer to chapter 6, "Large Knuckle Movement in Tandem with the Wrist." Second, zero in on the shifts: the ascending and descending motion of the hand on the fingerboard. Notice whether any of the knuckles pop out of alignment during transport, disrupting the continuity. Refer to chapter 13, "Lateral Movement." Finally, connect primarily to the lifting and dropping of each finger without lowering the arm or dropping the hand in its entirety. Refer to chapter 6, "Knuckle Support for the Articulating Finger."

63. Next, play the scale while maintaining the circular shape of the hand's tunnel. You may find that you have greater success navigating the scale if you avoid leaning the hand against the neck. Refer to chapter 9, "Securing the Hand's Tunnel."

64. Akin to the pole used in pole vaulting (a lever), the thumb can launch the fingers from a lower beginning position over the top of the thumb/pole into a higher end position. So when playing a three-octave scale, first visualize an upright thumb placement midway between the scale's ends. Then imagine the reverse on the scale's descent, with the thumb/pole hurling the fingers from a higher to a lower position. Picture the fingers traveling on these arcing paths from one destination to another. Refer to chapter 10, "Thumb and Fingerboard Usage and Imagery."

65. Then imagine that the left hand is an octopus, with the palm as the body and the fingers as the legs. On ascending shifts, the hand travels above the seafloor of the fingerboard, with its concave underside leading the trailing fingers. And on the descent, the palm shape becomes more convex (as does the octopus when backing up). Refer to chapter 5, "Palm Pliability."

66. When drawing a downbow on the scale ascent, picture holding a beach ball under your right arm. Now imagine the volume of the ball expanding while drawing the bow. Press the ball into the body to counter the ball's expansion. This image supports a healthy bow-arm structure, reinforcing the arm's dynamic relationship both to itself and to its foundation in the torso while protecting the elbow from lateral flexing (improper sideways deviation).

An Expanded Approach to Scales and Arpeggios

67. Imagine placing a ball (approximately softball sized) filled with helium under the left arm to maintain a good upper arm position relative to the body. During the three-octave scale, the ball creates a healthy resistance, allowing the hand to catapult into higher positions and drop back without the upper arm collapsing against the torso. Refer to chapter 16, "The Shoulder."

68. Now imagine that the arm is the body of a snake and the hand is the head. Encasing the violin inside a cylinder, coil the inner arm from the biceps of the upper arm to the palm of the hand (the ventral or anterior aspect of the limb) around the cylinder, like the snake around a branch. Doing so presents the arm with a good balance of strength and flexibility while connecting to its fullest sensitivity. Refer to chapter 3, "Setting Up without Tension."

69. Imagine the elbows as wings flapping, in the process displacing a semi-solid density of matter in the areas either in between or surrounding the arms. Refer to chapter 19, "Integrating the Arms through Visualization."

70. Divide the right hand in half with a line that we'll call the spine, extending from the first-finger large knuckle to the lower outside corner (refer to fig. 9.7). Now imagine that your right hand is a bird, with a wing balance of the thumb on one side and the fingers on the other. When the hand ascends with the bow, feel the hand's spine rising and falling in response to natural fluctuations, as would the backbone of a bird. Refer to chapter 18, "The Right-Hand Spine."

71. With your mental state meditative, each hand is a winged bird; the body of the violin dissipates, with the fingers playing only to the string. Refer to chapter 21, "Two Hands Ascend."

72. Imagine your fingers bending the E string sideways (refer to fig. 13.4) to leverage a move to the A string and passing the string from one finger to another (during shifts). Just as raindrops (or tossed-in pebbles) displace molecules on a pond's surface, similarly displace the string barrier as you articulate notes. Refer to chapter 13, "Guiding Imagery Using the Violin String."

73. When you want to convey a surrendered or an almost ethereal mood of playing, contemplate in the imagination that your legs are the bole of a weeping willow and that your body drapes sideways and backward, like a branch or sprig hanging down (refer to fig. 22.15). Accordingly, your body responds to movement like the tremor of a swaying branch.

74. Now merge your tools as the combination of your arms, the bow, and the neck outline the shape of a butterfly (refer to fig. 19.29 and fig. 19.30). Refer to chapter 19, "Integrating the Arms through Visualization."

75. Finally, think only of the left-hand fingers and the contact point of the bow to the string. Refer to chapter 18, "Projecting the Sense of Touch."

The scale practice for the day is complete. In your practicing, remember that consistency is your best friend.

The Thumb's Role in Supporting the Fingers

The thumb travels the same route with an arpeggio as with its scale companion, only in fewer moves. Because those moves are less incremental and therefore more dynamic, the arpeggio is an effective template for demonstrating the thumb's involvement. In the framework of the three-octave C major arpeggio (see ex. 23.2), extend the elbow to assist an upright placement of the forearm in second position, making it easier to balance the hand on top.

Example 23.2 Three-octave C major arpeggio.

With the thumb and fingers forming a tunnel, think of the neck as an axle running through its center (refer to fig. 11.13) and use the tip of your thumb to pivot the hand. Imagine affixing a string to the thumb tip so that when you pull the string toward the floor, the hand flips around the neck/axle centered inside the hand's tunnel to a position on top of the instrument. If, while directing the fingertips via the tip of the thumb, the hand folds or the knuckles collapse, the thumb loses its ability to direct the fingers and steers the fingers out of control. When playing second-position C-natural on the G string (as well as the note E in the arpeggio), draw the string downward, which lowers your thumb and positions your fingers above the G string. Release the thumb upward in increments to sink the fingers, positioning them above the D string (for the G note) and then above the A string (for the C). To complete the remaining second and third octaves of the arpeggio—the notes, E-natural, and G on the A string, and C, E, G, C on the E string—pull the thumb string down again, rotating the hand up and over the top of the violin. On the descent, allow the hand to drop back under the instrument into second position for the E-string notes, C-natural and G (with the thumb elevated again). Then pull the thumb string downward in increments, with the hand's spine cooperating by lifting the fingers to articulate with the A and D string enroute to the G, this dual awareness assisting the arpeggio's second-position E-to-G-string descent. To support a rapid descent, as the hand approaches the top of the arpeggio and the fingers are articulating the final notes, the elbow is at least anticipating or perhaps even beginning its turnaround.

CHAPTER TWENTY-FOUR

Mental Training and *Progressive Form*

On rocky terrain, your body is a responsive medium of navigation. Consider the musical life an inspirational journey into your natural disposition.

The Visually Balanced Violinist

As in the case of an athlete who gains an edge from mentally training without being in physical motion, so too is mental training integral to a musician's advancement. A classic example from athletics is the system developed by the Soviets, described in *Peak Performances: Mental Training Techniques of the World's Greatest Athletes* by Charles A Garfield, as a combination of mental training and hands-on practice. Our playing can similarly benefit from sitting in a chair with eyes closed, recreating the physical sensations and visual images of playing a passage, a scale, or even an entire piece.

Images in this book can be incorporated directly into your hands, even just approximations while reading. The main objective of this practice session, however, is to reaffirm your tactile connection to the violin using Progressive Form's system solely in the imagination, reinforcing technique for the actual playing. The following exercise recalls some of the images from the earlier chapters to build a vivid picture designed to inform the musculature. Try these and then experiment by creating your own.

To begin, sit in a chair with your feet flat on the floor, shoulder width apart. Place your hands on your lap, palms facing up, and then visualize standing with your feet similarly spread apart. Lift your left and right arms, each from their respective presentation points. Poise your left forearm as if it were a vertical pole and then place your elbow on an imaginary pogo stick at a level high enough to suspend both ends of the arm—the hand and shoulder. With emphasis on your left side, place a giant imaginary ball underneath the violin, the ball fully supporting the violin without impeding the left- or right-arm motions.

To experience the sensation of migrating the hand into position to play, think of the rotation as distributed between the hand and the arm as a whole. Envision a tunnel along the width—just inside the crease—of the wrist; then run a taut string through the opening (refer to fig. 7.14). Lifting the string drags the base of the palm up toward the fingers. The tightened string assists the palm in supporting the articulating fingers. While continuing these sensations, imagine that the violin is in your left hand; feel an ease of moving despite—even through—the neck as you articulate a descending, same-position scale. Trust that this approach will lend greater comfort to your playing.

Because the ultimate objective is for the fingers to fire easily, unimpeded in all positions, it helps to envision a vertical forearm position with your hand poised on top, free to make any playing motion. While maintaining that relaxed balance, articulate the notes on each string and within each tier of the scale in an optimal zone of comfort, always referencing that singular position of balanced neutrality. Afterward, when you practice with the instrument in hand, attempt to recreate that same feeling in the various locations on the fingerboard. Once you've achieved a peaceful sense of balance with the hand, transfer that feel and degree of finger stability to each segment of the scale while noticing the connection of the active fingers to the hand, wrist, forearm, elbow, and upper arm.

Imagine affixing an eye screw to the center of each palm and connecting the ends of an elastic string to each eye screw. Then in your mind's eye, see a vertical pole attached to the bridge with a (horizontal) pulley on top that guides the elastic around the pole, with the elastic forming an L shape (refer to fig. 22.14). Experience the relationship between the left and right hands and the subtle response of the concave and convex motion of each palm's center as they alternately pull and release each other.

On a scale ascent, imagine poking your thumb through the center of the neck (in between the D and A strings), bringing your thumb closer to the fingertips, with that close connection supporting finger speed (refer to fig. 7.15). Rather than consciously thinking of going over the top of the violin in the transition from third to fourth position, project the bottom of the hand on top of the E string first and then simply catapult the hand into a position where the fingers can drop easily.

Considering the substantial musculature that flexes the thumb toward various parts of the hand and fingers, all together biasing the fingers to their radial (thumb) side, experiment with articulating the fingers first from their radial side, then from their ulnar side, and finally from the middle of the finger. The articulating motions are usually most efficient when initiating motion from its radial side (refer to fig. 8.1), using backup support from the thumb, so imagine articulating each note of a scale with that emphasis.

Imagine the thumb as the contact point of support for the instrument's weight, sharing the job with the collarbone and with pressure into the neck. Without moving your fingers, experience the thumb's changing contact with the neck as it migrates along the path of a three-octave scale. Sense how the various aspects of the thumb cradle and balance the neck without holding on. Practice moving your fingers up and down to articulate notes with a sense of the large knuckles assisting in this process, at the same time staying conscious of your palm moving horizontally, maintaining a steadfast height.

Now picture an elastic band with one end attached to your elbow and the other to the back of your hand (refer to fig. 6.5). When the fingers are flexing toward the string, the restoring force of the rubber band urges the back of the hand upward, in that way dissuading the palm from dropping with the fingers to the point of articulation.

Experience the base of the palm energetically hugging the neck in all its rotations, and feel the liberating effect of its cozy support on the up and down motion of the fingers. Feel the weight of the large knuckles above the string played and how they lend backup support to the articulating fingers without creating a disruption of form.

On a scale descent, as the palm rotates clockwise for a need to engage the third or fourth finger, imagine a weight inside your first fingertip that does not allow it to lift fully off the string. Feel its stabilizing effect on all other fingers during descending shifts.

On a scale ascent, experience a sensation of the thumb and first finger tunnel formation catching or carrying your fourth-finger large knuckle in its center space. Ignore the presence of the neck and focus only on the hand's interaction with itself.

During the hand's ascent, observe in your mind's eye the scroll easing to the left, and on the descent, notice the scroll easing toward the right. In parallel, your hand and arm come in closer to your body in the higher positions and extend in the lower positions. When in first position and ascending from the D string to the E, think only of the sweeping motion of the fingertips during the hand's rotation. When catapulting from third position to fourth, feel the bottom of your hand direct the fingertips up and over the top of the violin. Once you have completed the ascent, descend back into first position on the E string. When in first position and descending from the E string to the D, imagine balancing the palm and fingertips on a snowboard. With heel and fingertips tight to the board, leap up and bounce the midpoint of the board off the string played, with the fingertips and heel staying with each other in the same plane and at the same angle to the string. The bottom center of the board aims for the D string destination as if the neck and other two strings (the E and the A) are nonexistent.

Envision yourself suspended on a horizontal axis, the spindle passing through the front of the body and intercepting your body's center of gravity just under the navel (refer to fig. 22.3), allowing rotation in the frontal plane like a pinwheel. When you imagine a different horizontal axis penetrating the center of gravity through the side of the body (refer to fig. 22.4), the rotation is in the plane of a head nod or formal, full-body bow. When a vertical line this time spears your body through the top of the head (refer to fig. 22.5), the body spins around it clockwise or counterclockwise in the horizontal plane. Finally, consider all the possible angles among these three fundamental axes, imagining all possible playing positions.

Visualization and the Bow Arm

The Bach Preludio presents a wide range of bowing challenges that can be generalized to apply broadly to the violin repertoire. Through mental practice using Progressive Form imagery, your right hand becomes a mime, dynamically expressing the full range of (e)motions in a dance, responding with appropriate gestures to all of its

Integration

required transitions. Sit in a chair again with eyes closed and imagine standing. This time, think only of the right arm. Place the facedown hand and forearm on a tilted platform with its angle shifting weight toward the fingertips. The board supports a continuous, even distribution of weight across the forearm that sustains a proper hand-arm formation (see fig. 17.1). Initiate the lift from the presentation point and then extend and direct your right arm forward and around your body as if to rest the energized forearm on a chest-high shelf out in front. Envision inserting an imaginary hinge into the back of your upper arm, several inches above the elbow (refer to fig. 19.1), with the hinge creating the feeling of a crook or second elbow to assist the arm in positioning itself out in front of the body. With it, you have more degrees of freedom in your arm, newly discovered elements that can be transmuted into forms of energy (weight, momentum, impulse) fed to the bow.

Play through the Bach Preludio from memory, first using the martelé stroke. On the downbow, feel the forearm's inner arrow hooking onto the string. Then as you draw the bow, you are also dragging the string. At the end of the downbow, anticipate how the hand leads with the second set of knuckles. Collaborating at that point with the restoring force of the string, fire the knuckles into the underside of the violin on the upbow. Imagine moving the position of the bow between the bridge and fingerboard in response to the change in sounding points proposed by the left-hand fingers.

Now imagine playing twelve measures of the bariolage starting at m.17 from memory (see ex. 24.1). First, hang your right arm over an imaginary horizontal pole, with the pole supporting your arm just beyond the elbow, leaving your forearm relaxed and buoyant (refer to fig. 19.3). Your fingers reach down from above. Then feel an imaginary axle cutting through the frog and held between your thumb and middle finger. In a moderato tempo, navigate the three strings by lifting the axle up and down with the frog rotating on the axle. The axle image allows bow rotation without disrupting the balance or shape of the hand.

Example 24.1 Bach's Preludio, mm. 17–28.

To handle the rapid string crossings, think of a rubber screw jutting out from the wall approximately chest high. At the place on the lateral edge of the arm closest to the balance point, press the arm against the screw (refer to fig. 19.24); then rotate the arm on that screw, with the forearm (knuckles to elbow) seesawing up and down. Despite being required to negotiate some rotation in the upper arm to support this motion, the elbow nevertheless remains poised above the D string.

Imagine drawing figure-eight-shaped loops in the air to represent the motions in the passage, all the same size. Informed by this observation, do not allow yourself to shrink the size of the circle or the motion of the bow stroke during the multiple string crossings simply because of fatigue or lack of concentration. The initiation is similar to pushing a swing: once the stroke is established, there is a certain sweet spot of balance you can find that gives you the efficiency and reliability of a pendulum. Add a second bow, frogs overlapping, this new one extending to the right of the other to help even out the stroke. By inserting a common axle, the imaginary bow mirrors the movements of the real bow. Navigate the three strings by lifting the axle up and down (refer to fig. 19.27 and fig. 19.28), with the two sticks flapping down and up like the wings of a bird.

This time, use detaché to increase the speed of the stroke, first by shortening the stroke itself and then by imagining a shortening of the arm while shrinking the length of the bow (imagine two poles, with one sliding inside the other). During this transition, use the image of the single bow in holding the axle while maintaining the elbow's suspension above the D string.

After the arm transitions from bariolage to the single-string passage, unless there is an even distribution of weight across the forearm, the forearm can't effectively fishtail side to side for the five-note sequence that follows on the D (see ex. 24.2). To transition the angle of the forearm from crossing strings to playing on one string (the D), after playing the last note of m.28 (tilted), picture bouncing the bones of the forearm at the balance point off the imaginary surface of a ball to restore the forearm's balance, which in turn stabilizes the hand. The hand is then able to fishtail easily on the level plane of the D string. Picture the bow hair as being tucked underneath the feet of the bridge to deepen your tone along with a feeling of suspending the violin (refer to fig. 22.16).

Example 24.2 Bach's Preludio, m.28 into m.29.

In m.78 the forearm is angled to include the A string. When transitioning from m.78 to m.79 (see ex. 24.3), the arm again reestablishes center balance and then fishtails the next five notes on the G string. In the remainder of the piece, it is helpful to

Example 24.3 Bach's Preludio, mm.78–79.

direct your focus to the fleshy part of the fingers at the tip and sense how the fingers feel against the movement of the bow, with the frog end of the bow propelling the point, just as rear-wheel drive propels a car. Now visualize that, akin to a needle, the string has an eye, so you can thread the eyes with the bow.

The last time through your dream practice, play the Preludio using a spiccato stroke. Recollect making your right hand into a sphere, curving it around a ball that is smaller than your rounded hand. On the downbow, your palm bounces against the ball (refer to fig. 20.2), and then the ball rebounds off the floor of the fingers and back into the palm (refer to fig. 20.3). Now release the ball visualization and imagine a circular indentation into the center base of the right hand. Slide the hand (palm down) onto a vertical pole projecting up from a platform; then fishtail the knuckles side to side (refer to fig. 20.8 and fig. 20.9). The first-finger large knuckle pushes the fourth-finger large knuckle via the knuckles in between, or the fourth-finger large knuckles pushes in reverse.

Toward the end, visualize that the right hand is a ball suspended on a rotisserie and that the spit running through the center of the tunnel formed by the flexed fingers and opposing thumb is the bow. Chuck the bow through the tunnel, one way or the other, propelling the full mass of the bow in a balanced format. Then imagine a rubber barrier at the thumb and fourth finger end of the tunnel that can catch and rebound the bow, the effect of which is to reduce the effort in long passages (refer to fig. 20.4 and fig. 20.5).

In mental training, you can practice without the intrusion of your own physical limitations and those of the instrument. The body can be fluid and the instrument ghostlike. And when necessary, gravity can become a nonfactor. At this point, trust that your body is aligned and balanced in relation to the violin, and release all semblance of structure.

Picture concentric circles on the fingerboard, and then while vibrating, plant your finger in the center of each to feel each finger joint dancing in circles. Sense either the motion of one finger or two motions side by side.

Ponder the existence of one note and then create a universe out of a passage. Or in your imagination, experience rain pounding on you and the pavement; then articulate your fingers on the fingerboard with similar, inevitable force—the wind carrying the rain, the sound of patter, and the quiet hum of a melody.

Visualize a galaxy with each ball—held in the flexed finger, in the palm, along the inside of the arm, under the upper arm, all the others—expanding and contracting, pumping life into your playing. Refer to chapter 16, "Rotational Interactions of the Arm and Hand." The structures dissolve, and your arms now embrace matter with the texture of quicksand, with your left-hand fingers moving to and fro, the wake of each action dissipating from sight.

To add buoyancy to the articulating finger, envision four tiny feet growing out of the bottom of your left hand, each foot corresponding to one of the four fingers above (refer to fig. 4.5). Picture a bungee cord wrapped around your (upright) hand just below the large knuckles; then suspend the bottom of your hand above the fingerboard. The feet, barely able to reach, kick off from the fingerboard, pushing the bottom of the hand up and onto the foot underneath the next finger to be articulated. Then that foot pushes the hand onto the next one, and so on. Step by step, the feet reposition the hand, creating continuity between the last finger articulated and the next.

While channeling the energy of your entire body into the fingertips, soar with the bow and fingers along arcing paths among destinations. Imagine that the notes in a piece of music are rubber balls, with the size of each ball determined by the note's length and its significance within the structure of a passage or phrase. Imagine each ball has the capacity to rotate on the string in the area between the fingerboard and the bridge (refer to fig. 20.7). Because a smaller ball spins more quickly than a larger one, envision a rubber-haired bow spinning smaller-sized balls that are quicker notes and rotating larger-sized balls that are longer notes. Spin each ball with the bow, applying weight and adjusting speed as needed. Sculpt tone, and then release it to the listener.

Appendixes

Appendix A

A fuller understanding of the relationship of the radius to the ulna is especially helpful for anyone without naturally good mechanics. The radius and ulna are the two parallel bones of the forearm. At the elbow the radius, on the thumb side, is the less prominent bone. And on the fourth-finger side, the ulna comprises most of what meets the humerus to form the elbow. The movement of the radius contributes the axial rotation of the wrist and hand, and it broadens at the far (distal) end to support the wrist and lend a solid platform to fingers one and two. The near (proximal) end of the ulna forms a hinge joint with the humerus, so it alone is involved with the flexing and extending of the elbow. The thinner distal end of the ulna at the wrist lends back-up support to fingers three and four.

The supinator is a muscle wrapped around the lower part of the radius, just beyond the elbow. In conjunction with the biceps in most cases, the supinator assists the turning up of the palm into playing position (supination).

Appendix B

In addition to eliminating a great deal of tension in the left arm, a feel for rotating the hand from the thumb side supports an awareness of a continuum of connection that runs along the sensitive, anterior aspect of the body from pectoral muscles to biceps to anterior surface of forearm to palm, altogether suggesting an embracing or cradling of the instrument. As a counterpoint to initiating motion from the inside out (an active function), this particular awareness invites the outside in (a receptive response). When setting up the left hand into playing position, start with an easy, balanced verticality and present the open palm in a simple gesture that keeps the supportive musculature of the torso and arm relaxed. Avoid any distortion and tension along the anterior continuum to keep the myriad sensory and motor (motion) connections alive and optimally available.

Appendix C

One end of the humerus is an enlargement, a ball that fits into the shoulder socket. The other end articulates with the forearm at the elbow. The latissimus dorsi (the lats) are large trunk muscles that attach in the back, wrap around the sides, and then insert on the head of the humerus to assist many arm movements.

Appendix D

The serratus anterior is a fan-shaped muscle, each of which originates on the superolateral (the angled top of the side) surface of the first to the eighth or ninth ribs. They insert mostly along the medial border (closest to the spine) on the anterior side of the shoulder blade (scapula). The serratus anterior assists with respiration by raising the ribs and conversely acts to pull the scapula forward around the thorax. Other muscles involved with arm movement include the biceps, triceps, coracobrachialis, pectoralis major, and deltoids, as well as the rotator group at the shoulder, especially the underestimated subscapularis.

Appendix E

For the purposes of violin playing, the forearm functions optimally with a fundamental orientation of the wrist and elbow in which horizontal lines representing flexion at the wrist and elbow are parallel and a line that bisects those two lines also bisects the forearm and the upper arm longitudinally. That framework, where the segments of the arm and hand are in alignment and from which the hand angles off minimally, is a configuration of both strength and relaxation, and it optimizes the continuous, sensitive connection along the anterior aspect of the arm and hand.

Appendix F

The forearm is a lever with the elbow as a fulcrum, and then there is a larger lever of the arm from the shoulder. Technically speaking, each is a third-class lever with the effort applied in between the fulcrum (the shoulder or the elbow) and the load (the arm or forearm). Awareness of the muscular forces that move the full arm and the forearm helps our understanding of arm extensions and rotations that are relevant to both sides of violin playing.

Appendix G

The hand is wonderfully complex with many joints that allow flexion and extension, adduction and abduction, and many others. Most of the movements with either hand that we make in violin playing involve intricate combinations of many motions across multiple joints that change, moment to moment. Together they constitute nuanced and powerful relationships of the hands to the bow and the violin.

Appendix H

Incorporating the thumb's metacarpal into the consideration of its motions is important in many ways for the full functioning of the hand. Those include strength and support through using the full frame of the hand, as well as freedom and relaxation through the proper use of the hand as designed.

Appendix I

When performing, the body is alive and in flux, and just as the beating heart communicates with the brain and body, the pulsating fingers awaken the voice of the violin, in turn supporting our heart connection to the instrument. Even though the heart transmits information through the transport systems of the body, it has been demonstrated that the heart's intelligence is autonomous. In fact, if you isolate heart cells and place them in a petri dish, they pulsate on their own.

Appendix Diagrams

Bones of the Upper Extremities

The relationship of the radius to the ulna is one of the body's most intriguing configurations, and an awareness of its mechanics is helpful in securing good formation and application of the left arm and hand. The ulna forms a hinge joint with the humerus of the upper arm, and then the radius has the ability to rotate the hand clockwise or counterclockwise, that range of motion contributing to carrying the fingers to their fingerboard destinations while minimizing arm distortion (see fig. A.1).

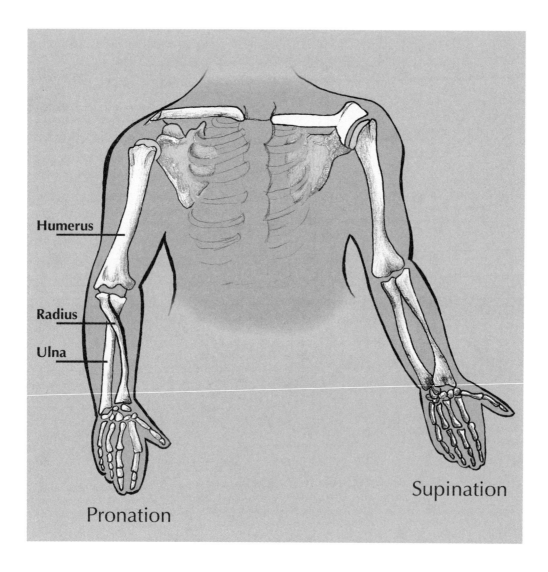

Bones of the Hand

The complex mechanics involving the hand's hard and soft tissues are eclipsed only by the sophisticated sensory and motor functions of its nervous wiring. The following chart exhibits the bony framework (see fig. A.2).

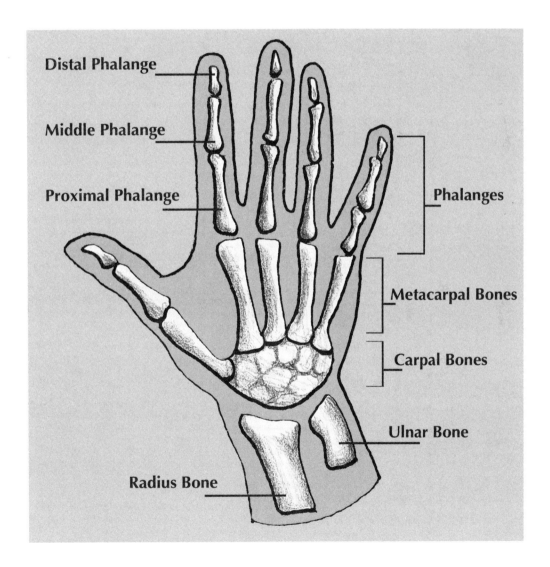

Appendixes

Planes and Directions

The human body develops in spirals, so with most motions involving rotations at multiple joints, rarely does it make sense to describe them as taking place in a single plane. The anatomical planes are a useful reference, however, because they form the framework for movement descriptions (see fig. A.3).

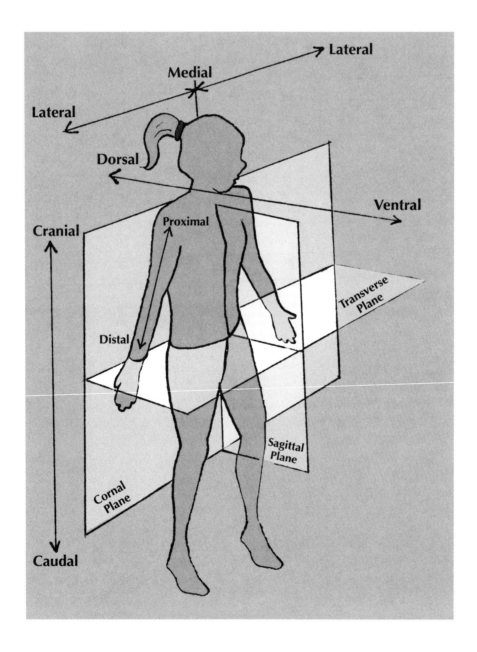

Glossary

abduction movement of a limb away from the midline of the body.

adduction movement of a limb toward from the midline of the body.

anatomical plane an abstract flat surface transecting the body used to describe position and motion (*see* appendix diagram A.3).

anatomical position standing posture with arms hanging and palms forward.

axis a line (one-dimensional) around which a rotating body turns.

carpal bones eight small bones that comprise the wrist and bridge the hand and forearm.

center balance the most naturally efficient configuration of a body part in a particular context.

cervical spine seven cylindrical bones (vertebrae) located between the skull and the thoracic vertebrae.

clavicle the collarbone; each one articulates with the sternum midchest and also with the scapula to form the shoulder girdle, often considered the first segment of the upper limb.

compressions combinations of forces exerted from the periphery either naturally or deliberately that collectively create a framework of strength and coherence.

distal farther from a reference point, often the center of the body (*see* proximal).

distal phalanges the bones that are the last segment of each finger.

dorsal/posterior the back of the body in anatomical position.

extension a movement that increases the angle between two body parts.

femur the leg bone extending from the pelvis to the knee.

flexion a bending movement that decreases the angle at a joint.

frontal (or coronal) plane a vertical plane running from side to side, dividing front from back.

fulcrum the point on which a lever rests and on which it pivots (*see* lever).

gravity the force that gives weight to objects. Becoming more conscious of weight is useful in negotiating our bodies with the instrument.

humerus the large bone of the upper arm, forming joints with the clavicle and scapula at the shoulder and with the ulna at the forearm.

lateral (external) rotation rotation away from the midline of the body (*see* medial rotation).

lever a rigid bar resting on a pivot (fulcrum) that helps move a heavy load on one end when pressure is applied to the other.

Glossary

leverage mechanical advantage gained with the use of a lever (*see* lever).

longitudinal on the long axis of the body or a body part.

lumbar spine five large spinal vertebrae located between the rib cage and the pelvis.

medial (internal) rotation rotation toward the midline of the body (*see* lateral rotation).

medial phalanges the middle bones of the four fingers.

metacarpal bones the cylindrical bones inside the palm.

pelvis the basin of bones in the lower trunk connected to the sacrum in back and the legs laterally.

plane a flat two-dimensional surface.

potential energy energy stored within a system. Think of a roller coaster accumulating energy while climbing higher, reaching its maximum potential at the very top of the hill.

pronation turning the palm down and away in the bow hand.

proximal closer to a reference point, often the center of the body (*see* distal).

proximal phalanges the finger bones that articulate with the palm at each metacarpal.

radius the bone on the lateral (thumb) side of the forearm; the radius contributes to the rotation of the wrist and hand.

restoring force a force that tends to return an object that has been stretched or compressed back toward some lower energy position. Elastic is a particularly apt image because of the elasticity of our soft tissue.

sacrum the triangular bone in the low back between the two hip bones.

sagittal (or longitudinal) plane a vertical plane running from front to back, dividing left from right.

scapula the shoulder blade and the clavicle's partner in the shoulder girdle (*see* clavicle).

solid a geometric or physical body existing in three dimensions.

supination turning the palm up in the bow hand or the left hand in playing position.

suprasternal situated above the sternum (breastbone).

thoracic spine twelve bones/vertebrae of the thorax, each articulating with a rib on each side.

tibia the larger and more prominent bone between the knee and the ankle.

transverse perpendicular to a longitudinal line, such as a cross-section of the forearm.

transverse (or axial) plane a horizontal plane dividing upper from lower body parts.

ulna the bone on the medial (pinky) side of the forearm that forms the elbow joint with the humerus.

ventral/anterior the front of the body in anatomical position.

Index

Abduction, 36, 37, 191, 300, 305
Active flexion, 50, 89, 91, 99, 141, 172
Adduction, 36, 37, 51, 300, 305
Anterior serratus, 22
Arc/curvature: arcing path of shifting hand, 54, 114, 145, 147, 151; bow stroke arc, 249, 250; contour of bridge and wrist, 196; fixed-elbow forearm motion, 15; thumb curvature, 98
Anatomical planes. *See under* Planes
Arm rotation: bow arm, 222–224; left arm, 8, 118; side arm, 225–226
Articulation: efficiency, 68–69, 87–88, 88–89, 107, 158, 159; finger action, 65–66, 84, 86–87, 90–92; heel support, 42; metacarpal support, 40–41; palm fluidity, 52–53; press-release touch, 179; restoring hand balance, 184
Axes: horizontal axes for the left hand, 101, 125, 145; horizontal axis for the frog, 227; long axis of violin, 7, 270; longitudinal axis of bow hold, 205, 206; neck as axis for legato bowing, 238; rotational axis for vibrating fingers, 183; spine of the lower outside corner, 134; three axes of rotation, 259–260, 293; vertical axis for bow stroke, 222; vertical axis of bow hold, 206; vertical axis of the left hand, 75, 112–113
Axle: avoiding axial rotation of the ulna, 20; bow arm as, 223, 224; frog rotating on, 227, 228, 294, 295; neck as, 98, 99, 290; tunnel of thumb and fingers as, 290; wheel, 112, 222

Bach, Johann Sebastian, works of: Partita No. 3 in E Major, Preludio, 143, 149, 195, 196, 204, 206, 208, 213, 227, 228, 229, 231, 242, 243, 245, 248, 249, 294, 295, 296; Sonata No. 2 in A minor, Fuga, 87, 200, 224, 251, 252; Sonata No. 2 in A minor, Grave, 75, 232
Balance: body, 259; bow arm, 233; bow hand, 205–206, 251; bow hold horizontal dimension, 209; bow hold vertical dimension, 209; core and arms, 17; finger, 70–71, 125; forearm and hand, 18; forearm lateral balance, 189; forearm longitudinal balance, 190–91; home position, 132; left hand, 50, 75, 95, 113, 168; lower outside corner, 132; octave fingers, 20; thumb and fingers, 94, 104; thumb to palm, 121
Balance point: capabilities, 192, 196; fundamentals, 192–194; location, 190; secondary balance point, 194; string crossings, 194–195
Ball. *See* Sphere/ball
Bariolage. *See* Crossing strings, right hand
Beethoven, Ludwig van, works of: Symphony No. 9, Movement II, 89; Symphony No. 9, Movement IV, 210, 236; Violin Concerto in D Major, Rondo, 150
Biceps: balancing arm and hand, 23, 24; energizing sound, 180; holding the violin 34, kinesthetic sense of the arm, 13; supporting the bow arm, 247; supporting vibrating fingers, 172, 174

Bilaterality: of the hand, 95; of the limbs, torso, neck, and head, 264

Bow hair: under bridge feet image, 270, 271, 295; at the frog, 234, 236; in middle to upper half, 234, 247; with a rubber strip, 237–238; to spin bicycle wheels, 219–220; with treadmill image, 246

Bow hold: autonomy, 231; chord progressions, 206; comparison with left hand, 106–107, 116–117; fingers balances, 208–209, 210, 211; four corners, 236; relaxed control, 245–246; right-hand spine, 206

Bow rotation, 226–227, 294

Bow stroke: bow changes, 191, 198, 205–206, 210; bridge and bow stroke curves, 251; detaché, 239; downbow, 193–194, 196, 198–199; fishtail motion, 192–193, 196; four-note chord bow stroke, 251; functional lengths, 223–224; legato, 237–238; longer strokes, 198–199; martelé, 232; quicker strokes, 195; right-arm suspension, 215; single-motion down-up, 196; spiccato, 234, 236; upbow, 198–199

Brahms, Johannes, Violin Concerto in D Major: Movement I, 26, 44, 152, 169, 224, 229, 235, 263, 268; Movement II, 245

Bridge: bridge feet mirroring real feet, 3, 269; drawbridge image, 155; lifting bridge feet, 270, 271, 295; playing to bridge feet, 247; scroll to bridge range, 14, 35, 38, 39, 144, 164, 185; suspension bridge image, 4, 217

Bruch, Max, *Scottish Fantasy*: Movement I, 12, 211, 239; Movement II, 54

Buoyancy/rebound: in the arm, 273; in articulating fingers, 64, 91–92, 135–136, 159, 161–162, 163, 165–166, 170, 171, 173, 179, 182; in the bow arm, 196, 199, 215, 216, 232, 234–235, 241, 272; in the hand, 56, 113–114, 125, 128, 131, 148, 163; in the palm, 54

Caprice No. 5 in A minor (Paganini), 24, 143

Caprice No. 7 (Kreutzer), 233

Caprice No. 15 (Kreutzer), 167

Caprice No. 24 in A minor (Paganini): Variation 3, 107; Variation 5, 108; Variation 7, 155

Carnival of the Animals (Saint-Saëns), Finale, 148

Center balance: of the body, 259, 305; of the fingers, 70; of the left hand, 51, 70, 75, 95, 111, 113, 251; of the right arm, 295; of the right hand, 251

Center of gravity: of the body, 259–261, 293; of the forearm, 4, 190–191; of the hand, 159

Chakras, 274

Chords: double-stop shifts, 96, 145; four-note chord bow strokes, 251–252; left hand, 87–88, 94–95, 132, 156; off-the-string strokes, 235; scooping motion, 251

Clavicle, 7, 264, 305, 306

Collarbone. *See* Clavicle

Compressions: arm, 172–173; cross-body, 268–269; dynamic balance, 50; elbow to palm, 266; forearm to hand four-way, 266; full body, 270; hand, 90, 91, 103, 114, 162; torso to arms, 257; trilling, 163, 165–167; vibrato, 185

Concerto for Piano and Orchestra in A minor (Grieg), Movement III, 241

Concerto No. 1 in D Major (Paganini), Movement I, 184, 199, 206

Concerto No. 4 in D Major, K. 218 (Mozart), Movement I, 19, 103, 109, 130, 141, 142, 143, 208

Containment: of the arm, 217; of the fingers, 64; of the torso, 261

Continuity/engagement: coiling gradually in ascending shifts, 11; core to periphery, 16, 21–22, 212, 257–258; forearm and upper arm, 27; forearm to hand, 18, 20, 39; initiating arm movement, 21–23; lateral rotation of the arm, 30, 118; progressively finer contractions, 29; shifting hand's continuous morphing, 141; torso to fingers, 10–11

Control. *See* Freedom/control

Counterrotation, 195

Crossing strings, bow arm: bariolage, 195, 208, 213, 225–226; counterrotations, 194–195; inner walls, 221; lower string orientation, 242; multiple string crossing, 213

Crossing strings, left hand: gradual full-arm rotation, 30; heel to fingertip balance, 58; leading with the wrist, 46; navigating a sphere, 10; rotating on an axis, 126

Deconstruction: body image, 3; left hand, 95

Detaché, 239

Dexterity. *See* Speed/dexterity

Directing point: for the left arm, 22, 23, 75, 277; for the right arm, 212

Double stops. *See* Chords

Downbow, 193–194, 196, 198–199

Dvořák, Antonín, String Quartet No. 12 in F Major, Op. 96 (*American Quartet*), Finale, 71

Dysfunction: decreasing full-body tension through posture, 16, 258, 261; deviated hinge joint, 20, 28, 218, 288; injury prevention, 20; joint dysplasia, 28; proper rotation of the hand on the forearm, 118; reducing strain in the joints, 30

Elasticity/pliability: of the arm, 13; of the hand, 48, 75; in the palm, 52–53, 96, 147, 172, 210. *See also* Restoring force

Elbow (joint): active flexion, 29–30, 172; the arm playing into itself, 28, 217; coordination with the wrist, 14; hinge mechanics, 20; radial rotation, 20; second elbow, 17, 212, 293–294; upper-arm-to hand balance, 23

Elbow (point): arm elevation, 8, 16, 33; arm rotation, 8; arm stability, 19, 14, 147–148, 244; lateral and longitudinal motion, 14, 20; lateral motion, 9; leading with the elbow point, 10; longitudinal motion, 9, 10, 12; supporting the hand, 66, 110; torso support of the elbow, 21–22, 136; upper arm support of the elbow, 21; weight transference to the fingers, 115, 203–204, 215–216

Elbow flexor. *See* Biceps

Elevation: of the left arm, 9, 21, 22, 29, 118; of the left fingers, 92, 98, 279; of the left hand, 73; of the left knuckles, 63, 151; of the left palm, 58, 83, 160, 162, 165; of the lower outside corner, 166; of the right arm, 213; of the right forearm, 196; of the upper body, 271

Endurance. *See* Stamina/endurance

Energy. *See* Readiness/energy

Fingerboard: aiming fingers through, 180; articulation with, 179, 236; balance of hand weight, 39–40, 57, 58; finger's relationship to, 23, 55, 64–65, 74, 82–83, 84, 86, 89; finger-to palm connection, 90; forearm's relationship to, 18, 281, 302; heel placement, 41; height of hand, 23, 55, 57, 123, 159; moving walkway, 35; palm weight, 128; projecting hand above, 48, 53; proximity of hand, 21; sinking into the fingerboard, 56; supporting platform for, 4, 31, 65; 108, 132, 134, 136; wrist navigation, 36, 37; wrist placement, 42–43

Fingernail: left hand, 72, 79, 84, 85, 142, 285; right hand, 208

Finger pad, 79, 85, 142, 144, 164, 285

Fingertips: balance in bow hold, 209; balance of, 70, 71, 76, 159; balance with heel, 57; balance with knuckles 66–67, 174, 175–178; balance with palm, 168–170; conjoining with wrist motion, 37, 39–40; drawing to the hand, 32; energy sent to, 274; engaging with the palm, 68, 80, 90, 157, 163; gravity, 127; leading with padded or nail side, 79; motion in bow hold, 211; placement/proximity, 77, 78; positioning/aiming 85, 148; rebound, 9, 92; relationship with thumb, 81, 85, 94–95, 98, 99, 102–103, 104, 106–107, 109, 111, 114–115, 150, 161, 178; supporting rapid articulation, 72; transferring weight to, 4, 26, 58, 64–65, 74–75, 137, 143, 159, 172, 205, 206–207, 218; using weight in shifting, 146

Fishtail motion: forearm/balance point, 14, 192–193, 196, 241 295; knuckles, 240–241, 296; wrist and hand, 193–194

Flesch, Carl, *Urstudien (Basic Studies) for Violin*, Exercise 1C, 88

Flexing fingers: left hand, 64–65, 84–85, 86, 158–159, 162; right hand, 210–211

Forearm (left): comfort zone in fourth position, 18; continuity with the hand, 20; fixed elbow motion, 15; integration with hand, 18; leading with the radius, 20; rotating the hand, 20; strength, 31–32; support for the hand, 19

Forearm (right): bending in all three planes, 192; compression with hand, 239; deconstructing, 194; lateral balance, 189; longitudinal balance, 190–191

Form/configuration: aligned arm and hand frames, 27, 28, 29; bow hand configuration, 203, 205, 213, 218, 231, 236–237, 239; bridge and bow stroke curves, 251; chords, 156; circular hand tunnel, 121; coherent frame of the palm, 50, 62, 100, 103, 137, 184; finger balance and shape, 70; frames of movement, 2; lateral range in the hand, 62, 67, 130, 162; left hand and arm, 31, 70, 301; left hand while moving, 148; left knuckles 124, 131; palm to fingers for vibrato, 168; right hand and arm, 198, 294; roundedness of a ball, 16, 286; shifting hand configurations, 183–184; square-shaped flexed finger, 65, 72, 92–93, 141, 159, 171, 178; thumb and fourth finger, 40–41, 52, 53–54, 57–58, 59, 82, 94–95; torso and arm, 257–258

Foundation/support: bottom center of hand, 36, 125–125; elevating the palm for trill fingers, 159; forearm for left hand, 19; metacarpals for fingers, 40–41, 158–159, 170; palm for active fingers, 50, 78, 80, 86, 157, 236–237; relaxed arm supporting articulating fingers, 16, 115; shoulders for arms, 25; stationary elbow for the shifting hand, 14–15; thumb for fingers, 108; torso for the arms, 218; torso for the head, 214; trunk muscles for the migrating hand, 9, 257–258, 261, 262; upper arm for the hand, 14, 27

Fourth finger, left hand: palm support, 147; positioning, 20–21, 27–28, 30, 39–40, 98, 118, 125, 147, 152, 155; strengthening, 30, 86, 118, 135, 184; thumb's role, 21, 96

Freedom/control: from forearm balance point, 192; in forearm musculature, 194; in knuckle response, 205–206; by lifting the heel of the palm, 80; from outside activating force, 10, 60, 153–155, 15; with palmar rotation, 1259; with palm hugging the neck, 58, 293; in patterns of tension and release, 52

Frog: balancing the bow from, 227, 245; curving away on a downbow, 238–239; finger placement, 206, 208; hand hold, 206, 207, 209, 240–241; improper transference of weight, 213; propelling/steering from, 247, 296

Fulcrum. *See* Leverage

Grasping. *See* Bow hold: comparison with left hand
Gravity, center of. *See* Center of gravity
Gravity, force of. *See* Weight as momentum
Grieg, Edward, Concerto for Piano and Orchestra in A minor, Movement III, 241
Grounding. *See* Stability/grounding

Hair. *See* Bow hair
Hand rotation: large knuckle involvement, 67; left hand, 59, 123–124, 125–127; right hand, 240; shifting, 146–147; three primary rotations, 39, 132, 139; thumb axle, 112; thumb to hand, 94, 98–101, 105
Handel, George Frederick, *Messiah*, Violin II, No. 16, 221
Heel: balancing with the fingers, 58, 205; energetically raising, 56, 115, 159, 169; leading with, 68, 142; proximity with the neck, 78, 90, 114; stabilizing against the violin, 51, 114
Humerus, 268, 302, 305, 306; left humerus, 12, 30, 299; right humerus, 191, 219

Injury prevention. *See* Dysfunction
Instrument position: chin and shoulder rest, 32; placement, 7, 21–22, 32–33, 34–35, 220, 260; support, 34, 270–271, 292, 305
Integration: arm's active flexion with fingers, 172; biceps-thumb-finger joint, 178–179; elbows, 229; fingertip to forearm, 180; fingertip to palm, 182; fingertip to wrist, 182; forearm-upper arm communication, 13, 21, 27; forearm with shoulder, 222; hand-forearm-upper arm, 27; hands, 249–250; hand with arm, 74, 217; large knuckle with fingertip, 65; palm with fingers, 157; shoulder with arm, 24–25; thumb with fingers, 94, 150; upper arm with hand, 23; wrist with fingers, 41; right-hand and left-hand symmetry, 116
Intonation: aiming the fingers, 75–76; interval spaces, 55–56, 62–63, 67, 130, 131

Kinesthetic awareness, 2, 12–13. *See also* Arm rotation; Flexing fingers; Hand rotation; Pronation; Supination
Kreutzer, Rudolphe, works of: Caprice No. 7, 233; Caprice No. 15, 167

Lalo, Edouard, *Symphonie Espagnole* in D minor, Op. 21: Allegro non troppo, 101; Andante, 201
Latissimus dorsi, 22, 268, 299
Leading: with the arm, 153; with the balance point/nock on the downbow, 198–199, 232, 246, 251; with the fourth finger on downbows, 211, 239, 247; with the heel, 36, 46, 68, 142, 151, 152; with the knuckles on the upbow, 198–199, 232, 246, 251; with the radius, 20, 144–145; with the right elbow, 213; with the tip on upbows, 247; with the ulna, 144–145
Left arm position: directing point, 21–23; elbow/humerus position, 8, 14, 115; forearm verticality, 18; initiating movement, 8, 22; lateral rotation, 8, 118; migrating motions, 9–12; presentation point, 21–22; radius suspending the ulna, 118; wrist placement to the strings, 30–31
Left hand position: balancing the hand, 118; curved thumb and fingers, 96; home position, 117–118, 132; lower outside corner, 134–136; motions on the wrist, 26, 117; muscular continuity, 29–30; non-grasping touch of thumb to the neck, 16, 110; palm support of fourth finger, 147; relaxed suspension, 142; stabilizing the palm, 50; tunnel formation, 98, 108, 121, 290; wrist placement, 42

Legato, 237–238
Level plane: of fingers, 144; of fingertips, 91, 159; of fingertips and heel 57; of forearm 189, 203–204, 205; of hand motion 9, 295; of palm, 59; of violin 7, 9, 33, 159, 221, 269–270; of wrist, 189, 203–204, 253
Leverage: balance point in right forearm, 190, 191; large knuckles as fulcrum, 62, 64–65; mid-left forearm as fulcrum, 31–32; shoulder as fulcrum, 25; thumb as fulcrum, 104, 105, 107; thumb as lever, 142
Lower string orientation: bow arm, 232, 246; left hand, 31, 80, 142; lower outside corner, 135–136; torso involvement, 263

Mahler, Gustave, Symphony No. 4 in G Major, Movement II, 109
Martelé, 232
Mendelssohn, Felix, Violin Concerto in E minor, Op. 64, Movement I, 13, 56, 58, 83, 101, 112, 115, 120, 133, 135, 142, 185
Messiah (Handel), Violin II, No. 16, 221
Metacarpals, 40–41, 45, 51, 56, 76, 86, 87, 96, 125, 158–159, 160–161, 167, 168, 169, 170, 182, 247, 285, 300, 306
Momentum. *See* Weight/momentum
Mozart, Wolfgang Amadeus, works of: Concerto No. 4 in D Major, K. 218, Movement I, 19, 103, 109, 130, 141, 142, 143, 208; Symphony No. 35 (*Haffner Symphony*) in D Major, K. 385, Movement IV, 100
Mussorgsky, Modest, *Pictures at an Exhibition*, Maurice Ravel orchestration: Gnomus, 15; Tuileries, 147

Oscillation: aiming the fingers, 180; hand support, 178, 179–180; knuckle involvement, 174; vibrating finger, 169, 174, 185; warped patterns, 18
Overextension: overextending a finger, 23, 41, 89, 142, 146, 161; overextending the bow, 203; overextending the thumb, 96; overflexing, 18, 204, 281; overrotating the bow hand, 206; overrotating within the left hand, 20

Paganini, Niccolo, works of: Caprice No. 5 in A minor, 24, 143; Caprice No. 24 in A minor, Variation 3, 107; Caprice No. 24 in A minor, Variation 5, 108; Caprice No. 24 in A minor, Variation 7, 155; Concerto No. 1 in D Major, Movement I, 184, 199, 206
Partita No. 3 in E Major (J. S. Bach), Preludio, 143, 149, 195, 196, 204, 206, 208, 213, 227, 228, 229, 231, 242, 243, 245, 248, 249, 294, 295, 296
Pectoralis major, 300
Pelvis, 261, 272, 305, 306
Perpendicular: balance point's inner arrow to the string, 232; collarbone to long axis of violin, 7; finger angle to the string, 73, 159, 178; horizontal line to the spine of the lower outside corner, 134; long bow strokes to the string, 246
Pictures at an Exhibition (Mussorgsky, Ravel orchestration): Gnomus, 15; Tuileries, 147
Planes: anatomical planes, 293; forearm bending in all three planes, 192; hand rotation in all three planes, 132; level plane, 35, 42, 45, 57, 110, 114; plane of the bow arm, 213; plane of the palm, 37, 59, 117, 132, 140, 155; torquing bow in vertical plane, 221; vertical plane motion of the left forearm, 14; vertical plane motion of right forearm, 196, 225–226
Pliability. *See* Elasticity/pliability
Position, body. *See* Standing position; Sitting position; Torso/trunk support
Position, instrument. *See* Instrument Position
Position, left arm. *See* Left arm position
Position, left hand. *See* Left hand position

Position, right arm. *See* Right arm position

Position, right hand. *See* Right hand position

Potential energy: ; in bow arm, 199, 202–202, 202, 218–219, 220–221, 246; in left hand, 72, 135–136, 158–159; with palm pliability, 53

Powering: metacarpal empowering the first segment of the finger, 158; powering the thumb, 96

Presentation point: left arm, 21, 27, 214, 277, 291; right arm, 212, 214, 291, 294

Pronation: left hand, 8, 36; right hand, 203

Radius, 20, 21, 27, 63, 73, 84–85, 118, 144–145, 184

Range: of articulating fingertips, 59; of hand rotation in home position, 132; of hand rotation on lower outside corner, 137; of palm extension, 130; of palmar rotation, 125, 171, 182; of wrist motion, 18, 39, 196

Rapid passage: left arm, 18, 38, 44, 57, 93, 114, 132, 144, 159; right arm, 184, 159

Readiness/energy: active flexion, 29, 50, 89, 99, 172; exuberance in rapid passages, 144; knuckles as hand's springs, 168; muscular continuity, 29–30; wrist-finger interaction, 41

Relaxation/expansion: acquiescence of the palm, 52–53; alleviating tension, 16; back expansion, 16; relaxed forearm for spiccato, 235; relaxed hand for trilling, 157; relaxed hand suspension for large shifts, 142; relaxed left arm, 42; shoulder compliance, 24–25

Restoring force, 13, 47–48, 53, 75, 163, 198–199, 200, 243, 266–268, 272, 292–293, 294. *See also* Elasticity/pliability

Right arm position: containing the arm, 217; directing point, 212; forearm suspension, 196; lateral forearm balance, 189; passive shoulder 212–213, 214; presentation point, 212; right-arm formation, 213; slope, 215, 219–220; squaring with the violin, 220

Right hand position: bow hand on wrist, 203; wrist suspension system, 203

Rocking motion of the hand, 37, 38

Rotation. *See* Arm rotation; Bow rotation; Hand rotation

Sagittal movement: bowing motion of the body, 259–260, 293; flexion to extension of the hand, 36, 39, 300

Saint-Saëns, Camille, *Carnival of the Animals*, Finale, 148

Scale passages: arcing paths, 151; clean articulations, 89; finger placement, 77–78; fixed elbow position, 14–15; heel of the hand, 151–152; knuckle momentum, 67; malleable hand, 150; thumb, 111, 114

Scapula, 300, 305, 306

Schumann, Robert, Symphony No. 2 in C Major, Scherzo, 64, 77, 106, 225

Scottish Fantasy (Bruch), Movement I, 12, 211, 239; Movement II, 54

Scroll: elevation, 164, 258; horizontal axis, 7, 270; support for, 9, 14, 32–33

Shifting: avoiding the shoulder of the violin, 120; descending shifts, 145–146; double stops, 75, 96, 145; function of speed, 148; gradual coiling of the arm, 11–12; large shifts, 46, 76, 106–107, 147; leading with the heel, 142, 151–152; maintaining a level hand, 59; momentum, 127–128; rapid passages, 144; sideways palm rotation, 155; third to fourth position, 23, 111, 127–128, 145; thumb-finger interplay, 150

Shoulder of violin, 51–52, 114, 118, 120, 148, 158

Shoulders, 24, 25, 214, 215, 268; left shoulder, 24–26, 28, 30, 31, 32, 33, 147, 158, 172, 173, 179; right shoulder, 189, 191, 192, 213, 214, 218, 218, 222

Sinding, August Christian, Suite in A minor, Presto, 241
Sitting position, 259, 269–270, 272; a new center of gravity, 260; sitting bones, 257
Sonata No. 2 in A minor (J. S. Bach), Fuga, 87, 200, 224, 251, 252; Grave, 75, 232
Sonata No. 3 in D minor (Ysaÿe), Ballade, 96
Sounding points 242, 247–249, 251, 278, 294
Sound quality, xviii, 206, 221, 237, 259, 266, 272
Speed/dexterity: with close fingertips, 77–78, 84–85; with compressions, 103, 130; in crossing strings, 152–153; with forearm support, 10; via images, 3–5, 89, 126; with instrument support, 33; with light touch, 79; with palm support, 81, 184; with rocking motion, 37; with thumb curvature, 98; in trilling, 159, 161–162; with weight added, 127–128
Sphere/ball: bow stroke support, 196, 215, 218, 239, 241–242, 246–247; controlling tension, 31–32, 172; full body support, 16, 34, 173, 212–213, 261, 271–272, 273; instrument support, 33; left-arm rotation, 10–11, 173; left-hand balance, 14; left-hand configuration, 58, 59–60, 62, 94, 182–183; left-hand rotation, 123–124, 125–126; left-hand strength/grounding, 50, 65, 73–74, 111, 128, 134–135, 167, 171; momentum to articulating fingers, 19, 90–91; navigating the fingerboard, 22–23, 60–61, 111; off-the-string bow strokes, 234–235; on-the-string bow strokes, 238–239; chakras, 274
Spiccato, 234
Spiral qualities: in arm support for vibrato, 180; in left arm and hand, 273; in left hand configuration, 72; in movement, 34; in torso and head, 274

Stability/grounding: base-trill metacarpal for continuity, 160; bow, 227; hand for the fingers, 73, 78, 82, 123–124; large knuckles for fingers, 67, 131, 165; lower outside corner, 52, 138–139; passages between shifts, 143; standing, 7, 259; third-to-fourth position changeover, 145; thumb for the fingers, 108; vibrating fingers, 180; weight imagery for shifting hand, 127–128
Stamina/endurance: in spiccato passages, 235; in string crossing passages, 242; to sustain trill, 161–162; to sustain vibrato, 179
Standing position, 7; balancing torso and arms, 257; creative bifurcation, 264–265; feet as foundation, 268, 269; integrating mass of violin, 260; three anatomical planes, 259–260
Sternum, 261, 265, 271, 305
Strength/cohesion: finger-palm connection, 161–162; forearm, 31–32; muscular continuity, 29–30, 262; thumb-finger, 103, 150–151
String Quartet No. 12 in F Major, Op. 96 (*American Quartet*) (Dvořák), Finale, 71
Suite in A minor (Sinding), Presto, 241
Supination, 8, 36
Support. *See* Foundation/support
Suprasternal notch, 7, 306
Suspension: fingers from thumb, 110; fingers from wrist, 129, 145; right arm, 4, 204, 215, 216, 217, 218–219, 235; shoulders, 25, 214; trill fingers, 161; vibrating finger and thumb, 183; wrist 203
Symphonie Espagnole in D minor, Op. 21 (Lalo): Allegro non troppo, 101; Andante, 201
Symphony No. 2 in C Major (Schumann), Scherzo, 64, 77, 106, 225
Symphony No. 4 in F minor (Tchaikovsky), Movement I, 109
Symphony No. 4 in G Major (Mahler), Movement II, 109

Symphony No. 6 in B minor (*Pathétique*) (Tchaikovsky): Movement I, 52, 115; Movement III, 38
Symphony No. 9 (Beethoven): Movement II, 89; Movement IV, 210, 236
Symphony No. 35 in D Major (*Haffner*) (Mozart), Movement IV, 100

Tchaikovsky, Pyotr Ilyich, works of: Symphony No. 4 in F minor, Movement I, 109; Symphony No. 6 in B minor (*Pathétique*), Movement I, 52, 115; Symphony No. 6 in B minor, Movement III, 38; Violin Concerto in D Major, Movement I, 175, 236
Tension: alleviating in left arm, 16, 80, 90, 94, 96, 103, 108, 115, 117, 124, 128, 129, 153–155, 157, 163, 172, 173, 174, 179; alleviating in right arm, 200, 205, 210; healthy pressures 83, 161, 266
Thumb functions: contact quality, 90, 98; foundation for fingers, 108; position, 94–95, 96; rotating the left hand, 94, 98–99, 100–101, 105; thumb and finger balance, 104, 121; thumb as fulcrum, 104, 105, 107; thumb axle, 112
Tone: quality, 52, 205–206, 220–221, 227, 237–239, 241–242, 247, 270–271, 272; sounding points, 247–249; volume, 238, 247, 270–271, 272
Torso/trunk support: bilateral foundations, 262; bow arm formation, 218; bow arm suspension, 200; engagement of trunk muscles, 22, 212; foundation for the head, 214; four-chord bow stroke, 251; reciprocity with the arm and hand, 257; separation from left arm, 16, 173; shoulder suspension, 25, 214; sitting bones, 259; spiral continuum of left arm, 16, 173; two-fold lateral arm rotation, 20
Touch: light touch of bow hold, 209; light touch of fingertips, 79, 144; light touch of left thumb, 32–33; nongrasping thumb, 16; press-release touch, 179
Triceps, 12, 23, 28, 33
Trills: compressions, 163; contrary motion, 160–162; finger to palm connection, 157; grounding, 160; large knuckle support, 162–163; metacarpal collaboration, 158–159; perpendicular orientation, 159
Trunk. *See* Torso/trunk support

Ulna: left arm, 20, 27, 30, 63, 73, 117, 118, 132, 144–145, 184; right arm, 189, 190, 203, 264
Upbow, 198–199
Upper arm. *See* Humerus
Urstudien (Basic Studies) for Violin (Flesch), Exercise 1C, 88

Vibrato: arm vibrato, 172–173; finger vibrato, 180; hand vibrato, 182; knuckle options, 174; new hand balance, 168; oscillations, 169, 174, 179, 180; palm flexibility, 171; quality of sound, 178–179; sustaining, 179; transfer of weight, 172; wrist vibrato, 182–183

Weight as momentum: to articulating fingers, 4, 56–57, 65, 74–75, 92, 159, 172; of the bow, 244, 246, 293–294; from bow arm to fingers, 203, 204–205, 207, 213, 215, 219, 220–221, 246–247; for left arm, 28; among left fingers, 104; for left hand, 24, 62, 67, 92, 127–128, 147, 148, 155, 159; in vibratory oscillations, 179–180;
Wrist functions: expanding the wrist, 45; foundation for the fingers, 42; leading the fingers, 36, 38; position, 42; powering the fingers, 40–41; range of motion, 39–40; sideways rotation in position, 37; suspension system, 203

Ysaÿe, Eugène, Sonata No. 3 in D minor, Ballade, 96

MAUREEN TARANTO-PYATT is a professional violinist and poet in the Boston area. She combined her love of imagery with a pursuit of elegant technique to create Progressive Form, thanks in part to her gifted teachers, each just a degree or two of separation from some of the great pedagogues of the twentieth century.

PETER STICKEL is a violinist, arts administrator, and longtime practitioner of Structural Integration.

For Indiana University Press

Tony Brewer *Artist and Book Designer*
Brian Carroll *Rights Manager*
Allison Chaplin *Acquisitions Editor*
Sophia Hebert *Assistant Acquisitions Editor*
Brenna Hosman *Production Coordinator*
Katie Huggins *Production Manager*
Nancy Lightfoot *Project Editor and Manager*
Dan Pyle *Online Publishing Manager*
Samantha Heffner *Marketing and Publicity Manager*
Jennifer L. Witzke *Senior Artist and Book Designer*